STOP THE KILLING TRAIN

STOP THE KILLING TRAIN

RADICAL VISIONS FOR RADICAL CHANGE

MICHAEL ALBERT

SOUTH END PRESS   BOSTON, MA

Cover by Bri McAlevey

Library of Congress Cataloguing-in-Publication Data

Albert, Michael 1947-
    Stop the killing train : radical visions for radical change / by
Michael Albert.
        p.   cm.
    Includes bibliographical references and index.
    ISBN 0-89608-471-x : $35.00. — ISBN 0-89608-470-1 (pbk.) :
$15.00
    1. Radicalism. I. Title.
HM281.A63   1993
303.48′4—dc20   ® GCIU   93-2147
                                                          CIP

South End Press, 116 Saint Botolph Street, Boston, MA 02115
    99 98 97 96 95 94   1 2 3 4 5 6 7 8 9

Table of Contents

PART ONE

Poison Headaches:

Thinking About U.S. Institutions And Ideology

PART TWO
The Present Now Will Later Be Past:
Thinking About The Future

PART THREE
Like Goliath, They'll Be Conquered:
Thinking About Change

Foreword

This collection ends with an essay entitled "We Can Win"—with an exclamation mark. The message is particularly appropriate at this moment. One has to go back a long time to find a period of such despair and hopelessness in the face of grave and mounting problems—a period in which, furthermore, so much can be done if only people find ways to escape from their isolation, fears, and sense of futility. The same message is what distinguishes Michael Albert's work over the past 30 years, a remarkable record of accomplishment, which offers valuable signposts for those who are not satisfied to contemplate a dismal future for much of humanity.

Albert asks, "Why does the U.S. left have nearly no self-sustaining infrastructure?" That's just the right question, and the one that he has sought to answer, not only in his writings but also in actions. He makes only brief and inadequate mention of some of what he has done. I'll add only a few words from personal knowledge.

When Mike arrived at MIT as a student, the world's leading university of science and technology—not to speak of coercive social policy—was overwhelmingly dedicated to service to power, including direct involvement in the US war in Vietnam, which was then rapidly escalating. Critique of this stand was limited, and faculty-based. Mike was one of a small number of students who sought to change the culture and nature of the university. Their Rosa Luxemburg collective was the source of what proved to be far-reaching changes. Well after the Tet offensive had convinced corporate America to liquidate the Vietnam enterprise as too costly, with educated sectors following in their wake and revising history accordingly, MIT remained tranquil and isolated in a growing ferment of activism and protest, by then, over a wide range of social and political issues.

In the fall of 1968, the few student activists agreed to organize a sanctuary in the student union for a marine who was deserting publicly in protest against the war. I have to admit that I was opposed, convinced that nothing of the sort could work in the climate of MIT. Fortunately, they disregarded my advice. It turned out that the passivity and conformism were paper thin. Within a few days, the university had virtually closed down. The student union became the site of a 24-hour-a-day mélange of seminars, public meetings, rock music (which I personally could have done without), and the kinds of human interactions among students, faculty and staff that were something new in this environment. One result was to open serious consideration of the place of the university in the larger society, of its responsibilities and proper role, and those of science and technology generally. The changes that ensued were substantial and have been lasting. The lives of many individuals were changed, and the institution too, much for the better.

While that single incident sparked much of the change, to focus too narrowly on it is misleading. The university was something of a cocoon, but not entirely, of course; and within it there was a background of organizing, discussion, and activism, which were to reach surprising levels of direct student-faculty involvement as events proceeded. Much as he may dislike the term and concept, Mike played a crucial leadership role throughout, and a highly constructive one. He later went on to devote himself to creating the infrastructure that popular forces seeking justice, freedom, and human dignity must have if they are to win—which is to say, if the world is to be saved from a bitter fate.

One very important success is the press that is publishing this collection, in which Mike played a central role from the outset. Not only has the press offered a voice to wide currents of the independent left, but it is also a model, in microcosm, of the forms of participatory economy that Mike, along with his co-author Robin Hahnel, have explored and elaborated in a series of important publications, including comments in the articles that follow here. When the press had become self-sustaining, Mike went on to found Z Magazine, with Lydia Sargent. How important that was, I can perhaps illustrate from personal experience.

Efforts of the large majority of the population to organize and enter the social and political arena were, naturally, unacceptable to elite opinion, and major efforts were taken from the early 1970s to reverse this "crisis of democracy" and to restore "governability"—meaning apathy and passivity, with power kept firmly in proper and responsible hands. The "sixties journals" soon succumbed to this cultural counterattack. By the mid-1970s, Ramparts and Liberation were no more. The "underground press" was disappearing or becoming commercialized. Even before, the one mainstream journal that had offered an opening to dissident opinion (the New York Review) had put an end to that deviation, hastening to join the reconstructing elite consensus. By the late 1970s, I found myself writing mostly in a journal of right-wing libertarians (Inquiry), which was open to a broad range of opinion, unusually so. Other outlets on the left remained, and new popular movements were forming and creating their own channels of expression and interaction. But a very noticeable gap had opened.

That was filled by Z Magazine, not only for me personally but for many others as well. Like South End press, Z Magazine also showed how much can be accomplished by dedicated, committed, intelligent effort, even without resources. I don't know of any real parallel. While the new technology of desktop publishing doubtless contributed, that's only a small part of the story. The press and the journal, and the offshoots that are now developing, are examples, in one realm, of the kinds of "self-sustaining infrastructure" that an independent left needs to bring people together, to offer them a voice and to help them develop their communities of understanding and action.

Mike's approach to understanding society emphasizes culture, gender, and politics, as well as economics. This breadth has characterized his political involvement from the start, the focus and priorities of projects like South End Press and Z, and, of course, the essays in this book.

The present era is new in many ways, but it has many resemblances—sometimes almost eerie ones—to important periods of the past. The enthusiastic resort to classical (now "neoliberal") economic doctrine as a weapon of class war is a striking example. Current debates about welfare-workfare can hardly fail to evoke memories of Malthus and Ricardo, whose new "science" allegedly showed that the poor majority could only be harmed by efforts to help them—a demonstration with the certainty of the "principle of gravitation," Ricardo declared. Someone who lacks independent wealth "has no claim of right to the smallest portion of food, and, in fact, has no business to be where he is," apart from what his offer of labor will bring in the market, Malthus proclaimed in highly influential work. Efforts to mislead the poor into believing that they have further rights are "great evils" and violations of "natural liberty," Ricardo held, as shown by the economic science of which he was the leading figure, and the unchallengeable moral principles on which it was based. As Karl Polanyi observes in his classic work on this period, The Great Transformation, "The wage system imperatively demanded the withdrawal of the 'right to live' as proclaimed" in earlier legislation; "nothing could have been more patent than the mutual incompatibility of institutions like the wage system and the 'right to live'." The latter therefore had to go, in the interests of all.

By the 1830s, the results of the "science" were becoming established in law, and the "right to live," an outmoded relic of earlier delusion, was succumbing to the wage system and the workhouse-prison. But widespread despair and suffering led to disorder and upheaval, first riots, later the rise of organized social movements that began to challenge the principles that raised capital accumulation to the supreme human value. The same happened in the United

States as the industrial order became established. Northern workers derided the hypocrisy of bosses "professing to be abolitionists...and making slaves at home." Workers began to organize "to abolish Wage Slavery before we meddle with Chattel Slavery," and bitterly complained that those who fought for freedom for the slaves were now subjected to a form of wage slavery that was hardly less abominable, as the industrial revolution based on "free labor" rapidly expanded.

In the face of riots and disorder—and worse, Chartist and socialist organizing—elite opinion shifted, and the "science" took new forms based on the discovery that the "right to live" had to be preserved. Laissez-faire doctrines fell into further disrepute as the new rulers came to understand that they still required state power, as in the past, to enhance their privilege and to protect them from market discipline. We move on to various forms of welfare state capitalism, at least in those societies that had won their place in the sun by terror, oppression, and robbery.

This history has, in fact, been relived over and over. There is little that is new in neoliberal programs, trickle-down theories, and the rest of the doctrinal baggage that serves the needs of privilege and power. The ideology of oppression may differ in form when applied to Third World service areas and domestic populations, but similarities are apparent, and current enthusiasms are hardly more than a recapitulation, often sordid, of earlier devices to justify the privilege of those who hold the reins. The present era is highly reminiscent of the moments of enthusiasm before the unseemly noises of the rabble had become too threatening to overlook, a fact that carries lessons that are not too obscure.

Current versions teach us that the best interests of all are served if decision-making power is concentrated in absolutist corporations, increasingly transnational, that operate in secret, with central management of production, commercial interactions ("trade"), investment, and speculation on a vast and growing scale. They are to be immune from public scrutiny, along with the network of institutions coalescing around them (the IMF, World Bank, World Trade Organization, etc.). State power retains its fundamental importance, as long as it is subordinated to their needs and interests. By pursuing economic virtue in this manner, we advance towards a low-growth, low-wage, high-profit future, with highly polarized societies worldwide and a huge and growing mass of superfluous people, who plainly have no "right to live," as their inadequacies in the market demonstrate.

As in the early 19th century, we are to understand that it is a violation of natural liberty and even science to deceive people into thinking that they have some rights beyond what they can gain by selling their labor power. Any effort to depart from such right thinking leads directly to the Gulag, leading thinkers soberly explain. Remarkably, they are assisted in their project by intellectuals of the left, who preach the "death of socialism," referring to the collapse of the tyranny instituted by the Bolshevik counterrevolution of 1917, which quickly destroyed every socialist structure that had arisen during the revolutionary period and instituted the brutal rule of the "Red bureaucracy," much as Bakunin had predicted many years before, and as leading Marxist and other left intellectuals observed at once.

Many of them also developed visions of a future society that could realize the traditional quest of the authentic left for freedom, justice, solidarity, and popular control of institutions: Anton Pannekoek's discussion of workers' councils is one prominent case, and there are quite a few others, often presented in some detail, with varying emphases. That the Soviet tyranny was radically opposed to this vision was obvious at once—to those who fashioned it, Lenin and Trotsky as well. The destructive and inhuman character of market systems, including the "really existing capitalism" that has always relied extensively on state intervention in the interests of the powerful, was no less obvious and familiar. The currently fashionable idea that these are the sole alternatives, and that only the latter is viable after the collapse of the anti-socialist Bolshevik tyranny, is a most remarkable feature of current dialogue, which departs radically from the authentic left tradition in this regard. Mike and his co-author Robin Hahnel have made an important contribution to this tradition with their careful studies of participatory economic systems, spelled out in technical and popular works and discussed in essays here as well.

There is not the slightest reason to succumb to the self-serving doctrines of the masters of the new world order. There is little doubt that, as in the past, popular forces will cast them aside and seek to take the future into their own hands, reversing the serious decline of democracy of recent years and the institutionalization of new forms of oppression. A look at very recent events signals some of the prospects, and the problems.

Compare two of these: south-central Los Angeles, and Chiapas, Mexico. There are similarities, but also striking differences. In both cases, the uprisings reflected the increasing marginalization of people who do not contribute to profit-making under prevailing institutional arrangements, and therefore lack human rights or value. People who live in the slums of Los Angeles once had jobs, in part in the state sector that is the core of advanced industry in what is called a "free market capitalist" society, in part in factories that have been shifted to places where labor can be more savagely exploited and destruction of the environment can proceed unhampered. By absolute measures, they are considerably wealthier than the Mayans of Chiapas, who recognize that what remains of their lives faces destruction as the investor rights agreements (NAFTA, GATT) extend their range. But the Los Angeles riots contrast sharply with the Chiapas rebellion. The contrast reflects the difference between a society that has become demoralized and devastated by external forces and one that has retained its inner cohesion and vitality. The specific problems that lie ahead are quite different; the crying need for solidarity and constructive participation could hardly be more clear.

The tendencies at work in the increasingly integrated world system are reasonably clear, as is their ominous portent. As to the right way to respond, my own belief, for what it is worth, is that traditional ideas and values of the libertarian left retain their power and significance, and that new opportunities are opening to revitalize them with the collapse of the Soviet empire and the illegitimacy of the state capitalist institutions—veiled by doctrine, but understood by growing numbers of people, at some level, from their own lives. That conclusion may be right or wrong, but one thing is evident: what is needed, as always, is intelligence and will, the will to become engaged, to seek, to think clearly, to join with others to change the course of history.

The essays that follow address a wide range of such concerns. The conviction that "we can win" is, I think, soundly based, despite the superficial appearance of Western triumphalism—in reality, narrowly-based triumphalism amidst general fear and despair. It is a task of historic importance to show that that is true.

—Noam Chomsky
1994

Introduction

This book is a compendium of articles from *Z Magazine*, 1988 through 1992. Each month my column, "Venting Spleen," was edited by Lydia Sargent and Eric Sargent, my co-staffers on the magazine, and their efforts have not only improved the articles' readability, but also their logic. Also, most months I solicited advice from Robin Hahnel, my co-author of numerous books and closest friend for the past three decades. His contribution exceeds even that, however, since the underlying intellectual framework guiding my writing was developed jointly with him. Also, on many ocassions nearly complete drafts of these articles were read to Noam Chomsky and/or Stephen Shalom, and, less frequently, Sandy Carter and/or Holly Sklar. All these friends helped with the logic, direction, and clarity of the articles. None, of course, are responsible for weaknesses.

Since these articles would not have been written without Z as a vehicle, I also want to thank the people who have made the magazine's existence possible, including fellow staffers; South End Press, where I developed skills and contacts essential to begininng Z and which has remained a source of aid for Z over the years; the many writers who have contributed their articles to Z; and our readers, who have not only expanded our circulation over the years, but also repeatedly answered our calls for help through difficult times.

South End Press's aims and mine are essentially identical because the press takes as its first priority the political impact of the books it publishes. South End assigns a coordinator to each title to work with the author, provide editorial advice, escort the manuscript through preparation and production, etc. My coordinator for this book was Cynthia Peters, who is also a good friend, and I thank her for her editorial help and corrections.

By way of a lengthier introduction to this book, it makes sense to say a little more about my political motivations. Luckily, I can do this through a contribution to Z (December 1992), "Glory Days," which uses some of my formative personal experiences to clarify my contemporary priorities.

Glory Days

In the summer following my senior year in high school, as I prepared to go off to college, I began being rushed for fraternities. Upperclassmen visited and befriended me in my home town, New Rochelle, New York. Months later, just before the official first semester, I arrived at school for Rush Week. I wanted to become a physicist. I was excited and eager.

I would go to one fraternity house after another to be wined, dined, and invited to stay for the night. I was shopping for a place to live. They were deciding who to invite to become members.

I became a brother at Alpha Epsilon Pi (AEPi), one of the predominently Jewish fraternities at MIT. Rush week initiated five months of pledging, which involved "pantsing," having to light cigarettes for upperclassmen, having to learn fraternity data, doing pushups, and other sundry silliness. Finally, every Friday night pledges were required to clean the place with a rigor that would have been extreme even at Paris Island.

These cleaning sessions would begin just after dinner and go as late as 4:00 AM. This meant we had no Friday nights and were often too exhausted to fully enjoy Saturday.

In February, there was a melodramatic ceremony with candles and pomp at which pledges became brothers. Immediately after the ceremony, our upper-class friends told us what had really happened during Rush Week.

The MIT fraternities carefully researched lists of all incoming freshmen, like for an NBA draft. When a freshman arrived, he either got the Bum's Rush—a quick tour through the first floor and a pushy escort out the back door to the alley—or, the Prospect's Rush, for which he was taken upstairs, intro-duced around, offered information, snacks, etc., and invited to stay for dinner. This was tacky enough, but the real news was that the fraternity's telephones were tapped and a number of its rooms bugged, so brothers could listen in and find out what pledge prospects were into.

For example, if I mentioned in a private conversation with another freshman or on the phone to my girlfriend, then at Simmons college in Boston, or my parents back in New Rochelle, that I would like it if there was more personal interest taken in my background or that I wished there was a bit more emphasis on physics or that some brothers were more into playing tennis or pursuing campus politics, next morning I'd be called into a bull session on personal histories or physics, invited for a game at the tennis courts, or given a tour of the campus student government system.

I knew when I was first told this news that had I discovered these policies during Rush Week, I would have gone berserk. Knowing that AEPi was tapping my personal calls would have driven me to frenzy, and no doubt the same was true for many other new brothers. But five months later, after giving up Friday nights, after making new friends, and after acclimating to a new place to live, *none* of us felt anger. Our investment was too great. The upperclassmen told us they had taken long hours to assess our personalities to decide where we best fit. Because Rush Week gave us no honest information to guide our choices, and because we were too inexperienced about college to know what we were doing anyhow, the brothers had to make our decisions for us. They used whatever tricks they could to get whomever they liked to join their house.

For the rest of the second semester, life went on at AEPi as elsewhere on campus. But that summer my contentment came undone. The new youth culture was gaining ground, I was into Bob Dylan and the Jefferson Airplane, and one year at college had not removed *all* gray matter. I came back the next Rush Week and quit the fraternity during the pre-planning period. When Rush Week started, I sat on the fender of a car outside AEPi, called over incoming freshmen about to enter the house, and told them what was going on. I still think this was my first overtly political act, though at the time I had no notion that the logic of the fraternities was connected to the logic of society. In any event, there was a wild brawl in the street—some brothers trying to get at me, others trying to hold them off for fear of repercussions. The school administration banned me from returning to the house and to future Rush Weeks, and simultaneously opened discussions about how to change policies. The invasive practices were negotiated away, though enforcement remains in doubt.

A couple of days before the fracas, my father came to town to help out, and we met at a hotel room rented by the fraternity. A daylong meeting with many brothers followed. First, junior and senior brothers argued I should stay in the House. Then came the House officers, until, by early evening, only some prestigious alumni and AEPI's president were left.

Finally, these "leaders" admitted that I was right. But so what, they said. Why couldn't I see that I would benefit from the lying and prying? Like them, I was going to be an AEPi success story. "It works for us," they told my father, "and since Michael can work to be one of us, he shouldn't give it up." At this point, my father changed sides, not real happy about it, but no longer trying to get me to reconsider my decision. We had both seen true elitism face to face. The kind that doesn't even bother to rationalize itself to itself.

Anyhow, in the ensuing months about half my class left AEPi. This was unprecedented, but what's more interesting is that all these folks became part of an emerging campus left, a significant working core of what we called Rosa Luxemburg SDS. What distinguished this group from a random selection of students at MIT was not knowing more about society, but *only* our reversal of attitude toward AEPi—a lifestyle switch away from duplicity and elitism.

Still at MIT but now out of AEPi, I lived with two friends in an apartment in Somerville, Massachusetts. Across the street, another friend lived in a smaller place, making four of us on the block. Among other activities, we used to play touch football with the local high school kids.

We got along well with our young neighbors, and enjoyed our games together. But a few months into our schedule, we began to notice a change in our neighbors' play. Quality went down. Attention went down. Soon, they wouldn't play at all. We'd see them, spaced out, and they'd pay only peripheral attention to us. Before long, we knew our young friends were sniffing glue.

Glue was then a popular escape in many working-class communities. It was readily available, cheap, and provided a special kind of high. Where marijuana heightened the senses, glue turned them off. Glue was also suicidal. The fumes destroyed brain cells. Some glue manufacturers, of course, were quick to notice the increased demand for their product. The market-wise among them naturally increased the deadly ingredients.

We got our neighbors together and tried to talk them out of their new habit. They told us they liked glue because it temporarily wiped away their problems. We told them sniffing was shortening their lives. They told us to look around and wise up. Their lives were already short. Their lives were already brutal. How much of a brain did it take to be a supermarket boxboy? To their eyes, early death was one more benefit of sniffing.

These teenagers were killing themselves, and we were powerless to stop it. Finally, one of my friends had the idea to tell them that sniffing glue would destroy their sex lives. This was a loss they understood. They gave up the glue, at least for a while.

A year later, I was elected undergraduate association president (UAP) of the entire student body at MIT. Our campaign, waged against other candidates as well as the nervous MIT administration, included as its programmatic goals: no more war research, a $100,000 indemnity payment to the local Black Panther Party, no more grades or course requirements, open admissions, a redistribution of MIT's technical resources to make them available to local community colleges, and so on.

After the election, the then second-in-command in the Institute's hierarchy, MIT's provost Jerome Weisner, came to visit me. He was a committed liberal, an ex-science adviser to John Kennedy, a figure of note in political circles, and destined to become president of MIT.

Weisner invited me to Hyannisport to spend a weekend at the Kennedy compound to talk about future possibilities. I said no thanks, I consider Hyannisport enemy territory, something that should have been obvious from all he knew about me. Yet Weisner was incredulous that I would ignore such an "opportunity," not realizing it didn't appear to me an opportunity at all. What Weisner saw as a big bribe, many in my generation now saw as obscene.

Weisner next reported that while he disagreed with my views, I had every right to hold them. He guaranteed that as long as I didn't do anything extreme, like burning down a building or assaulting another student, I wouldn't be hassled by the MIT administration. I thanked him for the sentiment and predicted that he would expel me within the year even though I would not have burnt anything down or beaten anyone up or done anything to merit such a punishment. He was indignant that I could think such a thing of him, and of MIT, and reiterated his pledge. He remained indignant, even as he witnessed and celebrated my expulsion about eight months later.

It was policy for the UAP to give a speech at the beginning of the semester to an auditorium full of alumni. First, the president of the university would speak. Then the UAP. When the time came for this, my first official act, I bounded onto the stage and had my say. By then I was calling MIT "Dachau on the Charles," carefully noting that while "our Jews" were in distant Indochina, they were being incinerated nonetheless. I spoke for about half an hour, giving what was, for the setting, an outrageous indictment of imperialism, capitalism, and MIT, admittedly enjoying railing at these corporate leaders. There was considerable turmoil, but no violence. After the talk, a number of alumni tried to get my attention. One succeeded, and asked me to come with him to West Germany to work in his successful chemical plant. I didn't even have to finish at MIT, he said. He would make me a vice president and my future would be glorious.

I had just savaged his values, his world, his domain, *everything* he stood for, indicating that for my generation his understanding of success held no appeal whatsoever, and still he made this offer. He thought I couldn't refuse. My pretense would disappear. My rhetoric would dissipate. He wanted to own my arrogance or some other horrible quality he saw, and he was convinced that the rest was posturing. I never forgot his limitless confidence or his inability to understand that a new culture and new values made his idea of success anathema to millions of young revolutionaries.

We all have our own collection of stories. These are a few of mine. In retrospect, the civil rights movement had pushed me, though peripherally, all during high school. A year and a half into college, the war in Vietnam had become my near and far horizon. Along the way, experiencing the gap between the kids sniffing glue and the MIT fraternities and administration and elite alumni, all during a cultural explosion, catalyzed my turn toward a new lifestyle. My journey mirrored that of many people in my generation. For widely varying reasons, we didn't just become irate at particular injustices or advocates of particular changes. We threw off one lifestyle and tried to evolve an alternative. We rejected not only this crime or that, but society's defining institutions. While risking jail was a hard choice many made, rejecting amoral suburbia or immoral mansions didn't involve a choice at all. We didn't forego success. We sought something better.

I write this not to revel in 1960s Glory Days, but to say that I wonder how many of us, myself foremost, have in part returned to sniffing glue or sucking up, protecting past investments or hoping for future returns instead of seeking a comprehensive alternative. To earn short-term rewards within oppressive circumstances is a necessary part of surviving. But in the process, haven't many of us taken our eyes off the real prize? Why are so many settling for lifestyles not so different from ones that we earlier, rightly, *easily* rejected?

In the 1960s, however young and apolitical we were, many of us not only opposed the war, racism, poverty, and sexism, we dreamed of a different way of living where all people could develop and fulfill themselves in their work and in their lives with equality, justice, and dignity. Our local fights were part of a bigger picture, and the bigger picture defined our being.

When we looked around for who to be, whether we examined the dead-end "failure" of the poor, or the hypocritical "success" of the rich, only revolution made sense. Fundamental compromises and lasting surrenders were inconceivable. At 45, regarding these same choices, I can't see how the 1990s are much different than the 1960s.

Is there some compelling new argument against being a revolutionary that I've missed? Is there some new evidence that private ownership, markets, bourgeois democracy, racism, and patriarchy offer a context for self-fulfillment? Does the recent return of tuberculosis, spread of AIDS, extinction of species, and dissolution of the ecology, mitigate the need for fundamental change? If not, why aren't we holding the banner of revolution higher, instead of behind our backs?

Is there some new argument against seeking diversity, solidarity, self-management, and equity? If not, why don't we create new institutions to foster these goals?

Is the degradation of living out of garbage cans or toiling for 40 years as a wage slave, and of economic alienation less now than 25 years ago? If not, why is the capitalist economy and competitive market system believed eternal, even on the left?

Is the allure of traditional success built on hypocrisy and amorality greater now than 25 years ago? If not, why don't we seek an alternative lifestyle?

Is there less reason to hope for success now than 25 years ago, despite the rapid fall of whole oppressive empires in the interim? If not, why not nurture objective assessment coupled with optimistic will, rather than subjective assessment coupled to pessimistic will?

Does having a single-issue orientation, a short time horizon, and an exclusively reformist attitude suffice now, though it didn't 25 years ago? If not, why are grassroots activists so hostile to agendas that transcend one focus and seek systemic alternatives *as well as* immediate reforms?

Finally, why am I more concerned with material comfort now than 25 years ago? Is it just age? Or has my revolutionary spirit atrophied for want of creative attention?

We have a new administration in Washington. The aura of hope and possibility that this has generated for many people across the United States creates a public context conducive to critique and change.

In response, social democrats and liberals will work with the Clinton administration to help implement its limited agendas.

The rest of us, however, must develop an uncompromising critique of our society and a comprehensive vision of a better future and we must communicate both the new analysis and new vision as clearly and widely as possible. But we must also create fulfilling and effective lifestyles that will help people put depression, false success, and sometimes even personal security aside.

We must help prepare the way for comprehensive revolutionary change. The 1990s need to become our kids' Glory Days, and ours as well.

—December 1992

PART ONE

Poison Headaches:
Thinking About U.S.
Institutions
And Ideology

A Triumphant New Year

Ten more years to a new century. Daily, one message reverberates: "Capitalism triumphs." For the moment, yes, but don't toss down too many vodkas at the celebration.

First, capitalism has beaten a moribund, decrepit, hypocritical Soviet system that was in any event never socialist, democratic, or egalitarian. Beating a social dungeon by virtue of the dungeon's dissolution hardly proves capitalism's lasting worth. Accompanied by parallel liberating changes in sexual, gender, political, and cultural forms, in due time a truly socialist economic option will *cause* capitalism's own dissolution. Celebrants, you'd better look to your left.

Second, the stain of capitalism's contemporary record ought to dampen triumphal celebratory spirits. To win a race as a hobbling, teetering, washed out, witless fool doesn't justify a flashy victory lap much less claims of future accomplishments. What is capitalism's condition in this self-congratulatory moment? Does Wall Street stand tall at the end of a well-run race? Or did the bottom line cross the finish line on its knees?

Last night I saw a TV ad for a network news show. Like the night before, and the night before that, the ad told how the upcoming news was going to reveal grisly facts about a grisly multi-victim murder—murder in the bedroom, murder in the alley, murder in the corner store, murder in the school, murder most foul. Network executives have apparently assembled compelling evidence that delivering more and uglier crime stories will boost their audience share. Capitalism creates hunger for criminality.

Violent crime is up 37 percent in the past decade. Even horribly understated official reports tell us that roughly one person in 20 suffers some sort of burglary, larceny, motor-vehicle theft, aggravated assault, forcible rape, or murder each year. And then the Neilson ratings tell us that that person wants to see more of the same on TV.

In response to this sign of how well our country is nurturing us into being the most humane people we can be, roughly 230 U.S. citizens out of every 100,000 rot in prison, and from 1983 to 1987 the number of people under "correctional supervision" in prison, on parole, or on probation jumped 40 percent and is still climbing. If you want to invest in the U.S. future, you would do well to invest in the manufacture of "containment and control products," since these will surely be among the most dynamic growth industries in this last decade of capitalism's century of triumph.

The U.S. has approximately 250 reported rapes each day. That's one every six minutes. And for every rape reported, there is another one, another two, another three, that go unreported. Moreover, for every rape, how many beatings occur? And for every beating, how many violent threats or assaults of the mind and spirit occur? And for every grown woman who suffers this type indignity, how many young girls get daily signals that if they don't learn their place this is their future too—or how many girls get molested by daddy or daddy's friends? And for every gay person that is bashed, how many are threatened and thereby put on alert that their lives are constantly "evaluated" by others who carry around with them the deep-seated fear and bias systematically ingrained by a homophobic society?

If for every rape reported there is only one other that goes unreported and if for every one that is completed another is warded off, then the odds are that whenever you get on a subway, at least one and probably more women in your car have suffered a rape or attempted rape, and many and perhaps most have suffered abuse. Likewise, nearly every gay person has suffered threats, and many have been bashed. This violence against women and gays and children is due principally to sexism, patriarchy, and homophobia, not capitalism. But capitalism has accommodated, rewarded, and aggravated sexual violence, and so this too is part of capitalism's record of triumph.

People fear the outdoors at night not because of stupidity or superstition but as a reasonable response to common mugging statistics or, often, to prior personal experience. Moreover, the less able to defend yourself you are, the more likely you are to suffer attack.

A year ago on Halloween I was attacked by a gang of young teenage boys out for fun. They ran after me pummeling me with eggs, apples, and rocks, one of which cut open my head. Luckily they didn't want to catch me anymore than I wanted to be caught, or it would have been much worse. In this case, and endless others like it, my political learning has taught me that what happened is the product of our schools, of class, race, and sex oppression, and of the angers, hostilities, oppositions, and destructive violence that these establish. But the easier conclusion for people without much political learning is that the cause lies in human nature, which is why the flip side of our society's anti-social decay is a growing belief by most citizens that people of other races, lower-class people, and women or gay people are genetically greedy, callous, and violent, or eager for violence to be done to them, and that this "human condition" is wired into our natures. This is the milieu in which people try to be happy, creative, and productive. People compete, suffer, and strike back until the general belief becomes that all humans are genetically shitty, greedy, anti-social, violent. Hope shatters. Trump triumphs.

The mortality rate for black infants is twice that for white infants. Life expectancy at birth is six years less for a black male than for a white male and five years less for a black female than for a white female. Racism has roots in cultural dynamics, but is certainly aggravated and not undone by capitalism. Another capitalist victory?

After heart/cardiovascular diseases and cancer, accidents (often on-the-job or due to unsafe cars and other shoddy capitalist products) are the leading cause of death. There follows pulmonary diseases, pneumonia and influenza, diabetes, and then suicide, one of which occurs every 20 minutes, with over 10 times that number of unsuccessful attempts. In short, once every two minutes some place in this country someone tries to kill him or herself, with a noose, a shotgun, drugs, or a high dive—and one out of every 10 of these attempts "succeeds." The suicide rate for those between 15 and 23 has nearly tripled since 1950. Capitalism is scorching our souls, triumphantly. Moreover, most experts agree that to protect families many suicides are labeled accidents. (How many traffic fatalities are also suicides?) And accidents, remember, appear third on the list of killers. Teen suicide. Capitalism triumphant. But I repeat myself.

Health declines, operations increase, medical consortiums prosper, Bristol Meyers and Johnson and Johnson celebrate. And since health care, such as it is, isn't free, to oversee its fiscal ebb and flow we need an insurance industry so large that the assets of the 10 largest U.S. insurance companies in 1988 totaled roughly $410.5 billion. How many houses for the homeless and beds for the sick could that buy?

In 1987 32.5 million people, or 13.5 percent of the population—not including those who no longer show up on any statistical report—lived below the poverty level. None of these people owns "a piece of the rock," but they nonetheless included 21.4 million or 10.5 percent of all whites, 9.7 million or 33.1 percent of all blacks, and 5.5 million or 28.5 percent of "Hispanics." In the same year, about 17 percent of all households had pre-tax incomes of $50,000 or more. These latter lucky individuals, *less than one out of every five of us*, controlled about 80 percent of all discretionary income, though even among these folks, buying power was largely the province of the top few percent rather than all 17 percent equally. This means that 17 percent of the population is the target of almost all the communicative messages sent out each day. They are the ones for whom malls are places to actually shop. In 1989, U.S. companies spent $125 billion advertising goods mostly to sell to people with "discretionary income."

Three million homeless people roam the streets of the U.S. At worst, they live in alleys, dine out of garbage cans, and carry their belongings in bags. At best, they endure shelters and perpetual violence and move to new "homes" every few days. Simultaneously, our country allots office space for 205,000 real-estate offices, over 100,000 banks and credit agencies, and 101,000 furniture and home-furnishing stores. These provide lovely accommodations for dealers of real estate, bankers, and sellers of furniture, all of whom leave their daytime work premises empty after dark. Of course this is profitable, if not for society, at least for real-estate agents, bankers, and furniture sales-people, and, more to the point, for their bosses, not one of whom has ever been homeless.

If this seems like stretching my point, try and reconcile the triumphant fact that in our country, while 3 million people are homeless, there are about 350,000 churches all dedicated to humanity's spiritual advance, all nearly empty most of the time.

Or consider that by a conservative estimate there are also 49,000 hotels and lodging places able to house 15 million business people making big deals day-in and day-out. Accounting for vacancy rates, how many of these hotels could be put to housing the homeless, with no loss in the number of rooms occupied by renters? Capitalism triumphantly uses all available housing opti-mally at all times, at least from the point of view of the hotel owners' bottom line.

Our national government spends just under $300 billion on the military, not counting additional untold billions that are really war-spending but mislead-ingly labeled "space-spending," "energy-spending," etc. Twenty-seven per-cent of the federal government's expenditures are directly on defense related purchases and staffing. Defense employment is about one million civilians plus 2.1 million active duty military personnel. That's over three million people who could instead put their talents to making life more livable. Meanwhile we vote for militarists, savor reports of power deployment, and buy toy warplanes and guns for our kids.

In Bolivia, tin miners have a life expectancy of 35 years due to tuberculosis and silicosis, and this is repeated in country after country to the benefit of Aluminum Company of America, Reynolds, Bethlehem Steel, etc. In the Third World over one million people yearly are severely poisoned by pesticides so that the land they "cultivate" can produce plenty of food for companies like Occidental Petroleum (the biggest food-producing firm in the U.S.) to sell in developed countries). Meanwhile, the indigenous population suffers malnutri-tion and is sometimes reduced to selling their organs or babies to avoid starving. Du Pont and Dow Chemical make out like bandits, of course—reverse Robin Hoods in the age of capitalism triumphant.

Multinationals pay 25-50 cents per hour in the Dominican Republic and local police keep the workforce free of organized opposition and then return to their barracks for another U.S. training film on how to use their graciously provided U.S. tools of the torture trade. Do CEOs discuss this with pride at the board meetings of GE, GM, and General Dynamics?

Capitalism rules most of the world's resources and is responsible for the allocation of most of its productive powers and talents. Meanwhile 50,000 children die unnecessarily of starvation and preventable diseases *every day* and 100 million children suffer protein deficiencies that threaten mental retardation. If capitalism wants to take credit for the flow of goodies this way and that, doesn't it have to take credit for the fact that some goodies never go in certain directions? Capitalism has climbed on the charts. It is now number one with a bullet. But capitalism is not only theft, it is also murder. Capitalism's chart, apparently, belongs in the post office. Celebration is premature.

And capitalism treats the earth with abandon too. Asbestos, carbon monoxide, formaldehyde, lead, nitrogen oxide, pesticides, radon, tobacco smoke, and organic gases from paints, solvents, aerosol sprays, and disinfectants corrupt the environment where we live and work and thereby reduce the quality of our health and our longevity. Waste dumps threaten our water and air. Acid rain depletes forest life. The greenhouse effect threatens all life. Meanwhile government agencies undertake to study the relevant problems yet again, while 50,000 people work in the tobacco industry alone.

Suppose all the above could be fixed. Suppose it was possible to have Sweden everywhere, social democracy for all. It would be better, to be sure, but not good enough. Even in its best Swedish designer clothes, capitalism still means that most people must work for others, following orders and not determining what and how they produce and how it's distributed. Wage slavery, commodity fetishism, and economic alienation in*evitably* characterize even Swedish social democratic-style capitalism. In short, capitalism's inevitable characteristics thwart human creativity, solidarity, and hope. Even at its absolute best, which can never persist for long simultaneously in all capitalist countries, capitalism deserves elimination, not celebration.

Yet while all of this characterizes our lives, our pundits, our scholars, the fruit of our educational apparatus, tell us that "everything is wonderful, Western civilization is great, and anyone doubting that is a demented ideologue." This shouldn't be surprising. After all, capitalism triumphant means that capitalism helps decide who gets degrees and what they learn. Contrary to myth, human talent and insight is crushed in most people and controlled in those few who are allowed to retain and exercise it. Out of 600,000 people in the U.S. doing scientific research, less than one percent choose their own research subject and less than four percent of research is aimed at other than immediate profit for some sponsoring and directing institution.

Does any dictatorship achieve that kind of regimentation? No wonder Eastern European elites are starting to agree that their system is an outmoded way to organize the lining of their own pockets.

You get the idea. At some level we *all* already know how disgustingly degrading and debilitating capitalism is. Not just leftists, but nearly everyone who lives in this society is familiar with its crimes. Not the details of course, not the scale, but the broad strokes. So why in the face of this grotesquery do so many do so little to eliminate it?

I believe the answer is that (1) we don't think there is any possibility of beating City Hall and its armies, Exxon and its minions, ABC and its tentacles, and (2) we have grave doubts that it would be worth the effort to beat them anyhow. We would just win a new world, the same as the old world.

If so, then the most disgusting thing about the current celebrations of capitalism is not that they disguise capitalism's ills. Everyone knows that these ills exist. No disguise would be sufficient. Instead, what the celebrations do is strengthen people's cynicism about the possibility of ever overthrowing capitalism and about the hope that any other system could be better. It is perfectly possible to know all of capitalism's ills and still think it is the best *humanly possible* option. All that is necessary is that you think people are genetically greedy, anti-social, and violent, which, of course, is exactly what capitalism makes us think.

That being so, while reassertions of the detailed truth about capitalism's ills are important, it is even more critical to address (1) what can be done to overthrow capitalism, patriarchy, homophobia, political authoritarianism, and racism, and (2) what we can replace them with and why and how something better really can work.

No amount of criticism of capitalism's failings will alone cause citizens to actively reject its defining relations. Only compelling visions of an alternative way to live and convincing formulations of how to attain it can turn knowledge of oppression into desires for change. We who write about the world need not only shift our focus toward vision and strategy, but also make sure our message is heard loud and clear.

—January 1990

History's End: A Drug Den?!

Bush is apoplectic. For him, the society that has successfully employed the free market to perfectly serve our human desires is becoming a drug-infested husk of humanity gone bad. How could this be? Bush says we must wage war on the drug scourge. He tells us he wants to lead the charge.

Bush has one thing right. Many people *are* being destroyed by addictive drugs that cause spiritual, mental, and material debilitation. Addictions do wreak havoc on friends, relatives, and workmates. They do induce criminal behavior to pay the piper.

However, determining just which drugs to wage war on presents more of a problem than Bush allows. For example, how about alcohol, which ruins tens of millions of lives, causes tens of thousands of auto deaths yearly, and disrupts millions of families at the hands of stupor-induced household violence? Did Bush mention martinis as bad stuff? Or how about cigarettes? They don't reduce competence or induce violence like alcohol, but if you add up all the smoke-induced cancers and cardiac arrests, they do plenty of harm. Has Bush turned in relatives for mainlining Marlboros? And how about TV, the nightly news, and sit-coms? In a serious discussion of addictions, certainly we ought to assess whether Peter Jennings or Alf belong in the drug category. Is two hours of TV a day enough to constitute addiction? Three, four, five, six?

And finally, what about advertising and consumerism? Does buying for the sake of the rush, regardless of the quality or usefulness of the product, indicate a psyche succumbing to addiction? Is Sears a den of drugged-out iniquity? Is there anything in this society not connected with "addiction"?

Between you and me, Bush is no dummy. And neither are his close advisers. Their drug policies are well thought out. Discovering what those policies will really do to society reveals much about the Bush administration's priorities.

First, Bush really does want people to be worked up about the threat of drugs to their end-of-history lifestyle.

Second, Bush increases police budgets, proposes new jails, and legitimates repressive laws. Obviously, he really does want to translate people's newly aggravated concerns and fears into a stronger police force.

Third, Bush portrays Colombian cartels as the prime purveyors of the drug scourge and thus the biggest current enemies of our national security. A reasonable deduction is that Bush wants a new excuse for Third World adventurism now that "anti-communism" is losing its appeal.

Fourth, despite an overflow of addicts unable to obtain desired medical help, Bush proposes only very moderate increases in funding for detox, prevention, and education. Apparently, Bush doesn't really care much about people who need help but can't afford to get it on their own.

And fifth, to pay for his drug war, Bush doesn't cut military expenditures, or tax corporations. He proposes slicing housing assistance by $50 million dollars. Clearly drugs are a scourge, but only when they cost corporations in lost productivity due to a doped workforce or when they threaten to infest suburban communities where little rich kids might get hooked before their time. Obviously, a solution to the drug problem can't be redistributive lest the solution has worse impact on Bush's friends than the drugs themselves. Bush doesn't want to give money or services to the poor. He wants to keep desirable deprivations of the poor from hurting the rich. Bush wants his cake (drug money). He wants to eat it (interventionism). And he wants to make sure that we get only crumbs (decreased social spending), even if he has to give us lung cancer (addiction) and false curatives (guns and jails) to keep us at bay.

Drugs are a national disaster because people abuse them, deal them, and fight over them. People abuse drugs because they suffer alienation, deprivation, abuse, and hopelessness. People deal drugs because they don't have a better way to make a living. People fight over drugs to get a piece of the action.

All this is not caused by Colombian drug-lords, or street-corner thugs, or even the Mafia. They only scavenge on the misery. The misery is caused by "legitimate" institutions that consign most of the population to deadening obedience and tiresome, often dangerous, and nearly always boring and undignified labor. It is caused by the poverty of unemployment. And it is caused by the indignity of racial and sexual abuse—all of which, remember—mark "the end of history" that is the triumph of capitalism.

But what about the availability of drugs, the supply problem, so to speak? Isn't the Medillín cartel the principal problem here?

No. Medillín is a means of widespread distribution, not its cause. Widespread distribution arises because drug-running is profitable enough to attract "entrepreneurs" out to make millions. Some, like the money launderers at the big banks, want the drug profits to finance their own haciendas in Columbia, Miami, or New York. Others, like Oliver North and George Bush, want the big bucks to surreptitiously finance gun-running, death-dealing, and general mayhem in Afghanistan, Nicaragua, and other "hotspots."

Bush says he wants under $10 billion to shut down a market worth hundreds of billions. Does anyone believe he expects to succeed? It is common knowledge that cutting off external sources just increases production within the U.S and that reducing access to less dangerous drugs just increases the distribution of more dangerous ones. Worse, cutting housing subsidies fuels drug demand. Bush understands this. He is implicated both in getting funds for projects he likes from drug sales, and in using the trade's existence to justify Third World adventurism. Rhetoric aside, Bush is a drug kingpin.

As profoundly venal as it is, drug use in the U.S. helps disempower downtrodden constituencies. This benefits elites too much for them to let their desire to reduce drug losses in workplaces and drug dangers in suburbia overly reduce drug addiction in the ghettos.

What would be a good anti-drug program? First, we should legalize drugs and use incentives to regulate drug use by taxing their purchase in proportion to their dangers. Tax nonfilter cigarettes higher than filtered ones. Tax hard liquor heavily and beer barely at all. Tax heroin, cocaine, and cigarettes heavily. By these means the illegal and violent element of drug distribution would be eliminated just as the criminality surrounding drinking was wiped out with the end of prohibition. Moreover, just as alcoholism was reduced significantly as a problem in England when taxes there favored beer, so alcoholism and all dangerous drugs would drop in use here as tax policies push use toward more benign options.

Second, if we want to reduce demand for debilitating drugs we should reduce the reasons why people prefer drug-induced unreality to reality. This would require reducing military spending and other boondoggles for the rich and introducing in their place redistributive programs to reduce poverty, racism, sexism, and other oppressions.

In the long term, to fully win the war on dangerous drugs, we will need to eliminate the source of their appeal, not by bombing Third World poppy fields but by replacing profit with human dignity as a motive force in U.S. production, by replacing spectacle elections and economic dictatorship with collective self management, by replacing racism and ethnocentrism and religious bigotry in U.S. community life with a diversity of cultures respectful of diverse solutions to issues of identity and celebration, and by replacing U.S. reproductive, sexual, and socialization institutions that denigrate and repress women and homosexuals with alternative diverse and equitable ways of living and loving.

In the short run, we need radical reforms—legalization, taxes in proportion to the danger of drugs, and income redistribution to better the lives of society's worse off. In the long run, we need revolution to create new institutions that do not breed despair. These are serious programs for reducing drug decay in our society. Bush isn't even offering Band-Aids. He just wants to make sure that the drug cancer doesn't damage organs he benefits from while it wreaks useful havoc elsewhere.   ٭

— October 1989

Live Outside The Law

W e call the Supreme Court "supreme" because it is the highest court in the land. But where rot rises rapidly, "highest" is also lowest. Have the supremos done their job?

- By returning abortion adjudication to the states, they have returned disposition of women's bodies to patriarchal authorities—again.

- By witholding public abortion money, they have slapped down the poor—again.

- By rejecting reproductive rights as favored by large majorities, they have reinforced the truism that "U.S. government" and "of the people" are opposites—again.

- By making affirmative action rarely implementable, barely enforceable, and a potential aid to whites, they have made nonwhite minorities and women easier targets for gross exploitation—again.

- By asserting that electrocuting a child can foster justice, they have legitimated the state's unrestrained use of violent retribution—again.

Does anyone doubt that before long our numero uno judges will reassert capitalists' rights to treat workers worse than machines—again?

I find all this as disgusting as the next person. It is not just abstract legalistic blather to justify inflated salaries. These supremely uncivil decisions throw us back to a near medieval time when unwanted children were thrown away with other disposables. Why is it happening?

Reported Motives

The *New York Times* tells us anti-abortionists want to "save lives and strengthen the family." The *Washington Post* tells us anti-affirmative actionists want "universal equality before the law." NBC tells us death-sentencers want "freedom for all from criminal assault." And media moguls and sensible citizens alike accept these rationalizations without first investigating how the words fit the behavior. So let's investigate.

First, anti-abortionists' claims that they want to save lives and defend human rights are negated by the fact that: (a) with few exceptions, anti-abortionists gleefully advocate policies that decimate millions of human lives—whether they be lives lacking housing, lives suffering AIDS, lives getting wiped away by death squads, or lives withering from hunger, and, (b) even if there are some who truly believe they are acting compassionately, the prevailing ideology among anti-abortionists is one of misogyny, i.e., one that devalues women's lives, attempts to control women's sexuality, and generally punishes women for acting autonmously.

Someone ought to check the percentage of anti-abortionists who support the death penalty for children. Someone ought to investigate how many of them advocate an end to multinational exploitation abroad. What, for example, do anti-abortionists demand when told that 10,000 children in India go blind each year from a deficiency of vitamin A that could be prevented by a nickel's worth of vitamins per child? Do they threaten to obstruct Congress until it coughs up these vitamins? Do they threaten mayhem unless our government and corporations stop imposing the elitist systems that bring on these ravages? Or, do they piously demand that the bearers of this type of unseemly news realize that it is just God's way and that we ought not intervene?

Likewise, the idea that electrocutionists want mostly to reduce criminal assault suffers dual illogic. First, most murders are unpremeditated and carried out by folks who never even consider the possibility that they will get caught. Deduction: Since the death penalty *doesn't* deter murder, clearly electrocutionists can't intelligently support the death penalty to reduce criminal assault. Second, if electrocutionists doubt the latter point and still support electrocution to reduce crime, shouldn't they also favor reducing poverty, providing free health care, improving public education, and expanding available housing, since these policies would obviously also reduce crime rates? Deduction: Since electrocutionists can easily learn that the death penalty doesn't deter crime and don't support other policies that obviously would deter crime, another motive must be at work.

And, finally, surely we can see that it is no accident that anti-affirmative actionists proclaim the need to attain "fairness before the law" only when brandishing that slogan can reinforce unfairness for everyone different from them in race or gender. To anti-affirmative actionists who deny this venal fact we ask, do you support a system of legal defense that would set universal fixed lawyer rates and provide public subsidies for anyone unable to meet their legal bill? Do you support any policy at all that would redress inequality and unfairness before the law, where the poor get shuttled like cattle and the rich walk free with their millionaire attorneys? No. Well then, QED, fairness before the law is not your motive.

So we have seen once again that why people do things and what they say about why they do things often differ, and that puncturing other people's silly hypocritical alibis is usually pretty simple. Yet the fact remains that one hypocritical anti-abortion claim—that is that "they want to strengthen families"—still befuddles many people. Many believe this rhetoric without realizing that anti-abortionists want to "strengthen families" only in the same self-serving way that the U.S. government wants to "spread freedom throughout the Third World"—that is, only when other higher and often contradictory priorities are met first.

How do I deduce this? Suppose you had some power in Washington and wanted to strengthen families as your highest priority. What would you do?

First, since obviously the pressures endured by women who lack the opportunity to undertake abortions can only disrupt families and lack of abortions can in no way strengthen families, you would *support* reproductive rights.

Second, understanding the logic of material incentives, you might also support major tax breaks for marriage and major tax penalties for divorce; substantial family subsidies for housing that would be withdrawn when families break up; and legislation to improve health care, public access, and education to reduce social pressures that disrupt families. You might even attack drug addiction and alcoholism and, in Bush's case, stop dealing this death yourself.

It follows that since anyone trying to reduce family breakup would support these or similar pro-family policies and since none of this, or anything like it, is advocated by anti-abortionists, anti-abortionists cannot be too pro-family. In fact, since anti-abortionists often support policies that decrease the material and emotional stability of families, to say that they seek to strengthen families can only be doublespeak.

Real Motives

So what is their goal? First and foremost, anti-abortionists want women subordinate to men. In the family, they want women in traditional roles. Outside the family, they want women poor and pliant. They prefer family to nonfamily as long as women are subordinate, just as corporate capital prefers democracy to dictatorship as long as Third World workers remain exploitable. No more, no less. Their revered values are the subordination of women, the sanctity of property, the subordination of "inferior cultures," the authority of the state, and even the profits of the liquor and drug cartels.

In the same way, the totality of their policy attachments indicates that anti-affirmative actionists want nonwhite cultures reduced to a status of inferiority to bolster the dominance of "white culture" and to ensure a steady supply of folks for the most menial, poorest paid, and most dangerous tasks in society, or to entertain whites. It doesn't matter that nonwhite constituencies are disproportionately poor due to historic *and* contemporary racism. It doesn't matter that due to today's racism they enjoy fewer and more degraded options than whites of comparable income. Racism needn't be redressed by affirmative action. That would treat people "unequally before the law."

Likewise, death-penalty advocates want a powerful state to defend the interests that the state always defends: private property of the rich and the prerogatives of male, white, legal, and economic elites to do whatever they want as long as no precedents that can be used against them are established. It is fine that policies that would really abate theft, drug dealing, rape, and even murder, aren't undertaken. It is even good, because so long as elite interests are properly defended by reinforced police bureaucracies and stiff enforcement for crimes against rich peoples' property, crimes against women and minorities and poor people serve useful dis-organizing, dis-empowering purposes.

But all this should not surprise leftists. It complies with our analyses of a capitalist, patriarchal, racist, authoritarian amalgam of institutions that interactively benefit various elites at the expense of everyone else. When 1960s and 1970s movements threatened this structure, the system grudgingly gave some ground to forestall additional losses. Now it wants everything back—and the number one court in the land is going for it.

Winning This War

In short, we are witnessing a war of position. On each axis—gender, race, class, authority—ground can be won or lost. Elites want to push the line of battle back over our bodies to a position of greater denial for us. We want to push the other way, over their bodies, to greater freedom and justice.

The fact that elites oppose reproductive rights shouldn't surprise feminists who maintain that reproductive rights not only affect women wanting abortions, but also women's autonomy and power vis-a-vis men, as well as how women's gains can interface with other progressive trends. And the same goes for affirmative action and freedom from state repression. Why should we be surprised when white culture and the state defend themselves and try to regain lost ground?

The irony of all this is that the court is a slowpoke. As the social movements of the 1960s grew tired and weak—partly from assault, partly from internal schisms—the right saw its opening and marched across the policy turf, pushing us back in the 1970s and 1980s. Three or four years ago they had us depleted and disgusted and they might have successfully legally sanctified their gains without spurring us into too powerful an opposition. By rightist logic, the supremos should have sought legal enforcement of right-wing gains then.

But they waited too long. They are seeking a knockout at just the moment when progressives are getting a second wind. Women are going to fight back, minorities are going to fight back, and working people are about to begin solidifying their own positions and organizations to fight back. So as bad as it looks in this round, if we have the necessary energy and courage, soon the war of position can be pushed forward in our direction.

When this occurs, different constituencies need to synchronize strategies, share resources, and not stop pushing until the society is transformed to its roots. For if our current temporary reversals teach us anything, it ought to be that in the absence of solidarity we are weak and that nothing less than complete victory will be comprehensive or permanent.

— September 1989

Uncle Thomas

In no particular order, here are a few thoughts about the Thomas hearings and Thomas's ascension to the Supreme Court.

(1) On the plus side, Anita Hill's accusations would have been dismissed without a thought had not women forced the Senate's attention.

(2) Nonetheless, feminists' inability to carry dissent about Thomas's nomination to the broader population has shown that, like the left in general, feminism has yet to gain significant support throughout society.

(3) Thomas's nomination began with a humongous lie: Bush claiming he chose Thomas because Thomas was the best candidate.

In fact, Thomas was chosen because he passed the administration's ideological litmus test (and because being Black would make him harder for liberals to attack). Having swallowed Bush's big lie before the hearings even began, the media revealed again their utter disdain for inexpedient truth. Moreover, no one, right or left, believed Thomas's sworn claim that he has never discussed *Roe v. Wade*, yet no commentator called this what it was, perjury.

(4) As a result, we now have a Supreme Court justice who openly and repeatedly perjured himself on national television. This is aptly despicable. The highest court is openly corrupt. The highest deliberative body is venal and stupid. Each exists to buttress elites at all costs.

(5) Thomas's/Bush's choice of the denial defense is instructive. I thought they would say he had made some jokes and otherwise teased Hill, but that she had greatly exaggerated his words and never indicated any discomfort. Thomas would tearfully apologize if he had caused her any pain, make evident that he thought he was only joking around with her participation, note that he didn't realize how prudish she was, note that he strongly opposes sexual harassment, and so on. But no. Thomas and Bush opted for total denial against all the evidence. They somehow knew that they could intimidate the Democrats. obfuscate the issues, reel in the media, and even convince most of the populace. Aside from venality, in the tradition of Goebbels, they showed an adroit astuteness regarding public opinion and the ease with which it can be bludgeoned into line.

(6) Getting to the facts, everyone had two choices:

- Believe that Anita Hill was telling the truth and that Clarence Thomas was lying to defend himself.

Statistically this would be a 50-50 proposition for any randomly chosen man even with no evidence. In this case, after the corroborating testimony, lie detector test, etc., it was a virtual certainty.

- Believe Thomas was telling the truth and that Hill dreamed up the sex-harassment scenario.

Remember, Hill not only didn't come forward this time, she didn't in the past either, even after reporting the harassment to her friends. For Thomas to be telling the truth, Hill must have fantasized it all.

Senators and media alike pilloried Hill to imply that she might fit this improbable mold but found no evidence for the claim. No one even questioned—much less pilloried—Thomas to see if he might fit the typical mold proposed for him. No one noted the relevance of his repeated lying to the committee on other matters, his history with pornography, etc. No one clarified that the only thing that had to have happened for Thomas to be unacceptable to the court in the eyes of *every* Senator is that he perjured himself on the stand, which he would have done if he so much as asked Hill out 10 years ago, since he denied doing so under oath.

(7) Given that a reasonable estimate of the number of men who have engaged in sexual harassment is one in two, and remembering that in this country garbage rises, it is overwhelmingly probable that:

- At least 30 or 40 Senators, including at least three or four and probably a good many more on the committee, are as guilty of sexual harassment as Clarence Thomas.

- Very few if any Senators care an iota whether an individual has committed sexual harassment.

- No Senators would like to legitimate the idea that sexual behavior can justify dismissal from the corridors of power.

All this helps explain why the questions asked of Thomas were so pathetic, though any good prosecutor could have ripped him to shreds.

(8) In any case, as an instance of investigation and evaluation, from start to finish, the hearing was a gigantic, hypocritical farce. The committee was a pack of wolves judging a wolf accused of nothing more than being a wolf. This is, of course, the norm for this type case.

(9) By voting Clarence Thomas to the Supreme Court, the Senate said that in a confrontation between a subordinate woman and her male superior,

allegations of sexual harassment, however well proven, have no bearing on the latter's career. Not only does our government prefer that, it will enforce it.

Coming forward continues to mean great pain and, nearly always, no gain. Everyone knows this. Along with rape and sexual discrimination, sexual harassment enforces male dominance. This is not easily overturned, even in a preposterous instance, much less systematically.

(10) Because of this clear message, we can expect that in the future from the about 5 percent of those harassed who currently file some sort of grievance, the number will drop even lower. Many deem this a horrible byproduct of the hearings. But I'm not so sure.

Do even half the women that currently file through existing channels get redress? A third? A tenth? In lieu of a better rate of success, what is the gain from more people making charges? Would we recommend that our daughters, mothers, and woman friends file through existing channels? Not filing means carrying around the pain that often reduces one's capacity to face reality. But filing in the absence of real change in gender relations means failing, which means suffering greater pain, again with ensuing self diminution.

The hearings showed the elite's response to women complaining about the conduct of better-connected, more powerful men. If Thomas had been rejected after the hearings, it *might* have led to a *temporary* willingness to address sexual harassment more equitably. But in the absence of a mass militant response enlarging these gains, it would also have sent *a false* message that sexual harassment is taken seriously by existing institutions. Instead of being pushed to confront the unchanging truth that existing channels crush women, women could have made believe all was well.

Sexism is structural. We can't overcome it solely by argument and evidence anymore than we can overcome class domination or racism solely by argument and evidence. Argument and evidence are necessary, but so is organization, movement, activism, pressure, and struggle. Since leftists all supposedly understand this, why are so many surprised at the outcome?

(11) Thomas will be a loose cannon on the court. He is a right-wing ideologue. His prior testimony already revealed that he is a consummate liar and opportunist. Now we can deduce that for him as for other mini-despots there are two kinds of people: those in his camp and those out to get him.

To have a Clarence Thomas on the Supreme Court bodes badly for women, the accused, the poor, Blacks, the environment, and just about everything worthy and just. *Roe v. Wade*'s days are numbered. But again, there is another side. Thomas now usefully symbolizes that while our government has power, it has no legitimate authority. Moreover, if Thomas had been rejected, his replacement would have been no better, only not so self-evidently horrible.

(12) Orrin Hatch is a right-wing thug. I suppose we already knew that, but many didn't know how easily he could get away with it in public.

Thugs like Hatch, David Duke, and others are surfacing and liberals are sometimes too ignorant, other times too compromised, and always too confused and cowardly to deal with them. One of the more frightening outcomes of this whole fiasco is the continuing accrual of influence to right-wing ideologues masquerading as politicians. In this regard, the only redeeming short-term hope, however slight, is that the affair might not be over. What if in the coming weeks more evidence regarding Clarence Thomas surfaces? Maybe further testimony? Maybe new instances of harassment? However sick the dynamic is, we can hope that those who supported Thomas will suffer as much as Thomas when he takes his great fall. The all-too-conceivable alternative, that we'll see Hatch running for the White House with Thomas at the head of the Supreme Court and Duke running the FBI, is truly scary.

(13) The sight of Clarence Thomas bullying Senators with his claims of lynching would have been amusing, were it not so sickening. Here is a man who attacked affirmative action as a "narcotic of dependency" and said of civil rights leaders that all they do is "bitch, bitch, bitch, moan and moan and whine," suddenly deciding that racism is so great that it has led white America to fabricate stories to legally "lynch" him.

Thomas has given new meaning to the term hypocrisy and everyone who bought his claims has given new meaning to the term gullible. Only the Republican Senators who claimed to be supporting Thomas on grounds of battling against racism can compete as hypocrites, and only those scoring the Republicans high for humanity are more gullible.

(14) And speaking of the intrusion of race into the deliberations, just where was Jesse Jackson during all this? Was he somehow shut out of the public debate? I find it hard to believe that he couldn't have gotten a national forum to assail Thomas as a hypocritical, reactionary, lying, sexist, sell-out who has no right calling Blacks to his defense after having so callously disregarded the needs and rights of Black people for so long.

Why couldn't Jackson lecture the Senators that their reticence to cross-examine Thomas was despicable? Why couldn't he provide questions that should be asked and analysis of ongoing revelations to provide context? Why couldn't he explain what legal lynching is, show when and where it occurs, and tell why Thomas was not subject to it? Why couldn't he defend Anita Hill when it counted, broadening the discussion and increasing its credibility?

It is hard to imagine that Jackson could not have gained a role as a commentator on one of the networks. Had he done so and used the opportunity to discredit Thomas and to help legitimate women's anger:

- Would Thomas have had a scintilla of support in the Black community?

- Couldn't there have emerged greatly strengthened ties between the women's movement and the civil rights movement?

I can't think of a single excuse Jackson could offer to explain how he could so completely avoid coming forward on this issue. As with undermining the Rainbow Coalition, Jackson's silence didn't make good personal political sense either. After all, Jackson could have cemented literally hundreds of women's organizations into his constituency. For Jackson, the cost of antagonizing Democrats like Biden, Leahy, Metzenbaum, and Kennedy was apparently too high a price to pay not only for being honest, not only for fighting for the truth and for fighting against Uncle Thomas and for movement legitimation and activism, but even for dramatically increasing the breadth of his own popular support. All I can figure is that the only prize Jackson's eyes are on is a favorable notice at Democratic cocktail parties. I hope someone can explain why my reading is wrong, for example that Jackson did try, but got shut out.

(15) The oft-repeated idea that men don't understand what hurts women and why women react so strongly is preposterous. What is so complicated about the idea that a weaker party can be cajoled, manipulated, denigrated, or maligned—sexually or otherwise—by a stronger party? What is so complicated about reticence to confront authority in a no-win situation? What is so complicated about the added dimensions of guilt associated with sexual harassment? Nothing. To say that men don't experience precisely the same form of degradation as women is, of course, true. But claiming to "not understand" sexual degradation and its roots is a way to defend sexist behavior without taking responsibility for doing so.

(16) The possibility of undertaking massive public political education via television has become more evident than ever. So is, therefore, the establishment's need to avoid such education. Imagine a week of open hearings on income inequality, homelessness, health care, the environment, or racial exclusion. Assuming substantial competing claims—for example, the health-care system is fine versus the health care system sickens us, or George Bush is racist versus he isn't, or homeless people deserve what they suffer versus homelessness is a crime against the homeless—in every case the country would be highly involved. U.S. citizens are literate enough to become highly politicized very quickly. The *existence* of a massive apparatus to preclude political and social debate helps prevent progress. Likewise, developing means of mass popular political and social debate could promote change.

(17) The case against Clarence Thomas was overwhelming before the issue of sexual harassment ever arose. The man was transparently opportunist and a liar, presumably sufficient reason for anyone to oppose him as a justice. Women, minorities, and poor people should have had little trouble discerning that Thomas deserved no support. Blacks, perhaps above all, should have been hostile. It is understandable why Blacks would want a Black on the Supreme Court. It is not understandable, assuming they had sufficient information to draw the conclusion, that they would want Uncle Thomas as much as polls

show they did. Either the U.S. public is the most highly educated and informa-
tion-glutted bunch of fools and followers, public-opinion polls are for shit, or
some very complex dynamics are driving people's preferences.

(18) The fact that no one on the left has the slightest idea which of these
interpretations is true says something quite depressing not only about the public
but about us.

Polls showed a negligible gender gap, more Blacks than whites, and an
overall majority believing Thomas. How do we explain that? What is causing
even white racists to support him? Do they recognize that race conflict is not
a conflict of species but of cultural communities and perceive that Uncle
Thomas is not a member of the hated Black community? Are they following
the government's lead? Are they just protecting the patriarch?

Are women who believe Thomas doing so because they don't want to ratify
Hill because of what that would imply for their future reactions toward
harassment, or, for that matter, for their past reactions to it? Having taken the
blame so long, was this process too abrupt to expect women to suddenly break
free of acquiescence?

Are men simply defending their prerogative by saying they believe Thomas
when they don't, but don't think it matters?

How many, if any, are merely rebelling against the Senate, sympathizing
with an underdog, or even resisting presumed racism? Why should we deny
Thomas, many might think, when he's no more guilty than the Senators?

Not being able to answer these questions means an organizer has little if
any idea how to communicate with the U.S. public. Once the sexual discrimination charges were levied and we were treated to Thomas the sexist, Thomas
the liar, Thomas the bully, the polls told us the public rallied to him in greater
numbers than previously. If this is false, why don't we unequivocally know it
is false by virtue of our thoroughgoing ties throughout the country? Answer:
Because we on the left have no such ties. And if it is true, what does it mean?

(19) NOW and representatives from labor, citizens' action groups, and
many other constituencies months back began the long process of founding a
new political party. Some suspected that NOW's break with the Democrats
was a facade to force greater respect before coming back into the fold. Others
felt that there would be insufficient willingness on the public's part to break
with the Democrats on the presumption that with them there was a better chance
to attain immediate gains. People are seeking something good from these
hearings. Barring fascism, further dissolution of respect for the government is
good. Specifically, it is hard to imagine leaders of NOW and other progressive
organizations who are considering a break with the Democrats not having their
resolve strengthened by the Democrats' incompetent spinelessness. Moreover,
public receptivity for a new party must have been enlarged.

— November 1991

Same Old (White Boy's) Song

This winter's *Whole Earth Review* is their 20th anniversary issue and includes 85 articles chosen by the editors to inspire and inform *Whole Earth's* readers on the general themes of its "maverick reporting." The one-page articles come from poets, new-age activists, anthropologists, hippies, consumer rights activists, reporters, Earth Firsters, social ecologists, economists, computer scientists, and other *Whole Earth* and "small is beautiful" counter-culture supporters ranging from Edward Abbey to Wendell Berry, Murray Bookchin to Jerry Brown, Hazel Henderson to Ralph Nader, Stewart Brand to Tim Leary, Ivan Illych to Gary Snyder, and Eric Utne to Anne Waldman. Of the 85 contributors, 100 percent are white and just under 90 percent are male.

The Nation, a progressive magazine publishing for more than 120 years and currently enjoying the second widest circulation of any left-of-center periodical, highlighted in its November 28 issue a symposium in which various *Nation* editors and editorial board members discuss "First Thoughts on the Election." Of the five participants, all are white men. Moreover, the group would have remained 100 percent white male had *The Nation* added all their regular columnists to the mix.

At the fantastically well-organized, well-attended, and well-funded anti-anti-communism conference held in Boston, Massachusetts, last November, talks, panels, and plenaries included speakers from all over the world. Though the focus was the dynamics and impact of anti-communism throughout the world, it also included its impact on foreign policy, public attitudes, on women and the women's movement, the black community, all kinds of politics, repression, etc. Of 151 speakers at the conference, 30 percent were women, and just over 20 percent were Third World (which reflects international more than U.S. participation). Of 32 speakers on major panels, there were 4 women, 28 men, and 11 people of color.

These are only three instances of racial and sexual imbalance that could be assembled covering the full range of left projects, publishing, and organizing.

My complaint is old hat, yes. But it is old hat because the condition persists—not because critics are knee-jerk nags.

Why should anyone care? Short answers include:

- Because sexual and racial imbalances are immoral no matter where or in what degree they arise;

- Because racial and sexual imbalances denigrate everyone who instigates or suffers their consequences;

- Because no movement that regards Third World people and women as fodder is morally worthy;

- Because most Third World people and women will not long support any movement that regards them as fodder;

- Because the left must build an inclusive movement if it is ever to win anything;

- Because diverse perspectives enhance understanding and their absence induces ignorance;

- Because much of what (some of) the old boys currently monopolizing the circuit say and write is already well known and getting a bit boring.

So why do imbalances persist? Here are some possible explanations of persistent racial and sexual imbalance and my replies.

(1) Imbalance is an accident.

Get serious! Accidents are random and go both ways. If sexual and racial imbalance were accidental, half the time there would be more women than men and more than a representative number of Blacks, Latinos, and other "non-whites." This hardly ever happens. The "accident" excuse displays either extreme ignorance of what the word "accident" means or an extreme lack of ingenuity at alibiing Neanderthal behavior.

(2) Imbalance derives from habit.

What?! Habitual imbalance is racism and sexism. If this is someone's answer, that person should fess up to fancying Klan consciousness á là excuse number 4 below.

(3) Imbalance arises when people reach out to folks they already know.

So why do publishers, editors, and conference organizers know mostly white men year after year? And why is this an excuse? Is laziness in the face of oppression a sign of political wisdom?

(4) Publishers, editors, and conference sponsors believe women, Blacks, Latinos, Asians, and Native Americans cannot write infor-

mative books or articles or give good speeches so it is a waste of
time to seek their equal representation.

Please, this excuse is only included for logical completeness. Anyone for
whom it applies needs more help than this column can offer, even if their
delusions stem from ignorance rather than venality.

(5) Publishers, editors, and conference sponsors aggressively seek gender and racial representation but fail to find qualified folks and rather
than reduce the quality of their product fall back on better trained,
more experenced, white men who are, after all, the experts.

This is the workhorse, all-purpose answer. Many give and believe this
answer. But it's bullshit on three counts. First, there are more than enough
readily-available, highly-proficient Third World and women writers and
speakers to provide excellent contributions on any topic any leftist might need.
Second, white men often demonstrate little insight into critically important
facets of topics they address—for example, about issues of gender, sexuality,
and race. Third, note that even if racism and sexism has so isolated women,
Blacks, Latinos, Native Americans, and others from writing and speaking
opportunities that very few were skilled at these avocations; organizers,
editors, and publishers should still seek racial and sexual balance even though
they would have to include less experienced and less polished writers and
speakers. Why? For the same reasons that apply when there are amply qualified
folks but, in addition, because under the more difficult conditions no practice
other than inclusion could as effectively inject new thoughts and experiences
into the radical political equation or provide experience and polish where it had
been previously denied.

I raise the issue of providing opportunity even to those who don't yet have
"exalted skills" (assuming we could agree on what those might be) because it
bears on the need to bring new people into the political circuit. The first few
times out, most new people do less well than some old-timers. Experience (up
to the point of inducing rote behavior) helps. But with a forward-looking
timeline, editors, publishers, and organizers should make choices that continually develop new talent and new skills in new people. Now, instead, a few
people are horribly over-extended, while new folks are not being developed.

But a question remains: Since many candidates do exist who would create
better balance in books, magazines, and conferences, why do imbalances
persist? Beyond special explanations of particular instances, I can find only
four widely applicable answers.

• First and most benign: Many women, Blacks, Latinos, Native Americans, and Asians are so suspicious of established largely white-male-

administered progressive institutions that they do not communicate with them and do not welcome their communications.

- Second: Women and Third World people often have a style that publishers, editors, and conference organizers don't understand/appreciate so that the publishers, editors, and conference organizers exclude whole ranges of insight not even realizing what they are missing.

- Third: Women, Blacks, Latinos, Native Americans, etc., often write and say things that threaten comfortable hierarchical norms that publishers, editors, and conference organizers favor, so that a disproportionate preference for white males is often a conscious choice to preserve favored policies.

- Finally, and most disturbing: Publishers, editors, and conference organizers don't seek gender and racial balance because, despite their own inclinations, they think (or even know from experience) that audiences who currently buy their products and attend their forums, and/or donors who currently help pay the bills for their efforts, won't support such inclusions, and because they know that they do not have the resources to reach out to wider audiences who would.

So, what's the solution? Within the rubric of the values and focus of their projects, publishers, editors, and conference organizers must meet representative participation goals no matter how they feel about what the new folks are saying. And to make these acts of political integrity fiscally wise, funders, readers, conference-goers, and everyone who relates to projects, institutions, and campaigns of the left must welcome sexual and racial balance and must vote for it with feet, funds, and support.

Highly noticed and excoriated for at least two decades, racial and sexual imbalance in communicative and organizing projects can be eliminated as soon as we really want to eliminate it rather than merely discuss it.

Then perhaps we will address another less noticed balance problem: How many union members and how many working people who are not professional writers, lawyers, doctors, or university academics are represented in the pages and forums of the progressive political circuit? And, of the professional people who are represented, how many transcend their social circumstances to communicate non-academically and eschew issues that concern only "conceptual workers?" Don't the answers to the "why care" question at the beginning of this article apply not only to gender and race but also to class inclusion?

—January 1989

Take What's Ours

The workers, Mr. Travail and Ms. Exertion, sell labor power. The capitalist, Mr. Moneybags, buys labor power and uses it to create commodities to later sell. With federal manipulation, monopoly massaging, and billions in advertising, markets allocate the results. Of course, capitalisms differ in population, levels of monopoly and empire, their entwined political, cultural and kinship relations, and in numbers of professionals, managers, and other "coordinators" operating "between labor and capital." But even skipping rampant inattention to these complexities, many activists rely too much on capitalists' non-existent largesse and not enough on worker militancy.

> *People suffer from oppression, and to save themselves from this oppression, they are advised to invent common means for the improvement of their situation, to be applied by authorities, while they themselves continue to submit. Obviously, nothing results but a strengthening of the power, and consequently intensification of the oppression.*
>
> *— Leo Tolstoy*

Class struggle is not just a rhetorical catch phrase uttered by suspender snapping, old-style lefties. In a capitalist economy, capitalists really do maximize their advantages. If workers are strong, they win more. If workers are weak, they win less. Workers get "good things" only as a byproduct of the capitalists' pursuit of profit and power or as a result of victorious struggle. In class struggle, relative power is everything.

For example, when Mr. Travail gets health care, it is not because capitalism respects Mr. Travail's health. If that were true, we would have the best possible health care for everyone, not solely for Moneybags and Co. No, Mr. Travail gets health care:

(1) to stay on the job and produce the wealth his bosses enjoy;

(2) to profit the people who sell him medicine at absurdly high prices;

(3) because other workers have previously organized and *won* good health care.

Workers also get education as a byproduct of capitalists' pursuit of profit or working-class victories, but never because the system wants workers to be fulfilled human beings. Schools teach prospective capitalists how to rule and prospective coordinators how to administer and conceptualize. Without a challenge, they teach prospective workers only what workers need to get along in a complex economy: how to withstand boredom and obey orders.

Likewise, workers' incomes are provided merely so workers will have means to persist in the work that capitalists hire them to do. Workers get more only when they win it.

Capitalists' education, upbringing, and self-identification permit them to care only for their own advance. Even if a particular capitalist's socialization breaks down, markets ensure that if he gives up greed and power he will suffer competitive losses and isolation from his peers. Thus, capitalistic moral behavior is rare and ineffectual—a kind of uncontagious ruling-class pathology. It is a waste of time to try to foster capitalist largesse by argument and/or supplication. No matter how good our arguments and no matter how righteous our petitions, we won't induce much moral behavior, and what we do induce won't accomplish much.

Short of toppling the economic system, to gain economic improvements we will have to get them from people in power. But that doesn't mean we have to regard capitalists' authority as legitimate or act like they have a right to their advantages. To ask capitalists to judge our claims or evaluate our pleas as if capitalists have some intellectual or moral stature entitling them to their authority legitimates a subservient position for ourselves and a domineering position for them, even if we extract some minor gains by doing so.

What do you suppose will satisfy the soul, except to walk free and own no superior?

— *Walt Whitman*

In general, Moneybags practices cost-benefit accounting. If giving us a reform costs him less then enduring our opposition, he will give it. Otherwise, he will cling to every last shred of advantage. Moneybags never institutes changes that increase working people's bargaining power and reduce the bargaining power of capitalists without a fight. Moral claims win nothing. Actions that reveal our growing strength win everything.

In this light we can usefully ask about areas of conflict within the economy: (1) What are the interests of capitalists and workers? (2) What is a useful approach in trying to attain beneficial changes?

Why should Moneybags or workers care whether each workplace will be more or less democratic?

• In a hierarchical workplace, workers start every battle from a position of institutional weakness.

Workers in hierarchical firms have no mechanisms of inter-communication, of assembling and developing their views, of expressing their positions, of knowing the actual circumstances of production, and of rapidly mustering their strength behind preferred policies.

• In a more democratic setting, workers can use votes to secure institutional reforms for immediate benefit *and* to aid future battles.

Democratically participating workers can institute a newsletter to publicize grievances and aims. They can establish assemblies to voice concerns and formulate demands. They can vote to open company books to formulate better pay demands and strike tactics. They can vote for changes in the pace and length of the work day, in product design, in investment choices. Eventually, they can vote to collectively administer their own jobs and to redefine tasks fairly. And if democracy is abrogated when worker preferences clash with capitalist preferences, it will be much easier for workers to know what is going on and to perceive their own rights and escalate their militancy.

But, of course, it is also well known that *partial* "democracy" can co-opt workers into disciplining themselves and conveying important information to management *without* affording workers significant powers over workplace design, organization, wages, timing, or investment.

Since workplace democracy is contrary to the interests of capital, it follows that if workers want workplace democracy but have no organized power, they will get nothing. If they have some organization and militancy, but insufficient understanding and staying power, then they may win partial workplace democracy but it will be massaged until it largely complies with capitalist dictates. However, if workers have powerful organizations able to threaten real losses to capital, they may win real democratic reforms, and may steadily expand these gains by further enlarging their militancy.

Notice that arguing with capitalists that worker democracy will increase worker on-the-job comfort, and thus workplace productivity, is beside the point. Likewise, arguing to capitalists that workers have a right to control their own lives in no way helps. Arguments and ethics are of first-rank importance when posed to fellow workers to win their militant allegiance. They are irrelevant when posed to capitalists concerned only with furthering their own advantages.

How can a rational being be ennobled by anything that is not obtained by its own exertions?

— Mary Wollstonecraft

Why wouldn't everyone benefit from having less unemployment? Capitalists wouldn't want to eliminate unemployment to benefit the unemployed, but why wouldn't they want to eliminate unemployment to benefit themselves?

After all, capitalists make profits by hiring workers, so why not hire all the workers? Why leave some unexploited?

If activists think the answer is that capitalists are being dumb when they permit unemployment, then to gain full employment activists will try to educate capitalists to its merits, and we will get nowhere. So what is the real reason for unemployment, and what must we do to get rid of it?

Every worker knows that when unemployment is high, workers are weak. It is *always* true that if the boss urges more work, more overtime, greater fealty, you must comply or risk being fired. But with high unemployment you can't afford to be fired, because you are unlikely to get a new job. On the other hand, with low unemployment, workers can take more time to do tasks, refuse extra assignments, demand better pay, and strike to get it. The threat of being fired is not so powerful since new jobs are readily available and now it is the employer who will have trouble getting new workers.

In capitalism, there is a constant battle over how much work will be done at what wages. Unemployment reduces all workers' bargaining power by reducing worker options and strengthening capitalist threats. Full employment has the reverse effect. For these reasons capitalists won't eliminate unemployment and, when it drops on its own, in due course they will intentionally induce new unemployment to reestablish their relative power.

So, again, carefully crafted arguments to capitalists (or their Congresspeople) about the productivity they could gain from hiring additional workers or about everyone's right to a job are beside the point. To win reduced unemployment, and particularly to win institutionalized full employment, workers must exert collective power. Because this gain would dramatically increase workers' bargaining power, it must be taken, not negotiated or begged. Moreover, the same can be said for welfare programs, unemployment benefits, increased minimum wages, a shorter work week, and even pay increases. Each of these gains directly redistributes wealth from capitalists to workers, and, more important, reduces the cost to workers of being fired thereby reducing workers' fear of pink slips and strengthening workers in their constant battle with capital.

I never would believe that Providence had sent a few rich men into the world, ready booted and spurred to ride, and millions ready saddled and bridled to be ridden.

— Richard Rumbold

Property is always for sale. Buy it, and then rent or sell it for a profit. That is the accepted capitalist mantra regarding property and in that light to house people who have no means to pay would require (1) redistributing wealth downward, and (2) making the worse-off more comfortable.

Capitalists do not want to set precedents that commodities should ever have any price other than the one they wish to place on them. Nor do they want to see wealth redistributed downward. Nor do they want to have the worse-off better off. So, up to the point where homelessness begins to interfere with business-as-usual, it is good business. Moreover, if homelessness does begin to impede "good" business, the capitalists' first inclination won't be to house the homeless, but to incarcerate them. After all, constructing jails can be very profitable and has none of the downside of benevolent social programs. New jails don't disrupt power relations. They reinforce them.

So how can movements to house the homeless (and thereby increase the bargaining power of all workers) win gains? Increasing the cost of homelessness to capitalists while creating alliances that guard against a wholesale incarceration of the homeless is the only way. Petitions will accomplish little. Coalitions with labor, with full employment movements, with civil rights groups, and with welfare rights movements, will accomplish much. Occupying buildings and squatting will win.

> A thing moderately good is not so good as it ought to be. Moderation in temper is always a virtue; moderation in principle is always a vice.
> — Thomas Paine

To understand how we can convert the amount we won't need to spend due to the dissolution of the Cold War—the "peace dividend"—into socially useful production we must know more about arms production in general.

Some production of armaments is certainly for use in the Third World or to ensure military superiority in imperial confrontations. But most has nothing to do with war and peace. "Defense" spending's other purpose is to channel excess productive capacity into creating "stuff" which, from the point of view of capitalists, will not adversely affect the society's balance of power.

Suppose we transfer hundreds of billions of dollars of productive capability from missile silos and high-tech tanks into hospitals, roads, schools, low-cost housing, and ecological cleanup. What will result?

Just as firms now sell "military hardware" to the government for a profit, in this hypothetical future, firms could theoretically sell socially useful items to the government, also for a profit. So the result wouldn't be that no one could make a profit off government buying. There would be firms that would lose, but others would gain. It follows that if having profit-makers were the only consideration, conversion could take place. And successful opposition to conversion is certainly also not a matter of fear about the effect of reduced job opportunities since social production would increase rather than decrease employment. No, strong opposition to conversion stems from the fact that the infusion of the products of greatly increased social production into society and associated increases in employment would alter society's relations of power and profit. With greatly increased social spending and higher employment, the life circumstances of working people would radically improve. Workers' bargaining power, their ability to organize, and their knowledge would increase. The idea that production should benefit the populace would attain credibility. In short, all sorts of dynamics disruptive of existing relations of dominance and submission would be unleashed.

The sad truth, therefore, is that military production is pursued largely in order to avoid pursuing socially useful production. Since World War II, the government has taxed the public via scare tactics and spent the revenues on high-tech defense industry boondoggles, generating huge profits for capitalists and spinning the system's wheels without disrupting existing hierarchies. From the perspective of capital, this approach has maintained their relative power, enriched their coffers, and kept workers in their lowly place. In contrast, to tax the public by appealing to desires for improved living conditions, and to then deliver real improvements via effective, bountiful social spending would drastically reduce the capitalists' relative power, impoverish their coffers, and elevate workers to a position of stature in society. From the perspective of capitalists, large-scale conversion of military to social spending would therefore mean a disastrous reduction in capitalists' advantage and power.

As a result, if the public doesn't demand a military expense reduction, the size of the "peace dividend" will be zero. After all, the military budget's primary purpose still exists: to provide a channel for unlimited profiting that won't otherwise rock the boat. On the other hand, if the post-glasnost public can no longer be scared into footing the bill for military spending, then there really will be a "peace dividend." In this case, capitalists will want to put the "peace dividend" to some new socially neutral but still profitable use. Perhaps a computer on every desk in every school, or an anti-drug army, or an endless proliferation of jails to house the homeless and other malcontents. Or, if they are really bright, capitalists might opt for a massive infusion of overseas expenditures in the Third World and in the newly opening Eastern bloc to bolster the U.S. world economic empire against Japanese and German incursions. Working people, on the other hand, should want to put defense savings to use in building hospitals, housing, schools, libraries, and new infrastructure, and in helping workers here and throughout the world boost their living standards and bargaining power.

The polarization over how to distribute a "peace dividend" therefore becomes a fight over whether changes should accrue primarily to capitalists (with a small trickle down) or primarily to workers generally, not only in the short term, but also in the increased bargaining power that can translate into additional gains in the future. Obviously, this is a serious fight. It cannot be won merely by arguing with capitalists or their representatives in Congress that conversion is technically possible, or that it would be abstractly good for people or even for the economy as a whole. Even those capitalists who aren't in immediately affected industries know that by definition of how the system works conversion will be relatively bad for them unless it is relatively bad for workers instead. Therefore nearly all capitalists will oppose desirable changes, however brilliantly we argue.

It follows that the only way to attain conversion, like the only way to reduce unemployment, or to get housing for the homeless, is to win it. And we will not be strong enough, nor militant enough, nor organized enough, unless we admit to ourselves and highlight to everyone we talk with all the reasons for defense spending and for opposition to conversion, as well as all the reasons to undertake conversion.

Capitalism is an abomination. Corporate cigarette manufacturers push death in the same way that heroin and crack dealers do, only more efficiently and for bigger bucks. The owners of Philip Morris, like arms dealers, are at the most disgusting end of the business spectrum, but all along the line capitalism promises only aggrandizement of the few, the rest be damned. To oppose a system as powerful as capitalism, we have to know the rules it plays by. They are not the rules of reason. They are not the rules of justice and human concern. They are the rules of the dollar and of power. We can win lasting gains only if we understand that we are not in a debate, but a war. And if we understand, as the capitalists do, that in this war, as in any other, when one side gains more ground, it is because the other side has lost the same.

Whether we're talking about winning a pay raise tomorrow or winning decentralized participatory socialist economic forms down the road, our arguments and ethics must always operate in our own minds and in all our discussions with potential allies. But for capitalists, we should have only disdain and regular reminders of our growing might.

— March 1990

Market Maladies

P rivate ownership yields grotesque inequalities, while markets:

- hide human relations, ensuring that economic calculations focus only on dollar profits;

- promote antagonism among buyers and sellers, yielding conflict and precluding solidarity;

- promote a class of intellectual workers dominating traditional workers, precluding democracy and self-management;

- bias against social goods, diminishing social and ecological concern.

Efforts to demonstrate these points have not yet convinced even progressive economists, much less the broad population. Perhaps this is because the discussion has been too abstract. If so, a couple of case studies may help.

Pile It On

In the February 8 issue of *The Economist*, there is a brief, boxed article titled "Let Them Eat Pollution." Ninety-five percent of the article reproduces parts of a purloined memorandum sent by Lawrence Summers, chief economist of the World Bank, to some of his colleagues. Summers is the picture of civilized accomplishment: a scholar, administrator, theorist, writer–dressed impeccably, exuding confidence—the fruit of our best breeding, the archetype, responsible, liberal Harvard economist. In his memorandum, this living ode to Western achievement argues, "Shouldn't the World Bank be encouraging more migration of dirty industries to the [Third World]?" He presents three supporting arguments, which, though it goes unstated, apply equally to dumping in urban ghettoes rather than wealthy suburbs.

First, Summers intones that "the measurement of the costs of health-impairing pollution depends on the forgone earnings from increased morbidity and mortality." Thus "a given amount of health-impairing pollution should be done in the country with the lowest cost, which will be the country with the lowest wages." In Summers eyes, markets, by definition, correctly value all factors in production. If markets set a low wage for Third World workers, they must be less productive than workers elsewhere. If we're going to dump toxic wastes, let's do it where those hurt by the dumping are not as productive. As Summers says, "I think the economic logic behind dumping a load of toxic waste in the lowest-wage country is impeccable and we should face up to that." Of course, the history of imperial domination and colonial and neo-colonial status, as well as the current imbalance of economic and military power, and how these affect wage rates and reduce the productive potential of Third World citizens are not part of Summers's "economic logic." Nor is the idea that the worth of a human is not measurable in the same way we measure the worth of a machine or a pile of copper. Nor is the insight that those who create poison ought to deal with it. None of these views enter a fully developed capacity for "facing the facts" so they are not part of "economic logic" markets operate by.

Summers's second argument is that "the costs of pollution are likely to be non-linear as the initial increments of pollution probably have very low cost." That is, if you let toxins build to a high level in one region there will be grave results, but if you spread the same load of toxins widely enough, no one will get enough of a dose to make a difference. Summers adds, "I've always thought the under-populated countries in Africa are vastly under-polluted; their air quality is probably vastly inefficiently low compared to Los Angeles or Mexico City." So why doesn't the vaunted market spread wastes more efficiently? Summers answers, "Only the lamentable fact that so much pollution is generated by nontradable industries (transport, electrical generation) and that the unit transport costs of solid waste are so high prevent world-welfare-enhancing trade in air pollution and waste." In other words, less-polluted countries can't offer to take our car exhaust, no matter how much we would pay, because its technically impossible, and they can't take solid waste for a fee, because, while technically possible, the costs of moving it make the fee exorbitant.

So, what's the solution? Summers doesn't offer a way out for toxins spewing from our cars. But to get rid of toxins coming from factories, Summers says we need only export the factories to the Third World. The products made in these factories can be shipped back to us even as the accumulating wastes, increased by the absence of expensive pollution-control machinery, flood into until now "inefficiently" unpolluted Third World countries. The moral question of why we needn't stew in the fruits of our own opulence need never be addressed. Indeed, the U.S. won't even have to pay a fee to Third World countries taking the pollution. It will be their's by "eminent domain."

Finally, for those not already convinced, Summers offers a third argument. "Concern over an agent that causes a one-in-a-million change in the odds of getting prostrate cancer is obviously going to be much higher in a country where under-5 mortality is 200 per thousand." That is, if the people in a country live a long time, they may die due to the effects of a toxic that, if they were to live shorter lives for some other reason, would have little or no effect on them. Summers's analysis does not cause him to worry that in some places people die younger than is biologically, technologically, and socially necessary, and to wonder why markets don't correct this particular "inefficiency."

Of course, if we let toxins accumulate sufficiently in our own backyard, the slow-acting ones will in due course also become irrelevant, as the faster-acting ones lower our own life spans below the relevant threshold, but again, that's a silly option because we're too productive to sacrifice.

The punchline of Summers's memorandum is its conclusion. "The problem with the arguments against all of these proposals for more pollution in [the Third World]," such as, "intrinsic rights to certain goods [like breathable air], moral reasons, social concerns, [and] lack of adequate markets could be turned around and used more or less effectively against every bank proposal...."

Summers's logic is the logic of the market. His mind works as the market works, and the market works that way regardless of what anyone, including Summers, says about it. Counter-arguments to Summers's proposal that we dump more pollution on the Third World—whether these counter- arguments are based on right, morality, power relations, etc.—are simply irrelevant. (1) These factors are not part of how markets operate and do not influence market assessments. (2) These factors are not part of how an advocate of markets thinks, since to think this way would undermine "every Bank proposal," which is to say, the entire market and private ownership system. Of course, Summers will not jettison capitalism, so instead he openly demonstrates his allegiances, by *a priori* excluding this kind of counter-argument from consideration.

If you look at letters indicating the mindsets of slave-owners in pre-Civil War America you will find similarly "cogent" accounts of why bartering human beings was the most civilized thing to do. Moreover, if you can restrain your anger, you will see that within the self-serving, and ignorant assumptions of the time, the "logic" of these defenses was "impeccable." Let us hope that when people look back at our time and read Lawrence Summers or any other economist on the virtues of markets and private ownership, they too will marvel that humans accorded the maximum of education and advantage could have been so grotesquely inhumane and ignorant.

Movie Time

Recently, I went on a fund-raising trip to Los Angeles. While there I spent an afternoon talking with a Hollywood insider. Our topic was the operating procedures of a movie production company that develops script ideas into screenplays in hopes of convincing a major studio to finance the final movie.

My insider friend explained that at any moment the company might have 10 or 15 projects underway. Each project begins with a plot idea, from a tidy paragraph to an already published book. In either case, someone is hired to write a first screenplay to submit to a vice president in charge of that project, who then claims a long list of horrible flaws and fires the first screenwriter. The product of the first writer's labors belongs to the production company, and the vice president sends it to a new writer, who rewrites it in light of the vice president's many suggestions. The cycle repeats itself, each time with a new writer, sometimes five or more, till the final screenplay incorporates contributions from numerous fired writers. The final screenplay becomes the basis for finding a director, actors, and, if things work out, a major studio underwriter. The whole process can take 10 years, from original idea to big screen portrayal.

As I listened to this description, I couldn't contain my incredulity at the absurdity of this scenario. I know screenwriters accept their lot because to work at all they must anticipate frequent dismissal and permanent lack of control over their work. But why does the company, which is certainly not weak and unorganized, accept long, expensive delays and a chopped-up script? Why doesn't the desire to minimize costs cause the company's owner to curtail the inefficient scrambling of the vice presidents? This is, after all, what capitalism is supposedly good at. My mentor replied:

(1) The owner needs vice presidents since there are too many projects for the owner to oversee without high-level, authoritative, help.

(2) The vice presidents don't want to maximize profits so much as to make themselves indispensable to the company, justify their large salaries, and lay grounds for further increases in their autonomy and better employment elsewhere.

(3) Thus, (a) the vice presidents almost never accept the first writer's screenplay, but instead find faults that don't exist and repeatedly demand new writers who they have to bring up to speed and motivate, and (b) the owners have to put up with it or close up shop.

But why doesn't the owner restructure the company so the vice presidents have more security and get a share of profits, giving them an interest in minimizing costs rather than maximizing their own role and indispensability? The answer, of course, is that capitalists, by definition of what capitalism is and by all its logic and implications, don't ever *give* anyone even a tiny piece of the profits. Not even to increase their own return.

Leftists have long understood that workers don't willingly help capitalists maximize profits but instead give as little of themselves as possible in the time they have contracted to work. To profit, capitalists must therefore coerce effort from their workers via struggles over the length of the work day, work intensity, and work conditions. Because of this, for example, a huge part of the country's productive energies goes to disciplining, coercing, and punishing workers.

At the same time, however, most people, including leftists, assume that management does use their skills and authority to maximize profits. A more sophisticated analysis recognizes that administrators also seek to preserve their own prerogatives against incorporation of their responsibilities into workers' roles. In this sense, managers guard their profession against encroachment from below by ensuring that managerial tasks are never usurped by workers. It is exactly like doctors (also in the coordinator class) obstructing increases in the skills of nurses, or the use of preventive medicine or popular remedies.

However, in this example of multiple vice presidents shuffling around multiple screenplays, there is another lesson. In the movie company, not only is the interface between coordinators and workers characterized by managers curtailing worker potentials and guarding against their usurping conceptual responsibilities, so is the upward looking interface between coordinators and capitalists characterized by coordinators redesigning production to make themselves as indispensable and valuable as possible.

So what? Well, this indicates still another reason why the so-called efficiency of markets is nonsense. Not only does tremendous energy go to exhorting work from deskilled, recalcitrant workers whose interest is to work as little as possible for as much pay as they can win, but also managers make work inefficient to advance their own pay and power, rather than the overall productivity of the firm.

The impact of this dynamic, like the impact of worker recalcitrance due to alienation and exploitation, is major. In the case of workers, the only solution is to give them a significant share of profits. Coordinators too need a share of profits to have an interest in frugality and productivity. However, they also need job security and a reduced job advantage over those below.

In short, the only path to having people interested in doing their jobs without increasing waste and other inefficiencies is to create a workplace where all actors have a shared interest in (a) having the totality of work be as fulfilling and efficient as possible and (b) having the product be as good as possible. In fact, to really do the job right, each actor's interest should be in maximizing the human worth of the economy's total product while making the involved total of work as fulfilling and minimally dislocating as possible. To achieve this, of course, *every* actor must share equally in both the increased rewards and reduced costs. An economy can accomplish this even partially, much less comprehensively, only by eliminating private ownership as well as the hierarchy of the capital/labor distinction and the market-bred coordinator/capital and coordinator/worker distinctions.

It follows that if they were funded at the same level and treated similarly by all other firms, a more participatory production company should outperform the traditional more hierarchical one, even in the presence of private ownership and markets. So why don't a few rich capitalists fund more efficient, collectively organized companies?

In fact, capitalism is not simply Marx's pithy: "Accumulate, accumulate, that is Moses and the Prophets." Instead, with very few exceptions, capitalists are also driven by the need to rationalize their past rapacity while playing by institutionally inscribed rules. They will not entertain that reducing their authority could somehow increase overall achievement.

People with $10 million don't seek $11 million and people with $100 million don't seek $200 million because they have their eye on a new bauble and need extra cash to make the purchase. Their motives to plunder beyond all possibility of consumption are more often to fulfill their destiny and increase their power. Accomplishing these ends requires respecting the rules of the game.

Suppose tomorrow you inherit a million dollars and don't have a rapacious past to rationalize. And suppose you want to expand profits only to fund worthy projects. You still won't use collective structures and other dramatic innovations to have a more successful company, because if you made such choices, the playing field would tilt as other capitalists (directors, actors, cinematographers, etc.) refuse to deal with you. And this is the point of the insider-critic: It doesn't matter that the vice presidential run-around is irrational when viewed *within* the production company. Within the *whole* system this run-around is the only workable way to play the game.

To what extent do these dynamics operate elsewhere? Do coordinators in the auto, shoe, education, and mining industries introduce procedures that enhance their status even at the cost of wasting time and diminishing the quality of cars, shoes, schooling, and extracted ores? This is a worthy topic for economic investigation.

No one ought to have any trouble seeing the broader and more obvious ills of markets, whether in the growing population of homeless people, in our crumbling infrastructure, or in the toxic waste spewing from high-productivity plants. But if that isn't enough, we also have the World Bank and Lawrence Summers's remarkable admission that "intrinsic rights of certain goods, moral reasons, social concerns...could be turned around and used more or less effectively against every [World] Bank proposal." Shouldn't this stem the pro-market tide?

— March 1992

Nobel Nerve

The 1991 Nobel Prize for economics was given to Ronald Coase, an 81-year-old retired University of Chicago Law School Professor. Coase got his prize for two papers written over 30 years ago.

For his first insight, Coase asked why people gather into corporations within which authority rather than markets mediate choices. Thirty years ago, economists didn't have an answer that preserved the pro-market mythology. Coase explained that if Henry Ford wants to produce cars he should buy a large plant in which all components can be assembled without the "transaction costs" of contracting with dozens of little firms making components by their own criteria. Why not get rid of markets entirely, with Henry Ford running the whole show? Coase replied that the "transaction costs" overcome by centralization do not warrant reducing market exchanges to nil. Entrepreneurs find the happy medium between free markets and large authoritarian firms.

Business people had no need of Coase telling them to accumulate. They already sought fiefdoms they could oversee with absolute authority. But if Coase's analysis didn't lead to different business behavior, it did buttress "politically correct" ideology. Markets are great, says Coase, and nonmarket allocation in firms just proves the point. So what if Coase ignores the costs of oversight, strikes, deskilling, etc.? So what if he ignores the alienation and denigration of workers in large plants? So what if he assumes away the pervasive ills of markets as his starting point of analysis? Coase resolved a conundrum for the powers that be. Thus, he's a genius's genius.

For his second stunt, Coase admitted that economic activities have two kinds of effects, those on the immediate buyers and sellers, and those that rebound "externally" on bystanders. Shoe production affects the owner via the accrual of profit and the consumer via the shoe bought. But it also affects the public via pollution from the plant's smokestacks. A train that spews sparks sometimes burns the cornfields of farmers whose land abuts the rail lines. The train owner gets paid by firms transporting items by rail. The farmers neither buy nor sell, but nonetheless suffer losses when their fields burn.

Before Coase, economists believed the only way to correct "externalities" like pollution and burnt fields was government intervention. But then, to maintain their celebration of unfettered markets, they had to assume such externalities were rare. Yet every economic transaction has external effects such as changing the ecology, social setting, and people's beliefs. Minimizing externalities was a bald-faced lie, so economists sought an alternative.

Coase offered the perfect escape. Every time a bystander is hurt, he suggested, we need only assign "property rights" indicating who can legally do what, and one party will always pay the other to correct for the otherwise ignored externality. If the train owner has a right to spew sparks, farmers will assess the costs they bear and offer some fraction of that to the train owner to use spark-free trains. If farmers have a right to have their fields not burn, the train owner will assess the cost of having to not generate sparks and offer the farmers some fraction of that to put up with the burning fields.

"Coase's Theorem" says that once we determine who can legally do what, externalities will vanish as actors pay one another off. This methodology— either the victims bribe the perpetrator to stop the distasteful behavior (when the perpetrator has a legal right to do it) or the perpetrator bribes the victims to put up with the distasteful outcome (when the victims have a right not to suffer the pain)—is considered an epochal innovation in American economics and jurisprudence. Even without understanding all the details and context, this tells us a great deal about our intellectual culture since, in fact, Coase's methodology doesn't work.

(1) Bargains made with only two parties, perpetrator and victim, will rarely if ever be efficient.

(2) Whenever the perpetrator is a corporation and the victim a far-flung collection of disparate individuals, the latter is at such a disadvantage in seeking recompense that without intervention correction rarely takes place at all.

(3) Coase's methodology provides a "bully incentive" for anyone able to muster the courts on their behalf. Suppose Z owns a train. If we have the legal right to spew sparks, we should create the most spark-spewing train we can. If we have the right to be noisy, we should create a decibel demon. Whenever anyone with the means to pursue legal claims has a right that could cause others pain, they should threaten to exercise it and then extort bribery payments to desist. In the absence of a specific legal prohibition, a bully walking down the street should spit on everyone, claiming that he will only suffer the pains of stopping if his victims bribe him to do so.

Not surprisingly, Coase's "extort the victim," "empower the powerful" analysis was welcome as soon as economists could understand its utility to elites able to make legal claims here, there, and everywhere, thereby profitably spitting this way and that with impunity.

Why the hoopla for Coase? First, Coase's Theorem, better named the Bully Theorem, reinstates markets and privatization as optimal, even providing an argument against unwanted government regulation. Second, it elevates "property rights" to the defining position in jurisprudence and establishes a logic for dealing with externalities perfectly suited to co-optation by capital.

What Coase's Nobel Prize and the associated commentary shows, therefore, is that mainstream civilized "intellectual discourse" is judged nearly entirely by "political correctness"—meaning subservience to elite interests. Save for their ideological and material utility to elites, Coase's two "insights" are entirely pedestrian. He is a whore of the mind, as are the great majority of other "intellectuals" in the modern academy. The pimp is Henry Ford.

— November 1991

Panama's Lessons

The U.S. has invaded a sovereign country—again. The only impediment to unfettered militarism has been international opinion and modest Panamanian resistance. Although there were dozens of local actions, large-scale resistance by U.S. citizens was absent. Where was the Vietnam syndrome?

Strategically, two components of the Panama events deserve special attention. Washington's "imperial methods" and our "resistance strategies."

Washington's Imperialism

The widespread claim that the invasion of Panama was the U.S. "helping others" by smashing drug dealers, crushing corrupt politicians, arresting criminals, deposing authoritarian leaders, or bankrupting money launderers is obviously a disgusting perversion.

(1) If the U.S. government intended to "smash drug dealers," Reagan would have ousted Noriega long before and Bush would not have heretofore supported Noriega's drug efforts as well as those emanating from Southeast Asia, Afghanistan, and wherever else the CIA has taken entrepreneurial responsibility for funding covert operations.

(2) If the U.S. army intended to "crush corrupt politicians," our embassies would not have provided sanctuary for the last two criminal heads of state, Marcos and Somoza, and our military would have to parachute into Washington to "crush" our own Congress.

(3) If the U.S. Department of Justice intended to "arrest criminals" it would not have underwritten Noriega's activities until now, nor would we continue underwriting the dozens of crooked Generals and finance ministers throughout the "Free World" merely because they support U.S. policies, nor would organized crime have the free ticket to ride that it does within the U.S. itself.

(4) If our State Department intended (in violation of international law) to "depose authoritarian leaders," it would not have employed Noriega as a CIA

asset nor would it bankroll three-fourths of his fellow heads of state in Central America who are far more repressive than he.

(5) And if our Treasury department intended to "bankrupt money launderers," since our own CIA and banking establishment have laundered drug money for decades, Treasury agents would be marching on Langley in Virginia and up Fifth Avenue in New York, pulling the plug on larger-scale profiteering than anything Noriega ever dreamed of.

It follows that Noriega's downfall was not that he was too criminal, but that he began to balk at his assigned ancillary role as a surrogate abettor of U.S. corporate and geopolitical priorities. First, unbeknownst to anyone reading the *New York Times,* Noriega showed an unseemly degree of (admittedly right-wing and opportunist) populism in continuing efforts of his predecessor (General Omar Torrijos) to incorporate nonwhite Panamanians into Panama's political life. Second, beginning around 1986 Noriega displayed an unwillingness to continue supporting U.S. organized counterrevolutionary terrorism in Nicaragua. Thus, on two counts Noriega violated the rules of the American neo-colonial game.

Considering the impending transfer of the Panama Canal to Panamanian jurisdiction, Washington policy-makers decided that to avoid a possible calamity: (a) Noriega's government had to be "decapitated" and then rebuilt in compliance with U.S. preferences, and (b) the Panamanian army, much too black and populist by our standards, had to be rebuilt as well.

So Bush and his boss, the "collective" Moneybags, sent the Marines to wipe out opposition, destroy existing political institutions, demolish the Panamanian army, and "rebuild" Panama to fit the U.S. neo-colonial image. The poor are ravished. Civilians die. The country is devastated. U.S. taxpayers foot the bill.

U.S. corporate capital and political arrogance invaded Panama to save it. This is entirely in accord with the reigning western idea that "freedom for third world populations" means they work for a pittance while "electing" U.S.-favored politicians in a setting where any indigenous electoral opposition has been methodically eliminated well before effective challenges arise. As a Panamanian professor, Cristobal Alfaro, put it: "This new government must owe their allegiance to the United States and not to the Panamanian people."

So how did Bush and his cronies pull this off? How did they invade Panama so blatantly and with so much support at home? For over 100 years, we have been committing this type mayhem, usually with an anti-communist cover. But by the time Reagan/Bush decided that Noriega had to go, the Cold War was already unraveling. Arguing in the age of glasnost that an ex-CIA asset was a communist dupe would no longer suffice. Bush needed a new cover. His advisers reconstituted a "victimize/demonize" approach to policing the world.

(1) Pick a target country for geopolitical, economic, or other reasons commensurate to robust imperial desires.

(2) Financially "victimize" the target country to undermine local leaders and reduce short-term opposition to U.S. intervention.

In Panama, we withheld fees for the Canal while we imposed the usual International Monetary Fund pressures. "For many poor people, the hatred of Noriega was based on economic reasons, not political ones," notes a Panamanian professor quoted in the *Boston Globe*. But where did the "economic reasons" come from? Even the *Globe* article adds that "it was the U.S. sanctions imposed on Panama two years ago that contributed the most to the economy's depression," though the *Globe* reporter predictably failed to draw the obvious conclusion.

(3) "Demonize" the opposed leaders to generate a U.S. domestic climate favoring an invasion by using the entire media apparatus to portray opponents as among history's most despicable and venal enemies of humanity, particularly poisonous to U.S. health and welfare.

NBC, the *New York Times*, et. al., inflated Noriega's all-too-real criminality until he seemed personally responsible for every strung-out drug addict wandering our streets. He was a butcher. A thug. He was without peer in the pantheon of detestable people. Sprinkled with racist, sexist intimations of Voodoo and prostitution, media reports about Noriega clinched the argument that we had to bring him to "justice" to be sure that he could not continue ravaging us.

(4) To stir up intervention fervor, provoke last minute incendiary events—like the killing under peculiar circumstances of a U.S. soldier and the hassling of another's family—and portray them as historically unprecedented provocations that finally crack our usually unlimited restraint against employing force.

(5) Having successfully crushed opposition, prepare the way for a U.S.-style democracy by destroying the necessary infrastructure for real democracy including independent unions, meeting places, and community organizations.

The U.S. cannot abide real alternatives in any third world "democratic" election (or our own, for that matter). Thus in Panama we can predict that in coming weeks and months U.S. troops will methodically transfer resources from a too-populist, too-black army to a much whiter and not-at-all-populist police apparatus able to "properly regulate" the new Panamanian "peace."

(6) Having installed a government and eliminated possible sources of opposition, cap the process by "schooling" the new government in

total subordination to U.S. agendas, down to staffing, policy formation, and protocol. Then, their job done, call the troops home for celebrations.

And what is the glorious outcome of the above six-point plan? A "friendly government," acceptable policies, a cowed populace, and no remaining infrastructure for electoral or institutional opposition—exactly what Washington wanted in the first place.

Our Resistance

What is the right way to combat "victimize/demonize" interventionism? Should we fight each instance by demonstrating that the particular ruler involved isn't as bad as is claimed and that in each case U.S. efforts are not motivated by desires for justice and democracy but by particular geopolitical or economic concerns, such as dominating the Canal or returning the local populace to acceptable servility? Or should we organize a more general awareness about U.S. institutions and general foreign policy principles that could translate easily from Vietnam to Nicaragua to El Salvador to Panama regardless of the details of each new atrocity?

U.S. peace and third world support movements have had an important weakness that has prevented their efforts around El Salvador and Nicaragua from translating more quickly and comprehensively into opposition to the Panama intervention, just as years ago the same weakness prevented widespread opposition to war in Indochina from translating more quickly and comprehensively into opposition to the anti-Sandinista war on Nicaragua.

To understand the problem we have to realize that U.S. peace efforts operate at two levels. On the one hand, they affect a widespread public, which in turn raises the social costs of hated policies and thereby pressures the government. On the other hand, peace and support movements affect a smaller number of new recruits who then become committed activists able to find time and energy to help enlarge current broad-based opposition and also tackle new problems as they arise.

New activists learn about U.S. political economy and thereby develop a commitment that transcends particular instances of aggression. Their initial opposition toward a *particular* intervention "matures" into a principled view that translates smoothly into equal activism in future cases. The new activists do not need to be reeducated, regalvanized, and recommitted every time a new problem arises. Their opposition becomes systemic, not episodic.

But the broader audience that the peace movement addresses never seems to undergo this type of experience. Instead, their opposition is episodic. They become furious about a *particular* situation based on horror over specific details—the pain endured in the rice paddies of Indochina, indiscriminate bombing of civilians, the murder of nuns or priests in El Salvador, the criminal funding of barbarous contras in Nicaragua—not an understanding of underlying causes nor an allegiance to general principles applicable in other contexts. As a result, neocolonialism that doesn't require U.S. military intervention goes largely unopposed by this broader constituency of the peace movement. Moreover, each time the U.S. retools for a new military intervention, this broad-based opposition must be organized more or less from scratch, with new rhetoric, information, and focuses.

Since the issue for the broad rank-and-file of opposition is in each case whether the particular intervention is justified, the particular rebellion is humane, or the particular policies are legal, all this has to be investigated, dissected, debated, and conveyed anew, a process that sometimes barely even begins before the intervention is over.

The alternative is that not only committed long-term activists but also the wider audience of rank-and-file peace-seekers should act on the basis of systemic understanding and positive principles rather than episodic outrage. When we organize around the details of each atrocity, to get even people who have previously supported peace efforts to respond to the invasion of Panama requires that we counter innumerable new media myths about Noriega, U.S. anti-drug motives, international law, etc. In contrast, if we had been more successful in previously organizing around systemic knowledge and principles, debates about the relative ills of Noriega, the jurisprudence of the intervention, and the magnitude of harm or "good" done during the days of the invasion itself would be ancillary. We would not have to regalvanize peace pressure. Opposition would be sustained and less subject to vacillations in the face of media propaganda.

I'm not saying no one has previously organized against crimes in Vietnam, Nicaragua, or other places by emphasizing principles and systemic knowledge of U.S. institutions. But I am saying that there has been a natural tendency for the systemic approach to give way to emphasis on priests being killed, peasants being bombed, and crooks funding thugs.

But the invasion of Panama reinforces the hard lesson we know but often ignore. To stop interventions before they occur and turn back neocolonialism, we must emphasize positive principles and comprehensive understanding rather than time-bound policies and particular atrocities.

The point isn't that we should ignore the legal and human details of Vietnam, Nicaragua, South Africa, or wherever else. It is that we should present these atrocious details in a context that explains U.S. policy and makes demands in terms of positive principles that could guide all future U.S. foreign policy. Using atrocities to set the context for urging time-bound policies like "stop the bombing" (and start search and destroy operations?), "bring the troops home" (and Vietnamize?), "cut the illegal contra funding" (and get another country to pay the bill?), "defend the priests" (and murder the union organizers?) does an injustice to tomorrow's cause and to today's as well.

We must give our analysis of U.S. corporate structures and geopolitical priorities the place they deserve in our thinking and in what we say and write for the broader public. As to positive principles, here are a few to consider as part of what we should be for:

(1) No unilateral intervention by any intrusive means into the affairs of any sovereign country.

No state has a right to police or otherwise coerce another for *any* reason. The excuse of "trying to do good" is no excuse at all since it will be employed in every instance regardless of how venal real motives may be. If we demand "no intrusion," not only are we taking a positive principled stand that will translate from one context to another, our demand automatically incorporates no aid to contras, no soldiers, no IMF coercion, etc., and, especially when this is joined with the principles below, our movements will not dissipate each time one strategy of control is replaced by another.

(2) Support for the UN as the only "police agency" on the international scene entitled to send troops on peacekeeping missions.

There is a place for concerted and effective efforts to curtail internal institutional violence against domestic populations and to curb acts of terror by one population against another. Thus when these functions cannot or will not be achieved by a directly involved government, if and only if the international community as determined by the UN General Assembly (where there is no veto) deems it wise, a UN peacekeeping force should be employed.

(3) No export of weapons to any government or military for any reason and no economic support for any country exporting weapons.

There is no excuse for munitions profiteering at the expense of human life and international stability. Such acts should evoke censure from all civilized countries, particularly the current major culprits, with the U.S. topping the list.

(4) No export of technologies or knowledge regarding terror tactics and police repression to any government or police apparatus nor aid for any country engaged in such export.

The process of repressing indigenous populations to make them compliant for manipulation by local elites and international corporations depends in large part on a vile and inhuman "export industry" that should not exist. Since it shouldn't exist, obviously the proper course of action is to eliminate it here in the U.S. and severely censure it elsewhere.

(5) Respect for Amnesty International, Americas Watch, and other similar organizations as indicators of the "repressiveness" of any state and, after a short period for rectification, a cessation of political relations and disinvestment of economic assets from any country that these agencies continue to declare engaged in gross denial of basic human liberties, particularly the arrest of political dissidents.

While intervention in the internal affairs of sovereign states can never be condoned, it is neither necessary nor sensible that repressive states engaging in the gross violation of their own citizens' rights should be supported. Should the price of domestic repression grow great enough, and political and economic isolation are virtually the only policies that can induce that result, such repression would sharply diminish. This is the logic of disinvestment in South Africa, and it should apply elsewhere as well.

(6) Reassignment of all currently budgeted aid that is cut off due to violations of the above conditions to reparations to UN General Assembly-sanctioned popular organizations or governments in every country in which U.S. companies have paid on average less than the U.S. minimum wage or in which the U.S. military or U.S.-supported dictators have acted in ways that reduced domestic standards of living and decency.

Everyone recognizes the idea of reparations at the close of a war. There has been a long-standing war by a few powerful countries against most other countries of the world. To transfer the resources presently going to support repression into reparations will not only redress grievances in afflicted countries and improve the lot of millions of people, it will stabilize world affairs, reintroduce the wisdom and talents of huge populations to the human community, and simultaneously cleanse the soul of our own country. The fact that reparations should greatly exceed currently misallotted funds can be a future additional demand.

It is easy enough to outline a program like that above. What is hard is to emphasize one as the context for *all* our demands about Nicaragua, El Salvador, South Africa, et. al., rather than merely talking about each case in splendid isolation. That is what the current invasion and past history teaches us we must do.

— February 1990

Post-War Roundup

August 2, Iraq invaded Kuwait. This was preceded by a period of threat and discussion in which Iraq made known its intention to reverse Kuwait's price reduction policies which were reducing Iraq's revenues and making it impossible for Iraq to recover from its recent war with Iran. Middle East efforts to resolve the dispute were unsuccessful. International outrage was immediate.

August 12, Iraq offered to withdraw completely from Kuwait if others too would withdraw from occupied Arab lands, Syria from Lebanon and Israel from the territories it occupied in 1967. This was "linkage"; that is, the idea that problems in the area should be addressed in full and according to one set of principles. This was derided by the U.S. as "appeasement" and dismissed.

August 19, Hussein proposed that the matter of Kuwait be left as an Arab issue to be resolved by Arabs. This was rejected by the U.S. as irrelevant.

August 23, Iraq offered to withdraw in return for the lifting of sanctions, guaranteed access to the Gulf, and full control of the Rumallah oil field which extends about two miles into Kuwait over a disputed border. Also mentioned were that Iraq and the U.S. should negotiate a mutually satisfactory oil agreement and jointly work on insuring stability in the Gulf. Despite attention by many U.S. officials at the highest levels calling the new stance "interesting and serious," the offer was ignored.

January 2, after a series of similar offers, many of which have not yet come to light, Iraq offered "to withdraw from Kuwait if the United States pledges not to attack as soldiers are pulled out, if foreign troops leave the region, and if there is agreement on the Palestinian problem and on the banning of all weapons of mass destruction in the region." The U.S. immediately rejected the offer, which was barely noted in the mainstream media.

January 14, France proposed that the Security Council call for "a rapid and massive withdrawal" from Kuwait along with a statement that Council members would bring their "active contribution" to a settlement of other problems

---

This essay was written for distribution during the Gulf War. It excerpted and amalgamated information from a number of Z articles by myself, Noam Chomsky, and Stephen Shalom.

of the region, "in particular, of the Arab-Israeli conflict and in particular to the
Palestinian problem by convening, at an appropriate moment, an international
conference" to assure "the security, stability, and development of the region
and the world." This proposal was supported by numerous countries, but
rejected by the U.S. and Britain.

Negotiations in late February to end the ground war once it had begun
likewise failed. The offending "conditions" seemed to be Iraq's desire for a
ceasefire *before* they retreated. Last minute peace offers, brokered by the
Soviets, were ignored. No ceasefire took place, and the Iraqi troops were
bombed mercilessly even as they sought to retreat.

Parallel to these events we had a crescendo of news coverage of: (a) the
fantastic power of the Iraqi army, (b) the intransigence of Hussein, and (c) the
unending U.S. efforts to find a diplomatic solution. In fact, however, a
diplomatic solution is exactly what the U.S. was laboring tirelessly to avoid.

Given a Chance, Could Sanctions Have Succeeded?

The UN reaction to Iraq's violation of Kuwait's sovereignty was to employ
international economic sanctions. Could this have worked, thereby eliminating
need for a military solution? The critical factor in assessing whether sanctions
would succeed was the extent of international support. This was virtually
universal since the usual blockade-busters, the U.S. and England, were leading
the enforcement. As a result, the sanctions were immediately effective.

General Schwarzkopf, on October 28, 1990, said,

> *Golly, the sanctions have only been in effect about a couple of months...
> And now we are starting to see evidence that the sanctions are pinching.
> So why should we say, OK, we gave them two months (and it) didn't
> work. Let's get on with it and kill a whole bunch of people? That's crazy.
> That's crazy. You don't go out there and say, OK, let's have a nice war
> today. God Almighty, that war could last a long time ... and kill an awful
> lot of people. And so we've just got to be patient.*

On December 19, 1990, a Congressional Joint Economic Committee held
hearings on sanctions. The staff report stated:

> *There was a strong consensus among the witnesses that: (1) The sanc-
> tions against Iraq are extremely comprehensive, have a great amount of
> international support, and will do extensive harm to Iraq's economy and
> military in a relatively short time. (2) The chances are good that the
> sanctions will achieve their stated objectives including convincing Sad-
> dam Hussein to remove his military forces from Kuwait.*

According to the CIA, by December 1990, the sanctions cut off over 90 percent of Iraq's imports and 97 percent of its exports. "Most importantly, the blockade had eliminated any hope Baghdad had of cashing in on higher oil prices or its seizure of Kuwaiti oil fields."

James Schlesinger, former secretary of defense and energy and former director of the CIA, said on November 27:

Since the original estimate was that the sanctions route would require a year, it seems rather illogical to express impatience because they have not produced the hoped for results in six months…. Saddam Hussein … has forfeited $20 billion of foreign exchange earnings a year…. To allow our own political rhetoric to obscure the severe punishment that has already been meted out or to suggest that our current policy is in some way unsuccessful and that Saddam's position is now or is potentially enviable strikes me as misconceived.

Adm. William J. Crowe Jr. said on November 28: For a country the size of Iraq to lose $30 billion "is not chopped liver."

It's curious that some expect our military to train soldiers to stand up to hostile fire, but doubt its ability to train them to wait patiently…. I cannot understand why some consider our international alliance strong enough to conduct intense hostilities but too fragile to hold together while we attempt a peaceful solution. Actually, I sense more nervousness among our allies about our impetuousness than about our patience…. It would be a sad commentary if Saddam Hussein, a two-bit tyrant who sits on 17 million people and possesses a GNP of $40 billion, proved to be more patient than the U.S., the world's most affluent and powerful nation.

These sentiments were widespread among U.S. foreign policy "experts."

- Brzezinski: "Sanctions are not a blunt instrument for promptly achieving total surrender."

- Harold Brown: "I would continue with diplomatic and economic sanctions for some time."

- Robert McNamara: Give sanctions 12-18 months; "We have not by any means proven that they will not achieve their objective."

It is obvious from the sequence of events leading to war that the sanctions had already worked. The Iraqis, almost from the moment they invaded Kuwait, sought a diplomatic way out. It was U.S. policy, however, that a diplomatic solution had to be avoided at all costs.

Why Did the U.S. Pursue War Instead of Diplomacy?

Iraq could have been forced out of Kuwait by a combination of sanctions plus diplomacy. Yet the historical record shows that at every turn the U.S. rejected diplomacy and favored war.

Offered reasons were that beyond getting Iraq out of Kuwait, we had to punish Hussein's violation of national sovereignty, respect international law, avoid "appeasing" Hitlerite aggression, and avoid legitimating "linkage."

As we will see below, each of these reasons is false. The U.S. frequently violates national sovereignty, ignores international law, and appeases aggression. And the U.S. never thought Hussein was another Hitler and also understands that "linkage" is just another name for diplomacy.

When Bush sent 400,000 troops to the Persian Gulf instead of 15,000, which could have been just as effective in preventing further Iraqi aggression, he did it to scuttle negotiations and leave only military might as the arbiter. Bush's worst nightmare was a negotiated solution that would legitimate the role of international law rather than U.S. power. He did everything possible to forestall that nightmare and legitimate war instead of diplomacy. The carnage that resulted was his preferred scenario.

Does the U.S. Respect National Sovereignty?

George Bush claims that in the Gulf "America stands where it always has, against aggression, against those who would use force to replace the rule of law." If so, then in the past the U.S. would have consistently opposed violations of national sovereignty. Otherwise, Bush was lying.

The U.S. invaded Panama in December 1989 to oust General Noriega and impose a puppet regime under U.S. control. As a result, Panama is now an occupied country undergoing the worst political and economic crisis in its history. A representative of the Families of the Victims of December 20 says:

> One year after the invasion, the dead call out to us from the mass graves, demanding justice. Our orphans grieve for their parents who will never see them grow up, who will never have the privilege of knowing their own children. None of the crimes of the invasion will be forgiven, and none of our victims will be forgotten.

Earlier the U.S. had invaded Grenada, ousted its government, and installed one more in tune with U.S. priorities. The results were similar to Panama, including subsequent dissolution of the economy. The excuse was that Grenada was about to become a base for Soviet militarism (which would *seem* to be their right). When asked about this, a CIA official noted that the military cost of allowing Grenada to go its own way would be re-targeting one or two missiles. In this view, therefore, we violated Grenada's national sovereignty to avoid re-targeting a missile. Even the U.S. government is not moved to violence by such minuscule factors, so what really provoked U.S. violence was that Grenada's government was planning to marshal Grenada's resources to serve Grenada rather than U.S. elites. If this effort succeeded, the international lesson would be that if even tiny Grenada can escape U.S. economic dominion, why can't other nations? Grenada was thus invaded to curtail this dangerous "showcase effect" before it went too far.

These cases alone demonstrate that for the U.S., recognition of national sovereignty is not a principle. But there are many more examples, including the U.S.-organized and financed contra war against Nicaragua, the U.S. war in Indochina killing over 2,000,000 people, the U.S. installation of a violent dictator, Pinochet, in Chile, and similar actions throughout Central America. But these instances only reveal U.S. willingness to itself violate national sovereignty. Perhaps what Bush meant to say when asked about the U.S. attitude to national sovereignty is that we oppose violations of national sovereignty by any other country, like Iraq, as a matter of principle. So what was/is the U.S. attitude to recent violations of national sovereignty by other countries?

- When Turkey invaded northern Cyprus, broke it up, killed 2,000 people, tried to destroy relics of Greek civilization, and drove out 200,000 people, the U.S. approved.

- When Israel attacked Lebanon, killed about 20,000 people, bombarded the capital, and occupied (and still occupies) southern Lebanon, the U.S. vetoed a series of UN Security Council resolutions to terminate that aggression. Israel still holds onto the occupied territories and has annexed some of them.

- When Indonesia invaded East Timor, killed 200,000 in the worst slaughter relative to the population since the Holocaust, the U.S. provided aid.

- When Morocco invaded the Western Sahara and annexed it, the U.S. approved.

- When Iraq attacked Iran violating its national sovereignty in a seven-year war in the 1980s, the U.S. backed Saddam Hussein and Iraq because, at that time, Iranian fundamentalism was the force deemed more likely to interfere with U.S. plans for Middle East oil.

Continuing with the highly relevant Iraq/Iran case, Texas Congressperson Henry Gonzales, chair of the House Banking Committee, charged that one Atlanta-based bank alone extended $3 billion in letters of credit to Iraq, $800 million of it guaranteed by the Department of Agriculture's Commodity Credit

Corporation. Gonzales charged further that armaments, possibly including chemical weapons, were obtained by Iraq under the deal. "There is no question but those $3 billion are actually financing the invasion of Kuwait," he said. "There is no question that the greater portion of that was dealing with armaments."

According to 1987 data, over 40 percent of Iraq's food was imported from the United States and in 1989 Iraq received $1 billion in loan assurances, second only to Mexico. The Reagan and Bush administrations scarcely reacted when Iraq purchased U.S. helicopters and transferred them to military use, used poison gas against Iranian troops and its own Kurdish citizens, and relocated half a million Kurds and Syrians by force. Iraq was our ally against Arab fundamentalism. Iraq was therefore good and its acts acceptable. Arab fundamentalism was bad, not because it was Arab or fundamentalist, but because it was not properly subordinate to U.S. agendas for the region.

August 2, Hussein and Iraq became our enemy for the same reason, not being properly subordinate to U.S. agendas for the region.

The evidence shows that, as a matter of principle, the United States pursues U.S. elites' interests. When these interests conflict with another countries' national sovereignty we, or one of our clients, violate that sovereignty. When these interests coincide with support for some other country's national sovereignty, we and our clients support national sovereignty and claim virtue in doing so.

In the Middle East, first the U.S. worried about Mossadeq in Iran, then Nasser in Egypt, Khomeini in Iran, and finally Hussein in Iraq. In each case, these leaders were subjected to U.S. ire despite having nothing in common other than that they were all nationalists—right or left, ex-ally or not—who believed that the Middle East ought to control Middle East resources.

Does the U.S. Respect International Law?

- On December 23, 1990, the U.S. vetoed a UN Security Council resolution condemning the invasion of Panama and ignored the December 29 General Assembly resolution demanding "the withdrawal of the U.S. armed invasion forces from Panama" calling the invasion a "flagrant violation of international law and of the independence, sovereignty, and territorial integrity of states."

- Roughly a year later, the U.S. lauded UN Security Council resolutions condemning Iraq's aggression against Kuwait. At the same time, however, it continued to ignore 11 resolutions condemning Israeli aggression against Lebanon and other Mideast countries, and vetoed four others.

• August 9, the UN Security Council rightly declared Iraq's annexation of Kuwait "null and void" under international law. The U.S. applauded and prepared to go to war. But in August 1980 the Security Council declared Israel's annexation of Jerusalem "null and void" and in December 1981 declared Israel's annexation of the Syrian Golan Heights "null and void," both under international law. The U.S. hindered all efforts to act on these legal determinations.

Regarding Iraq, the U.S. supported and extended UN resolutions. Regarding itself, Israel, and other allies, the U.S. vetoes, obstructs, or ignores UN resolutions. Defenders of these policies contend that U.S. intransigence toward disliked UN resolutions is often just resistance to the fact that other nations use vetoes to dominate the UN. Is this accurate?

From 1981 to 1986 the U.S. vetoed 36 draft resolutions of the Security Council. The Soviet Union rejected two. The U.S. is far in the lead in the past 20 years of Security Council vetoes, Britain is second, France a distant third, and the USSR fourth.

Moreover, the situation is similar in the General Assembly, where the U.S. regularly votes against resolutions on aggression, international law, human-rights abuses, disarmament, and other relevant issues, often alone, or with a few client states.

Some influential Americans, of course, are proud of their country's rejection of international law and the United Nations. As George Will put it after the invasion of Grenada, "it is bad enough we pay for the United Nations; surely we do not have to pay attention to it." But other, more moderate voices claim to be calling for U.S. attention to law and the UN. It pays to look at what these U.S. "advocates" of international law have to say.

For example, Richard N. Gardner, a former State Department official and diplomat, currently the Henry L. Moses chair of Law and International Organization at Columbia University, wrote an article in 1988 making what he called "The Case for Practical Internationalism." Gardner urged the U.S. to take up Gorbachev's "extraordinary" challenge to enhance the role of the United Nations and he prodded Washington to end its illegal war on Nicaragua. But Gardner warned that we should not go too far. We must not follow those "who decry any unilateral use of force and would subject our country to the international 'rule of law' on all matters as determined by the World Court or other UN bodies." Such a policy, he cautioned, neither makes good sense nor serves our national interests.

Another voice allegedly pressing the United States to follow international law is Senator Daniel Moynihan. In 1984 he lashed out at Reagan administration hypocrisy. The president had said: "I do believe in the right of a country when it believes that its interests are best served to practice covert activity...." Moynihan sharply replied that this was "a wholly normless statement." A nation has such a right, the Senator declared, only "if it is the right—which is to say, if its behavior is consonant with international law."

Moynihan explained that this meant U.S. covert operations against Canada would not be justified, but "given the behavior of the Nicaraguan government toward at least one of its neighbors, there is, I believe, a right of action there."

Moynihan charges that the Reagan administration went on to ignore this Congressional view by mining Nicaraguan harbors. But the World Court not only found the mining illegal, but also the entire U.S. covert war against Nicaragua. Moynihan, who served as vice-chair of the Senate Committee on Intelligence, presumably was aware of the absence of any evidence of Nicaraguan interference in El Salvador since January 1981.

At a press conference following Iraq's annexation of Kuwait, Bush was asked whether the U.S. policy against the annexation of captured lands in the Middle East was an across-the-board policy. Bush evaded the question. He had to, because if international law or the UN were to become the basis for determining when international aggression has occurred then the United States would not be able to undertake its own invasions or arrogate to itself the right to judge international behavior solely on the basis of U.S. elites' interests.

Was Hussein Another Hitler?

Saddam Hussein's a thug: But he was also a thug before August 2 when he got $1.5 billion in U.S. equipment that helped his nuclear and chemical warfare efforts; when he got billions of dollars of U.S. loans and loan guarantees; when he got U.S. satellite intelligence and military advice during his war with Iran; when he used chemical weapons against the Iranians and the U.S. responded by reestablishing diplomatic relations with him; when he used chemical weapons against his own Kurdish minority and the Reagan and Bush administrations opposed any U.S. sanctions against him; when the State Department ordered that a Voice of America broadcast critical of Hussein be taken off the air; and when, a week before his invasion of Kuwait, the U.S. ambassador told him he had been treated unfairly by the U.S. media.

Saddam Hussein began his political career as an assassin for the Ba'th Party, whose ideology bears some frightening parallels with fascism. The Ba'th first came to power in 1963 and carried out a horrendous massacre of Communist Party members. There is some evidence the CIA collaborated in this atrocity, providing the Ba'th with the names and addresses of Communists to facilitate their extermination, a pattern the U.S. repeated on a vast scale two years later in Indonesia.

So Saddam Hussein is a ruthless thug. But to call Hussein a Hitler and use analogies with World War II Europe to justify attacking Iraq one has to demonstrate that Hussein had the capacity to run rampant throughout the Middle East, and that we had to assume that he would use that capacity, so that diplomacy would in due time equate to appeasement.

However this analogy has no basis in reality. Just prior to its invasion of Kuwait, Iraq—with help from the U.S., Western Europe, the Soviet Union, and the Arab oil producing states—couldn't even conquer Iran.

The U.S brags of having spy satellites able to read license plates on cars and to determine if someone had recently shaved. With this capacity, and also knowing what military hardware Hussein actually had since it was all bought on world markets, and often with U.S. funds, the U.S. certainly knew the extent of Iraq's military capability. And what was that capability? Nearly nil, at least against an industrialized super-power. The "allies" claim about 100 casualties in military conflict, less than were lost in operational accidents in the six prior months of the "campaign." Iraq lost over 100,000, likely over 200,000, and perhaps far more. This "war" was a cowardly slaughter. The enemy was virtually defenseless, not a superpower like Hitler and Nazi Germany.

In the period leading up to the massacre, major media in the U.S. provided maps, drawings, and detailed analysis of fortified bunkers, miles and miles of razor wire fields, deep channels of moats with burning oil, and miles of minefields that the "allies" would have to courageously cross to get at the Iraqi military. Yet none of these existed, and there were no chemical weapons anywhere in the military theater. This masterwork of media manipulation was not to fool Iraqi military leaders, who certainly knew what they did and didn't have, but to fool the U.S. public into believing wildly inflated estimates of Iraqi military might so that we would buy the "Hitler analogy" as a moral justification for avoiding a negotiated settlement.

Why Did the U.S. Oppose "Linkage?"

Since linkage refers to the notion that in settling disputes diplomatically it is fitting that all matters the disputants deem important are brought to the table, opposing linkage means opposing diplomacy. In the Gulf crisis, for example, two central issues were at stake: The Palestinian's treatment at the hands of Israel and claims regarding a state of their own, and Iraq's occupation of Kuwait. The U.S. was not interested in "linking" these issues, that is, in treating both diplomatically simultaneously, because it was not interested in dealing with *either* issue diplomatically *at any time*.

Regarding the Palestinian question, President Bush likes to describe how James Baker has labored for peace, but Bush remains silent about the terms of the famed Baker plan, whose basic principles ban an "additional Palestinian state"; bar any "change in the status of Judea, Samaria, and Gaza other than in accordance with the basic guidelines of the [Israeli] government"; preclude any meaningful Palestinian self-determination; reject negotiations with the PLO, thus denying Palestinians the right to choose their own political representation; and call for "free elections" under Israeli military rule.

These views fly in the face of international opinion. Long before Iraq's invasion of Kuwait, the U.S. consistently opposed an international conference on the Middle East (where we would be in a tiny minority), and vetoed Security Council resolutions calling for a political settlement.

So Why Did the U.S. Want Iraq Out of Kuwait?

In the 1940s the State Department described Mideast oil as "a stupendous source of strategic power, and one of the greatest material prizes in world history," "probably the richest economic prize in the world in the field of foreign investment." Eisenhower called the Mideast the most "strategically important area in the world" with good reason. Much of the world's known oil reserves are located in the Persian Gulf. It is U.S. policy that we should have a dominant say over the price of oil, that we should have favored treatment regarding access, that we should own as much of the accruing profit as possible, and that as much of the remaining profit as possible should be invested in U.S. or allied banks to prop up our economies.

As far back as the 1920s, the U.S. ambassador in London—Andrew Mellon, the head of the Gulf Oil Corporation (named for the Mexican, not the Persian, Gulf)—was instructed to press the British to give Gulf Oil a stake in the Middle East. At the end of World War II, when immense petroleum deposits were discovered in Saudi Arabia, Secretary of the Navy James Forrestal told Secretary of State Byrnes, "I don't care which American company or companies develop the Arabian reserves, but I think most emphatically that it should be American."

In 1928, Standard Oil of New Jersey and Mobil joined British and French oil interests in signing the Red Line Agreement, under which each pledged not to develop Middle Eastern oil without the participation of the others. Nevertheless, after World War II these two U.S. firms (together with Texaco and Standard Oil of California) grabbed the Saudi concessions for themselves, freezing out the British and French. When the latter sued on the grounds that the Red Line Agreement had been violated, Mobil and Jersey told the court that the agreement was null and void because it was monopolistic.

In the early 1950s, oil was used as a political weapon for the first time—the United States and Britain against Iran. Iran had nationalized its British-owned oil company which had refused to share its astronomical profits with the host government. In response, Washington and London organized a boycott of

Iranian oil which brought Iran's economy to the brink of collapse. The CIA then instigated a coup, installed the Shah, and effectively un-nationalized the oil company, with U.S. firms getting 40 percent of the formerly 100 percent British-owned company. This was, in the view of the *New York Times*, an "object lesson in the heavy cost that must be paid" when an oil-rich Third World nation "goes berserk with fanatical nationalism." Going "berserk" with "fanatical nationalism" is the *Times* way of describing a third world nation seeking to benefit from its own resources.

In 1956, the oil weapon was used by the United States against Britain and France. After the latter two nations, along with Israel, invaded Egypt, Washington made it clear that U.S. oil would not be sent to Western Europe until Britain and France agreed to a rapid withdrawal. The U.S. was not adverse to overthrowing Nasser—"if they had done it quickly, we would have accepted it," Eisenhower said later—but the clumsy Anglo-French military operation threatened U.S. interests in the region.

In October 1969, the Shah of Iran asked the U.S. to purchase more Iranian oil to boost his revenues. But the Shah's request was rejected because, as an assistant to then President Nixon explained, "a substantial portion of the profits from these purchases would go to non-American companies if Iranian oil were bought," while if Saudi oil were purchased, the U.S. share would be larger.

By the end of the 1960s, the international oil market was far different from what it had been two decades earlier. Oil supplies were tight, the number of oil firms had grown, and the producing countries, joined together in the Organization of Petroleum Exporting Countries (OPEC), were seeking to improve their financial position.

Crucial talks on oil prices began in 1970 between U.S. companies and the government of Libya. Significantly, Washington did not weigh in on the side of the companies, and in fact, the companies themselves did not put up much resistance to the price increases. In truth, for U.S. oil companies, higher prices would be beneficial, making profitable their growing investments in the developed nations (for example, in Alaska and the North Sea). Moreover, higher prices could be passed on to consumers—and in 1972-1973 oil companies raised their prices to a greater extent than higher crude costs warranted.

In 1972, the Nixon administration advocated higher oil prices. According to a study by V. H. Oppenheim, based on interviews with U.S. officials, "The weight of the evidence suggests that the principal consideration behind the indulgent U.S. government attitude toward higher oil prices was the belief that higher prices would produce economic benefits for the United States vis-à-vis its industrial competitors, Western Europe and Japan, and the key Middle Eastern states, Saudi Arabia and Iran." Henry Kissinger has since confirmed that this was U.S. Government thinking: "The rise in the price of energy would affect primarily Europe and Japan and probably improve America's competitive position."

In late 1973 and into 1974, the Arab oil producers cut production and imposed an embargo against the U.S. and the Netherlands for their pro-Israeli position. The U.S. public has memories of long lines at the gas pump, rationing, and a crisis atmosphere. However, in Kissinger's words, "the Arab embargo was a symbolic gesture of limited practical impact." The international oil companies, which totally monopolized petroleum distribution and marketing, pooled their oil, so the shortfall of Saudi supplies to the U.S. was made up from other sources. Overall, the oil companies spread out the production cutbacks to minimize suffering, and the country most supportive of Israel—the U.S.—suffered among the least. From January to March 1974, U.S. oil consumption was off 5 percent, compared to 15 percent in France and West Germany.

In the aftermath of the embargo, U.S. allies tried to negotiate their own bilateral petroleum purchase deals with the producing nations without going through the major international oil companies. Washington opposed these efforts indicating once again that the well-being of U.S. allies has never been the key consideration for U.S. policy-makers.

Nor for that matter has their crucial concern been the well-being of the average U.S. citizen. One former Defense Department official has estimated that it cost U.S. taxpayers about $47 billion in 1985 alone for military expenditures related to the Gulf; former Secretary of the Navy John Lehman put the annual figure at $40 billion.

These expenditures have been necessary for the survival of the West. According to former CIA analyst Maj. Gen. Edward B. Atkeson, if all Gulf oil were cut off, eliminating recreational driving (which in the U.S. accounts for 10 percent of total oil consumption) would reduce Western petroleum needs to a level easily replaceable from non-Gulf sources. Even in wartime, Atkeson concluded, Gulf oil is not essential to Western needs.

But the billions of dollars are a good investment for the oil companies, given that they don't pay the tab. To be sure, the multinationals no longer directly own the vast majority of Gulf crude production. But they have special buy-back deals with the producers whereby they purchase, at bargain prices, oil from the fields they formerly owned. According to former Senator Frank Church, U.S. firms "have a 'sweetheart' arrangement with Saudi Arabia, notwithstanding the nominal nationalization of their properties...." Radical regimes want to sell oil as much as conservative ones do, but a change of government in any Gulf state might eliminate the privileged position of the U.S. oil companies.

The internal security of regimes like Saudi Arabia against their own people depends heavily on outside, particularly U.S., support. Many Saudis believe that in return their country has been overproducing oil to please the United States, to the detriment of their nation's long-term interests. Selling oil beyond the point at which the proceeds can be productively invested is economically irrational, particularly given the fact that oil in the ground appreciates in value.

More democratic or nationalistic governments in the Gulf may not be so willing to sacrifice their own interests. And such governments will also be less willing to accommodate a U.S. military presence or to serve as U.S. proxies for maintaining the regional status quo.

For these reasons and to ensure continued flow of oil profits into investments in the U.S., for more than 40 years, through many changed circumstances, there has been one constant of U.S. policy in the Gulf: support for the most conservative available local forces in order to keep radical and popular movements from coming to power, no matter what the human cost, no matter how great the necessary manipulation or intervention.

And now, in the aftermath of the Gulf War, what is the U.S. status in the region? "By virtue of its military victory, the United States is likely to have more influence in OPEC than any industrial nation has ever exercised." American officials are just beginning to discuss how they might use their new franchise. The U.S. wanted Iraq out of Kuwait for reasons evident in 40 years of U.S. Gulf policy: We wanted no reduction in our relative control over oil prices, in the beneficial arrangements with Middle East governments, or in the share of oil profits invested in Western and particularly U.S. and British banks.

Was the Gulf War a Just War?

U.S. motives were the geopolitical and economic interests of elites, not law or ethics or anyone's freedom. Nonetheless, Iraq's violation of Kuwait's sovereignty was real and therefore wasn't the war just, even if U.S. aims weren't? Doesn't UN authorization make it right?

A useful way to think about the potential of the UN is by considering the analogy of domestic politics in the U.S. Though the U.S. has well-developed democratic institutions, the inequalities between rich and poor severely circumscribe true democracy: Those with money purchase political influence, not just by direct vote-buying, but through campaign contributions, control of the media, lobbying, threatening to withhold investment, and the like. Americans concerned with social justice have accordingly had a three-fold task. First, to have as many social decisions as possible brought under the control of elective institutions, rather than being left to the arbitrary authority of those with wealth and power. Second, to broaden democracy by extending political rights to encompass all disenfranchised groups. Third, to point out the inherent limitations of democracy so long as resources are unequally distributed.

The attitude of supporters of world legality toward the United Nations ought to be guided by the same principles as in the domestic analogy. We should strive as much as possible to shift responsibility for the maintenance of international order from the arbitrary power of individual states to the UN and we should seek as much as possible to democratize the UN. At the same time, we should be aware of the limits of such democratization—no amount of structural and voting changes in the UN will eliminate the power that wealth provides—and we should be prepared to denounce those instances where the UN clearly serves as the cover for that power.

And the way the U.S. used the UN in this crisis was clearly an instance of bought votes: Washington dangled the prospect of eased trade restrictions and a $1 billion loan from Saudi Arabia in front of Moscow; Beijing was offered a meeting at the White House, ending its international isolation after the Tienanmen Square massacre; Romania, in difficult financial straits, was desperate for U.S. aid—as Thomas L. Friedman of the *New York Times* reported, the Bush administration "never hesitated to let other nations know" that their support for the resolution authorizing force "was vital to Washington, which would remember its friends, and its foes." As soon as the Yemeni delegate voted against the resolution, "a senior American diplomat was instructed to tell him: 'That was the most expensive no vote you ever cast'—meaning it would result in an end to America's more than $70 million in foreign aid to Yemen."

UN compliance was also obtained by U.S. threats to use force unilaterally if not approved by the Security Council, and by U.S. monopolization of information. (The "UN committee charged with overseeing the sanctions has no staff, no money, and no clout to coax data out of international intelligence agencies" and was thus unable to independently judge the embargo.)

If UN ratification didn't make the war just, what about Iraq's violation of international law? It is logically true that the U.S. government could have the wrong motives for fighting a war that is, for other reasons, just. But what made the Gulf War unjust is not solely that the motives of the U.S. were self-serving, and that the brutal, virtually unanswered violence the U.S. employed would have been cowardly even if it had been a just war, but that the crisis was pursued militarily only to legitimate militarism instead of diplomacy. A war undertaken to legitimate war is not a just war.

What Is Bush's New World Order?

In the final days of the slaughter, the *New York Times* published a fragment of a national security review from the early days of the Bush administration. It reads: "In cases where the U.S. confronts much weaker enemies, our challenge will be not simply to defeat them, but to defeat them decisively and rapidly." Any other outcome in disputes with "small countries hostile to us" would be too "embarrassing" and might "undercut political support." The reporter who released the review suggests that the U.S. population must appreciate "the stark and vivid definition of principle ... baked into [George Bush] during his years at Andover and Yale, that honor and duty compels you to punch the bully in the face." He then quotes Bush: "By God, we've kicked the Vietnam syndrome once and for all." No longer, Bush exults, will we be troubled by "the sickly inhibitions against the use of military force," as Norman Podhoretz puts it.

Bush said the Mideast crisis should lay to rest talk about a "peace dividend" from cuts in the defense budget. What he meant was that he thinks the U.S. is now free from the two major hindrances to its exercise of brutal military might in the world. The Soviet Union has disappeared as a super power opponent. The U.S. public has lost its moral opposition to war.

Thomas Friedman of the *New York Times* declared that the Gulf crisis had shown that "even in this new multipolar world, only the United States is able and willing to be the policeman." Police officers, however, are supposed to be agents of the community as a whole; citizens who unilaterally try to maintain order are usually called "vigilantes."

Friedman's colleague, R.W. Apple Jr., explained that the U.S. "show of force was useful ... precisely because some people had begun to doubt American will in the post-Cold War era." According to administration officials, General Colin Powell, chair of the Joint Chiefs of Staff, "was not entirely certain after the Kuwait invasion that Iraq was going to move on to Saudi Arabia," but the United States nevertheless had to rush troops to the region "to demonstrate that it was still a superpower."

Columnist John J. Farmer made the point explicitly: "At bottom, the cause for the United States in the gulf crisis is ... Washington's determination to retain its place as the world's last superpower, as arbiter, in effect, of a kind of global Pax Americana." In the London *Financial Times* of November 21, 1990, a respected commentator describes the Gulf crisis as a "watershed event in U.S. international relations," which will be seen in history as having "turned the U.S. military into an internationally financed public good." In the 1990s, he continues, "there is no realistic alternative [to] the U.S. military assuming a more explicitly mercenary role than it has played in the past."

The financial editor of the *Chicago Tribune* put the point less delicately at about the same time: "We must exploit our virtual monopoly in the security market ... as a lever to gain funds and economic concessions" from Germany and Japan. The U.S. has "cornered the West's security market" and will therefore be "the world's rent-a-cops."

Some will call us "Hessians," he continues, but "that's a terribly demeaning phrase for a proud, well-trained, well-financed and well-respected military"; and whatever anyone may say, "we should be able to pound our fists on a few desks" in Japan and Europe, and "extract a fair price for our considerable services," demanding that our rivals "buy our bonds at cheap rates, or keep the dollar propped up, or better yet, pay cash directly into our treasury." "We could change this role" of enforcer against the Third World, he concludes, "but with it would go much of our control over the world economic system."

What Is the War at Home Really About?

People in the U.S. who are suffering its violence have long recognized an ongoing "war at home." It is against people of color, poor people, women, the homeless, the unemployed, and all working people. It takes the form of the dissolution of services and welfare programs of all types, including health care, housing, and education, and an accompanying reduction of income. The domestic infrastructure is deteriorating, the economy is declining, housing is not affordable, schools are like jails, streets are dangerous—but the wealthy suburbs, business districts, and resorts remain comfortable and opulent.

It has always been true that massive military expenditures are only partly designed to develop military might. Much of their logic comes from a desire to cajole huge sums from the public in taxes which could then be profitably spent on militarism without disrupting hierarchies of wealth and power.

Now the situation is further aggravated. Having put so much into militarism for so long, the U.S. is no longer able to compete in non-military markets with Europe and Japan. To do so again, we would have to develop a workforce far better educated and more secure than ours now is. But this would require solutions to social problems causing a redistribution of wealth and power. From the perspective of U.S. elites this scenario involves immediate losses and threatens greater future losses as working and poor people become better educated and more materially secure and therefore better able to fight for further gains.

The New World Order is the preferred, alternative way for U.S. elites to remain at the top of the international hierarchy of wealth and power without having to risk solving U.S. domestic ills. We export violence and extort payments for committing it. War at home and war abroad are therefore connected. It's not just that a militaristic foreign policy reduces resources available to solve pressing problems at home. It is that because elites *prefer* to ignore domestic problems, they must pursue militarism and war at an ever increasing scale. As we become a mercenary state the fact that our city's are failing and our workforce undereducated becomes not a debit, but a good breeding ground for military enlistment. Growth industries become police repression at home, arms exports, international demolition and also, ironically, international construction. We no longer destroy cities to save them. Now, for a fee, we destroy whole countries and then profit from rebuilding them.

— February 1991

TV Guide

W hat if the videotape of LA cops beating up a Black man had been fabricated to undercut the legitimacy of the LA police? Or, what if Jesse Jackson vigorously opposed government policy using film footage of unemployed people, who later turned out to be Hollywood extras assembled for the purpose? Such manipulation would be big news. The perpetrators credibility would be reduced to zero.

The *TV Guide* of February 22 featured a cover story titled "Fake News," by an otherwise unidentified David Lieberman. The article describes how private companies hire public-relations firms to produce tapes that look like independent news reports. These high quality, self-serving clips are then made available to television news shows that carry them without any special identification. The result, says Lieberman, is that an already large and rapidly increasing percentage of what we see on the nightly news is from private sources. Lieberman calls this "fake news."

Accompanying Lieberman's article is a lengthy sidebar by Morgan Strong, identified as a freelance writer who covers the Middle East. The title is "Portions of the Gulf War were brought to you by ... the folks at Hill and Knowlton." Strong's story repeats a relatively familiar revelation that the reporting of Iraqi atrocities against Kuwaiti babies was fabricated and that related testimony given before the UN and Congress and widely shown and reported throughout the U.S., was also false. But the new claim that makes Strong's piece worth reading is that this duplicity was orchestrated by "the public relations firm of Hill and Knowlton headed at the time by Craig Fuller, former chief of staff to George Bush when he was vice president."

Strong details a variety of techniques used by Hill and Knowlton and lists some of the more extreme examples used in the PR firm's effort to build public support for the Gulf War.

It's important to realize what is and what isn't new about all this. The practice of presenting compromised material as if it were objective is of course as old as the media. The material prepared by news staffs of TV stations, newspapers, etc., is not independent. After all, their employer is a corporate giant not an independent, objective, socially responsible actor. For decades, corporations, the Pentagon, and the government have been providing a large portion of the news that appears on TV and in daily newspapers, through press conferences, position papers, news leaks, and the like, all usually reported without any scrutiny, analysis, or indication of the compromised source. The idea of consciously orchestrating a counterfeit image of reality to galvanize support for heinous acts is also nothing new. In recent history countless media lies exist; the best archetype is probably the phoney Gulf of Tonkin "story" about North Vietnamese militarism against the U.S. Navy.

So what is new in the Gulf War case? There is no longer a serious effort to fake the fake news. It is now okay, after the fact, to let everyone know that the news was fake. After all, the fake news did its job. Later revelations only produce more cynicism and more public attention to form and appearance rather than a hidden reality. Revelation also removes the onus and costs of long-term secrecy, and generally jades the population to its own oppression. And with no need for permanent secrecy, the government and corporations can use private PR firms, the best in the business, despite almost guaranteed leaks.

Is this exaggeration? The best way to tell is by assessing the response to the *TV Guide* story, which many millions of people will see. Will the "fake news" story galvanize a militant movement to reclaim the media and restrain government and corporate elites? Will it spur a new law requiring indication when news reports are public-relations projects? Will the presidential candidates take up the cry? Or will the story disappear through the cracks, save for the herd of new clients who will no doubt flock to Hill and Knowlton?

There is no more wide-reaching print media message-bearer than TV *Guide*. The cover story, "Fake News," says not only that the government lied to pursue its Gulf War aims, but also that the government and corporations lie regularly to pursue their aims, and do it with the connivance of the media so the lies appear as honest reports. OK, the *TV Guide* articles aren't a detailed Noam Chomsky exegesis, and *TV Guide* isn't a place people turn for critical social analysis, but the articles make an important, revealing point to the widest possible print audience. Those interested in using their own or mainstream media to affect public consciousness need to seriously consider the response, or lack thereof, that this article engenders.

— March 1992

Stop The Killing Train

Suppose a hypothetical god got tired of what we humans do to one another and decided that from January 1, 1991 onward all corpses unnaturally created anywhere in the "free world" would cease to decompose. Anyone dying for want of food or medicine, anyone hung or garroted to death, shot or beaten to death, raped or bombed to death, anyone dying unjustly and inhumanely would, as a corpse, persist without decomposing. And the permanent corpse would then automatically enter a glass-walled cattle car attached to an ethereal train traveling monotonously across the U.S., state by state, never stopping.

One by one the corpses would be loaded onto the cattle cars and after every thousand corpses piled in, higgeldy piggeldy, a new car would hitch up and begin filling too. Mile after mile the killing train would roll along, each corpse viewed through its transparent walls, 200 new corpses a minute, one new car every five minutes, day and night, without pause.

By the end of 1991, on its first birthday, the killing train would measure over 2,000 miles long. Traveling at 20 miles an hour it would take about five days to pass any intersection. By the year 2000, assuming no dramatic change in institutions and behavior, the train would stretch from coast to coast about seven times. It would take about six weeks from the time its engine passed the Statue of Liberty to when its caboose would go by. God still wondering when pitiful, aspiring humanity would get the message.

Think how a young child sometimes points to a picture in a book or magazine and asks for an explanation, "Tell me about a tree?" A car? A boat? Or a train? A big train? The killing train? Go ahead, answer that one.

If the ecologists are right that this planet is a single super-organism, they are wrong that pollution, toxic waste, and other human-created garbage is the most deadly virus attacking it. The killing train is worse.

Think about the pain that radiates from the Vietnam War monument with its 50,000 names in Washington, D.C. Imagine the lost opportunity and lost love and the network of negative influences that radiate from the unnecessary deaths enumerated on that monument. Now think about the killing train stretching from coast to coast and back and forth and back and forth and back and forth. Consider its impact, not only on those on board, but on every person that any of those corpses ever loved or would have loved, fed or would have fed, taught or would have taught.

Who rides the killing train? Citizens of the "Third World," selling their organs for food, selling their babies to save their families, suffering disappearances and starvation. They live in Brazil, the Philippines, El Salvador, and New York. They are headed for the killing train. Every day. Millions.

Is this exaggerated? When 10 million kids die yearly for lack of basic medical aid that the U.S. could provide at almost no cost in countries whose economies Exxon and the Bank of America have looted, what can you call it other than mass murder? Bloated diseased bodies are victims of murder just as surely as bullet-riddled bodies tossed into rivers by death squads. Denying medicine is no less criminal than supplying torture racks and stealing resources.

Evolution has given humans the capacity to perceive, think, feel, imagine. At a time of war—as now in the Gulf—if we get aroused to action we begin to see the whole train as it persists day in and day out. When this happens, what do we do about it. Become depressed? Cynical? Anguished? Cry? Daydream of Armageddon? Daydream of justice? Hand out a leaflet?

Once we begin to see it, how do we face the killing train? Part of me says these crimes are so grotesque, so inhumane, that the perpetrators deserve to die, now. A little tiny killing train for the killers and no more big killing train for everyone else. An eye for a million eyes. What other step makes more sense? But, of course, that's not the way the world works. People give the orders, wield the axes, withhold the food, pay the pitiful salaries, but institutions create the pressures that mold these people. When an institutional cancer consumes the human patient, what kind of surgeon can cut it all away? Is the weight of repression so intense it can never be lifted?

At first, becoming attuned to our country's responsibility for the corpses stacked behind transparent cattle-car walls makes handing out leaflets, or arguing for peace with a co-worker, or urging a relative to think twice about paying taxes, or going to a demonstration, or sitting in, or even doing civil disobedience seem insignificant. But the fact is, these are the acts that the hypothetical God, tired of our behavior, would be calling for if she were to actually parade the "free world's" corpses down our mainstreets in killing trains. These are the acts that can accumulate into a firestorm of informed protest that raises the cost of profiteering and domination so high that the institutions breeding such behavior start to buckle.

The fact is, "You lose, you lose, you lose, and then you win." Every loss is part of the process that leads to transforming institutions so that there can be no people as vile as Hussein or Bush, as hypocritical as Aziz or Baker. No more "Good Germans" or "Good Americans," cremated Jews or decapitated peasants.

War in the Middle East is a horrendous crime against humanity. It is an orchestrated atrocity that mandates our militant, unswerving opposition. There should be no business as usual until this war is ended and all U.S. troops leave the Midle East.

But even after the Gulf War ends, the on-going U.S. war against "free world" people destined to ride the killing train will, if it continues, remain a tremendous crime against humanity. The killing train transcends the Gulf. Ultimately, so must our opposition. The killing train—poverty, disease, starvation, death squads, and terror—stems from basic institutions. These too must become our target.

—February 1991

The Canon

It is currently all the rage to attack the universities and especially "radical faculty" on the grounds that they are being too subjective. The claim is that leftists are violating a sacrosanct, heretofore operative norm of apolitical objectivity, instead attempting to impose "political correctness."

The main focus of this raging debate is the literary canon. "Traditionalists" claim that the canon is just fine. That it is composed entirely of white male writers from a European tradition indicates only that that tradition and those people have been the source of the most enduring and valuable work. "Revisionists" claim the canon is overly narrow and discriminatory and not properly descriptive of the actual diversity of American culture.

The traditionalists claim the canon, and with it most of Western civilization, is "under siege." Moreover, at stake is not only literature's required readings, but whether the university will continue to be an apolitical zone of disinterested study, or fall victim to "totalitarian urban guerrillas" imposing politically correct behavior.

Revisionists, surprised at the vehemence of assault against their modest demands, actually do not want to replace the current canon of required readings. They merely want to enlarge it by including works by writers other than white, Eurocentric men. For leftists this is not much of a debate. As the old slogan goes, one side's right, one side's wrong, and anyone not racist and sexist is likely to support a victory for the revisionists, even if he or she finds many other views of left literary theorists more problematic.

But it is surprising that, as far as we know, no one has as yet made the obvious point that on "apolitical objectivity": The traditionalists are completely devoid of integrity. The university is not now and never has been a place of disinterested, politically unconstrained study or research in other than the hard sciences, and arguably not even there. Thus the revisionists' campaign is not against a norm of objectivity and reason, but for loosening prior lockstep ideological conformity.

Take English, for example. The traditional reading list has reflected the racist, sexist, and classist character of the defining institutions of society and the interests of the elites that control those institutions. This has been so because (1) the universities are among those institutions and reflect the same norms, (2) the administrators of universities are among those elites and pursue the same interests, and (3) selection and advancement procedures within university departments have as much to do with being liked and serving one's elite employers as with the quality of one's intellectual work.

As a result, opinion within university departments is self-censored. In literature this means the canon at Stanford University includes 33 white male writers, only the tip of the university's ideological conformity iceberg.

The degree of ideological homogenization of economics, politics, government, and other departments is so great that, as Noam Chomsky puts it, "certain ideas, however natural and well-supported, do not even come to mind or, if noticed, can be dismissed with derision."

How does academic conformity arise? Partly prior training and socialization outside academia. But additionally a selection process operates within the university. Some young scholars are "hard to get along with," are "too strident," "show poor taste in their choice of topics," "don't use the proper methodology," or in other ways don't meet professional standards that insulate ideologically constrained scholarship from challenge. They disappear or struggle in virtual isolation while those easier to get along with, less strident, and with better taste and methodology determine canons.

Consider an example that Chomsky raises, the investigation of the hypothesis that "corporations have some influence, perhaps significant influence, in setting foreign policy." Certainly this is plausible, given the extent of corporate profit that arises from foreign operations. And certainly it is worth investigation, assuming one is disinterestedly concerned to understand the roots and dynamics of foreign policy. So, in an ideologically unconstrained university, we would anticipate that the hypothesis would be thoroughly investigated.

In fact, when Dennis Ray did a 1972 study of "respectable literature" of admired, influential scholars, he found that less than 5 percent of 200 books granted even passing attention to the role of corporations in U.S. foreign relations. In his words, "There is virtually no acknowledgement in standard works within the field of international relations and foreign policy of the existence of influence of corporations."

To top it off, Ray himself, after having uncovered these results, deems the people in academia who obscure or deny critical truths "respectable scholars," while he views those who reveal and study the same critical truths as engaged in "advocacy" rather than scholarship. This is how people like Gabriel Kolko move from being respected scholars to being "essentially pamphleteers" as they dispense with ideological blinders.

The university is a factory for producing rationalizations of elite behavior while curtailing investigations of why society works as it does, what its effects are, who benefits, who loses, and what alternatives might exist. Any breach in the wall of ideological conformity is viewed as a catastrophic assault—first, because it stands out like a single black dot on a uniformly white background, and second, because any breach threatens that the academic Emperor's nudity will be revealed, if not to cohorts who lack even rudimentary sight, at least to students and perhaps those beyond academia's walls.

Thus, here's some unsolicited advice to revisionists in the canon debate. Forgo the defensive; go on the attack. Make the whole disgusting charade of academia's objectivity your target. And don't ignore class in your rightful efforts to pay serious attention to race and gender.

—May 1991

Post-Modernism

A little over two years ago, preparing to ride from Boston to New York to attend the Socialist Scholars Conference, I asked a scholar friend to explain "post-modernism" in the four to five hours we would spend on the road. He accepted, and we rode—he lecturing and me listening.

When we got to New York if someone had walked up and asked, "What is post-modernism?" I could not have answered. Four hours and I still didn't know what "post-modernism" referred to. Three interpretations spring to mind.

- My tutor was an idiot incapable of explaining one concept in four hours.

- I am an idiot incapable of understanding one concept in four hours.

- The concept is idiotic, a vague pastiche of mush covering a range too broad to clarify in four hours.

The third possibility, as you might guess, is my favorite. But how could a concept which engenders shelves of books be nearly empty? Here's my hypothesis: Literary theory is largely a sham literary theorists use to cajole regal treatment from their professional cohorts, bosses, students, and broader intellectual community.

How can I commit such blasphemy?

First, calling an academic discipline phony is often common sense, not blasphemy.

Take mainstream economics. Nearly the entire "neoclassical" economic edifice is constructed to legitimate the rewards of economists by pleasing the corporate piper who pays the bills. Thus, mainstream economists mainly "prove" capitalism's worth or indicate how capitalists can better pursue their own ends and rarely try to understand how the system works, who benefits, who loses, and why.

Or take academic political science. Again, the idea is not actually to understand the government—who would pay scholars to do this?—but to "theorize government" in ways that justify official behavior.

I doubt that Z readers would recoil in horror at these condemnations of mainstream economics and politics. I even think most Z readers would probably find supporting evidence quite convincing. For example, surveys reveal that economics graduate students accept these horrible assertions about their own profession, and the best first-hand documentation of the inner workings of the U.S. government, such as the Pentagon Papers, are exactly the materials that political science departments never bother to study.

But literary theory? Surely this can't be phony. After all, the most obscure practitioners of literary theory are often radicals and self-serving mystification is never radical.

Nonetheless, suppose you are an English literature teacher and you want a high salary, intellectual status, and tenure. How does reading and discussing literature warrant receipt of such goodies? Wouldn't admitting that such matter-of-fact activity was the essence of teaching English literature make it hard to justify big bucks, big status, tenure, and paid trips to distant conferences? To justify these rewards there must be a "theory" that takes years to master and that some people employ better than others, at least in their own eyes.

Enter literary theory, an incomprehensible tangle of concepts and phrases made so dense and vague that:

- No one who isn't willing to suspend rationality can use it.

- No one can possibly get enough of a grip on it to counter or refute it.

- Anyone who attempts to can be ridiculed on the grounds of not understanding the theory in the first place.

Thus, with their incomprehensible "discourse" in place, literary theorists have a defensible academic niche. The fact that many students feel like dummies because they don't have a clue what's going on is apparently insufficient reason for anyone in the club to rock the boat.

Now I admit that the above is very harsh and no more than an undefended hypothesis. And I also admit that the reason for the lack of supporting textual evidence is because my attempts to find a literary theory book that I can comprehend sufficiently to assess have been futile. Here's the kind of "discourse" you have to comprehend to read even what the less obscure literary theorists say about novels, movies, MTV, modern architecture, pop songs, and modern literature: post-modern moment, binarisms, overdetermined conflict, pure systematicity, post-structuralism, hermeneutic, metanarrative, deconstruction, irreducible materiality, semiotics, and dialogism.

Not understanding these tangled terms and doubting the need to use them to comment sensibly on pop music's Talking Heads, TV's "The Young and the Restless," Hollywood's *Star Wars*, baseball's Dodgers Stadium, or literature's Ishmael Reed, I more than happily grant that my hypothesis that these terms mean nothing may be wrong. Perhaps "irreducible materiality" and "pure systematicity" are exactly the concepts needed to "theorize" Madonna. But if so, it still ought to be possible for literary theorists to describe, popularize, and generally make understandable what their results are so the rest of us can know there is something real going on behind all the obscure terminology. Even the most difficult physics can be described so average persons get a good idea of the main results and questions. If it can be done for theories about quarks, gluons, big bangs, and black holes, it ought to be able to be done for theories about everyday culture and communication.

So, please, someone tell me what I can read to understand literary theory so that I can withdraw my hypothesis and write an informative summary. I'll bet not one percent of Z's readers can define the earlier listed terms. So wouldn't it be sensible to let the rest of us in on the action, assuming there is any?

— May 1991

Conspiracy ... Not!

Nowadays, wherever they go, leftists encounter many questions from newly political folks about this or that political episode—the October Surprise, the BCCI scandal, Irancontra, David Duke—with an emphasis on who did what, when, and with what knowledge and intent. They field far fewer questions about the *systemic* causes of trends and events. People study the membership of some rogue group. They ignore the structure of government and corporations. How did this trend come about? Where is it taking us?

Conspiracy Theory

A conspiracy theory is a hypothesis that some events were caused by the intractable secret machinations of undemocratic individuals. A prime example is to explain Irancontra as the secret rogue actions of Oliver North and co-conspirators. Likewise, another conspiracy theory explains the hostage-holding in Carter's last presidential year as the machinations of a "secret team" helping Reagan win the presidency. A conspiracy theory of Karen Silkwood's murder would uncover the names of people who secretly planned and carried out the murder. Bending usage, we could even imagine a conspiracy theory of patriarchy as men uniting to deny women status, or a conspiracy theory of the U.S. government as competing groups seeking power for their own ends.

Conspiracies exist. Groups regularly do things without issuing press releases and this becomes a conspiracy whenever their actions transcend "normal" behavior. We don't talk of a conspiracy to win an election if the suspect activity includes only candidates and their handlers working privately to develop effective strategy. We do talk about a conspiracy if the resulting action involves stealing the other team's plans, spiking their Gatorade, or other exceptional activity.

Conspiracy theories may or may not identify real coteries with real influence. Conspiracy theories:

(1) claim that a particular group acted outside usual norms in a rogue and generally secretive fashion;

(2) disregard the structural features of institutions.

Personalities, personal timetables, secret meetings, and conspirators' joint actions claim attention. Institutional relations drop from view. We ask, did North meet with Bush before or after the meeting between MacFarlane and Mr. X? Do we have a document that reveals the plan in advance? Do phone conversations implicate so and so? How credible is that witness?

Institutional Theory

In an institutional theory, personalities and personal motivations enter the discussion only as results of more basic factors. The personal actions culminating in some event do not serve as explanation. The theory explains phenomena via roles, incentives, and dynamics of underlying institutions. An institutional theory doesn't ignore human actions, but the point of an institutional explanation is to move from personal factors to institutional ones. If the particular people hadn't been there to do it, someone else would have.

An institutional theory of Irancontra and the October Surprise would explain how and why these activities arose in a society with our political, social, and economic forms. An institutional theory of Karen Silkwood's murder would reveal nuclear industry and larger societal pressures that provoked her murder. An institutional theory of patriarchy explains gender relations in terms of marriage, the church, the market, socialization, etc. An institutional theory of government emphasizes the control and dissemination of information, the dynamics of bureaucracy, and the role of subservience to class, race, and gender interests.

Institutions exist. Whenever they have sufficient impact on events, developing an institutional theory makes sense. However, when an event arises from a unique conjuncture of particular people and opportunities, while institutions undoubtedly play a role, it may not be generalized and an institutional theory may be out of place or even impossible to construct.

Institutional theories may or may not identify real relationships with real influence on the events they explain. Institutional theories:

(1) claim that the normal operations of some institutions generate the behaviors and motivations leading to the events in question;

(2) address personalities, personal interests, personal timetables, and meetings only as facts about the events needing explanation, not as explanations themselves.

Organizational, motivational, and behavioral implications of institutions gain most attention. Particular people, while not becoming mere ciphers, are not accorded priority as causal agents.

The Difference

For a conspiracy theorist, the implicit problem is to punish or "impeach" the immediate culprits, a general point applicable to all conspiracy theory. The *modus operandi* of the conspiracy theorist therefore makes sense whenever the aim is to attribute proximate personal blame for some occurrence. If we want to prosecute someone for a political assassination to extract retribution or to set a precedent that makes it harder to carry out such actions, the approach of the conspiracy theorist is critical. But the conspiracy approach is beside the point for understanding the *cause* of political assassinations to develop a program to prevent all policies that thwart popular resistance. Conspiracy theorizing mimics the personality/dates/times approach to history. It is a sports fan's or voyeur's view of complex circumstances. It can manipulate facts or present them accurately. When it's done honestly, it has its place, but it is not always the best approach.

For some who favor an institutional analysis, the problem is to discern the underlying institutional causes of foreign policy. The *modus operandi* of the institutional theorist would not make much sense for discovering which individuals conceived and argued for a policy, or who in particular decided to bomb a civilian shelter. To understand *why* these things happen, however, and under what conditions they will or will not continue to happen, institutional theory is indispensable and the motives, methods, and timetables of the actual perpetrators are beside the point.

Take the media. A conspiracy approach will highlight the actions of some coterie of editors, writers, newscasters, particular owners, or even a lobby. An institutional approach will mention the actions of these actors as evidence, but will highlight the corporate and ideological pressures giving rise to those influences. A person inclined toward finding conspiracies will listen to evidence of media subservience to power and see a cabal of bad guys, perhaps corporate, perhaps religious, perhaps federal, censoring the media from doing its proper job. The conspiracist will then want to know about the cabal and how people succumb to its will, etc. A person inclined toward institutional analysis will listen to evidence of media subservience to power and see that the media's internal bureaucracy, socialization processes, and interests of its owners engender these results as part of the media succeeding at its job. The institutionalist will then want to know about the media's structural features and how they work, and about the guiding interests and what they imply.

The conspiracy approach will lead people to believe that either:

(1) They should educate the malefactors to change their motives, or

(2) They should get rid of the malefactors and back new editors, writers, newscasters, or owners.

The institutional approach will note the possible gains from changes in personnel, but explain how limited these changes will be. It will incline people

(1) Toward a campaign of constant pressure to offset the constant institutional pressures for obfuscation, or

(2) Toward the creation of new media free from the institutional pressures of the mainstream.

The Appeal of Conspiracy Theory

Naturally, conspiracy theory and its associated personalistic methodology appeals to prosecutors since they must identify proximate causes and human actors. But why does it appeal to people concerned to change society?

There are a many possible answers that probably all operate to varying degrees on people who favor conspiracy theory. First, conspiracy theory is often compelling and the evidence conspiracy theories reveal is often useful. Furthermore, description of the detailed entwinements becomes addictive. One puzzle and then another and another need analysis. Conspiracy theory has the appeal of a mystery—it is dramatic, compelling, vivid, and human. Finally, the desire for retribution helps fuel continuing forays into personal details.

Second, conspiracy theories have manageable implications. They imply that all was well once and that it can be okay again if only the conspirators can be pushed aside. Conspiracy theories therefore explain ills without forcing us to disavow society's underlying institutions. They allow us to admit horrors, and express our indignation and anger without rejecting the basic norms of society. We can even confine our anger to the most blatant perpetrators. That government official or corporate lawyer is bad, but many others are good and the government and law *per se* are okay. We need to get rid of the bad apples. All this is convenient and seductive. We can reject specific candidates but not government, specific CEOs but not capitalism, specific writers, editors, and even owners of periodicals, but not all mainstream media. We reject some vile manipulators, but not society's basic institutions. We can therefore continue to appeal to the institutions for recognition, status, or payment.

Third, conspiracy theory provides an easy and quick outlet for pent-up passion withheld from targets that seem unassailable or that might strike back. This is conspiracy theory turned into scapegoat theory.

Where Are Conspiracy Theories Taking Us?

It would be bad enough if endless personalistic attention to Irancontra, the October Surprise, Inslaw, etc., were just attuning people to search after coteries while ignoring institutions. This was the effect, for example, of the many Kennedy assassination theorists of past decades. At least the values at play would be progressive and we could hope that people would soon gravitate toward real explanation of more structural phenomena.

But the fact is, the values inspiring conspiratorial ways of trying to explain events are beginning to drastically diverge from progressive values. Even some left activists have become so hungry for quick-fix conspiracy explanations they are beginning to gravitate toward any conspiracy claim, no matter how ridiculous.

Thus the field of conspiracy theorizing has become attractive, and new entrants are no longer always progressive and sometimes even tilt toward reaction or downright fascism. The presentation of conspiracy theories has moved from little newsletters and journals to large audience radio talk shows and magazines and, at the same time, from identifying "secret teams" of CIA operatives to all-powerful networks of Arab financiers and worldwide Jewish bankers' fraternities.

There is an ironic analogy here to some recent analysis of national Republican Party politics. In that arena, many journalists now claim that the Republican Party's manipulations of race in prior years paved the way for David Duke by reacclimating the public to racial stereotyping and increasing its appetite for more. In somewhat the same way, isn't it plausible that the relatively huge resources thrown into progressive conspiracy writing, organizing, and proselytizing over the past decade is now coming home to roost? Of course, the changing times are partly responsible for growing public interest in conspiracies, but doesn't past behavior by progressives bear a share of responsibility as well?

What to Do About It

Leftist institutionalist theorists generally ignore conspiracy theorists as irrelevant. To confront their arguments is to enter a miasma of potentially fabricated detail from which there is no escape. Nothing constructive emerges. But perhaps this view needs some rethinking. When Holly Sklar, Steve Shalom, Noam Chomsky or any of many other left analysts talk about events, even about Irancontra or the October Surprise, they pay attention to proximate facts but also the institutional context. That's as it should be, but apparently it's no longer good enough. Now, those who have an institutional critique may have two additional responsibilities. First, perhaps they should point out the inadequacy of left conspiracy theory, showing that at best it does not go far enough to be useful for organizers. Second, perhaps they should debunk and castigate rightist conspiracy theory, removing its aura of opposition and revealing its underlying racist and elitist allegiances.

Likewise, when progressive radio talk shows and left journals and magazines invite people to communicate with their public about world and national events, it is good to be sure the guest is coherent, has effective speaking or writing style, talks about the issues, identifies actors accurately, and knows about the relevant history. But that isn't enough. Fascists can fulfill these standards and still spout made-up statistics as if they were facts, disgusting allegations about social groups as if they were objective commentary, and nothing at all about real institutional relations, passing this whole mess off as a useful way to look at the world. Left media, even strapped as it is, should take responsibility for its offerings. People expect that if commentators appear on our shows and in our publications they have a degree of integrity, honesty, and sensitivity. We should not lend credence to right-wing garbage, whether it is blatant or so well concealed as to be civil but malicious. Even regarding progressive and left conspiracy theory, while it often uncovers important evidence, left activists ought to indicate its limits and augment it with institutional and contextual analysis.

—January 1992

Irrationalism

An "anti-rationality" trend is sweeping our society. It's hard to specify its scope or breadth but it seems most pronounced in parts of the left. Consider the following experiences:

- At a talk to a group of activists and academics eight months ago in Amherst, MA, a speaker is repeatedly called "too logical." He is told he offers too much evidence, hypothesis, and argument, and too few emotive descriptions. His "scientific style" renders his words worthless. *A priori,* his ideas are dismissed.

- A few weeks later, a Midwestern anarchist editorial advises activists to henceforth doubt the writings of a heretofore highly respected commentator. The fellow accepts too many of "western technology's" offerings and by this allegiance his utterances are made suspect.

- More recently, a New York leftist attends a conference and is criticized for being "too forthright" in expressing strong disagreement with a presentation. When she protests that forthrightness is honest and therefore good, she is told that forthrightness is "too fractious." Rather than confront people she should simply "reinterpret their words to make them more acceptable to her own views." This will reduce disagreement and "show respect."

- Next, an exchange occurs at a meeting in Chicago because someone asserts that some claim about our culture is true. She is told by another activists that there is no such thing as truth—neither her claim nor any other. It is better to discuss competing interpretations, possibilities, or stories than truth. Truth is too final, too closed, too imperial. There is no one truth, no one angle for knowing, and therefore no single right answers.

- Finally, we have JFK and Vietnam. First, a view is posited: "JFK wanted to end the war and was killed for it." Then, when some data can be "reinterpreted," "massaged," or manufactured to fit that view, it's done.

On the other hand, when all other evidence contradicts that view, it's ignored.

I could go on with specific instances and broader trends including aspects of conspiracy theory, especially on the West Coast, and, of course, the miasma of post-modernist theory throughout academia. The point isn't that all these phenomena are identical. They aren't. But they are part of a growing trend elevating anti-rationality to a virtue and demoting rationality to a sin.

When I first encountered this new "anti-rationalism," it seemed to be just another arcane, academic fad that would quickly fade. Now, however, seeing how many tributaries feed anti-rationalism, I worry that my optimistic reaction may have been wishful thinking.

Roots of Anti-Rationalism

Anti-rationalism arises, in part, from many insights about science, the most self-consciously rational pursuit. These insights include feminism's assault on scientific machismo, multiculturalism's rejection of scientific racism, social ecology's advocacy of wholeness as against scientific reductionism, anthropology's respect for experience as against scientific abstraction, humanists' regard for diverse inquiry as against solely following the "scientific method," common sense's rejection of scientific propaganda, and the working class's hostility to coordinator class (managerial, professional, academic) elitism.

- Source 1. Feminism. Feminist critics are right that the questions scientists ask and even the answers they give frequently incorporate sexist assumptions. Moreover, women scientists have certainly been excluded, relegated to lesser opportunities, or cast in a peculiar light if they succeed against the odds. U.S. science is often sexist.

- Source 2. Multiculturalism. As multiculturalists point out, efforts to homogenize cultural differences, whether by assimilation or annihilation, have often had the support of scientists arguing for cranial differences between the races and the like. Likewise, the scientific establishment has certainly incorporated almost exclusively Eurocentric culture, largely excluding or at least greatly discomforting third world scientists. U.S. science is often racist.

- Source 3. Ecological Activism. As Greens claim, reductionist, technological approaches to "fixing our environment" are often as much a part of the ecological problem as the polluting chimneys or leaking pipes they try to correct. Likewise, scientists often ignore the interconnectedness of reality and frequently emphasize parts to the exclusion of highlighting holistic ecological insights. U.S. science often pollutes.

- Source 4. Anthropology. As anthropologists report, scientists do frequently run roughshod over people who lack scientific language and methods but who, nonetheless, have acquired great wisdom and insight. Moreover, their historically accumulated experience is then often lost forever under the scientific onslaught. Tribal knowledge of the medicinal powers of various herbs or sustainable farming are obvious examples of wisdom often denigrated, ignored, and finally lost forever. U.S. science often colonizes.

- Source 5. Humanism. Humanists are right that scientists often denigrate nonscientific ways of knowing that ignore rules of evidence and even logic (such as mimicry, fictionalization, poetic expression, dramatization, experience, etc.), without admitting that huge realms of experience well addressed by these approaches entirely defy scientific analysis. U.S. science often exaggerates its own power.

- Source 6. Common Sense. Popular common sense correctly tells many folks that a nuclear physicist arguing that fission reactors are safe, or a biochemist arguing that cigarettes don't really cause cancer, or an engineer arguing that work must be organized in a hierarchy of jobs differentiated by skill and empowerment, are all hypocrites. Their expert, "statistically ratified" testimony is pure bunk, packaged for the highest bidder. U.S. science often sells out.

- Source 7. Class Consciousness. Finally, of course, working people are right when they feel it is unadulterated self-serving ideology when doctors, managers, scientists, and other representatives of the "coordinator class" claim that their advanced knowledge entitles them to assert what is true and false and good and bad about everything from the nature of the atom to the meaning of hope or love, and then to decide how our lives ought to be lived. U.S. science often exploits.

Science—meaning verified knowledge—is sometimes limited, biased, or just plain propaganda. Science—meaning the practice of accumulating verified knowledge—is often distorted in its questions and answers, often dominates those with different agendas, and is often just plain bought and paid for. Scientists—meaning the people who accumulate verified knowledge—are sometimes narrow, mechanical, colonizing, or hypocritical. Moreover, all these problems exist primarily along the familiar axes of class, race, power, and gender. Science can therefore be an illegitimate totalizing project, can marginalize less scientifically presented knowledge, and can argue, seemingly quite rationally, for the most odious projects, just as its critics claim.

At Los Alamos during the massive multidisciplinary effort to develop the atomic bomb, biographies indicate that not one influential scientist morally questioned the project. Worse, a significant number of the scientists present thought that an open-air detonation of their new weapon might conceivably ignite the atmosphere thereby terminating all earthly life. They ignited the bomb anyway, afterward expressing relief to be alive to assess the devastation.

So What's Wrong With "Anti-Rationalism?"

When I was a student at MIT (1965-1969), I spent considerable time struggling against the nearly overwhelming arrogance and hypocrisy of science. I called the school "Dachau on the Charles," and I would rail at its noted scientists for having despicable values and for so often imperially usurping the rights of others. Because of the particular character of the place, I repeatedly urged, by logic and emotive example, that there was nothing wrong with strong emotions and that feelings and values should have a priority in deciding what to do with the insights that more sober analysis produced. My hostility for the majority of the world-class scientists around me easily kept pace with what contemporary ecologists, feminists, multiculturalists, and sensible citizens and workers feel for today's experts. Moreover, nearly a quarter of century later, my views on this score are, if anything, even more militant. Yet I have *never* criticized rationality or logic, and though anti-elitism and anti-coordinatorism are part of my project, anti-intellectualism is anathema to me.

These distinctions are important. (1) To critique scientific knowledge and scientists is part of understanding the world to make it better. Indeed, that kind of critique is a core activity of science itself. Moreover, (2) to suggest methods that people could use to avoid excessive reductionism, to ward off sexist, racist, and classist biases, or to guard against exaggerating the scope of scientific insights is a useful way to aid scientists (and political activists as well). But to then (3) criticize reason, logic, and the rules of evidence as being at the root of science's many evils is a misconceived act of self-denial. It is both wrong and has no role in making the world better. It is consistent, instead, with the worst kind of religious, Stalinist, bourgeois, and fascist demagoguery.

Yes, the faults critics find with science are mostly there. In fact, nearly everyone from every background exhibits variants of the same sexist, racist, classist, and ecological faults. But these faults do not arise in science from the fact that all scientists follow the rules of evidence, make deductions, or argue strenuously for their beliefs, any more than they arise throughout society from the fact that all people breathe, eat, sleep, or procreate.

Instead, just as for the rest of us, overarching institutions establish boundaries for what scientists must do to garner rewards during their lives, upbringing and schooling limit their concepts and feelings, and the immediate institutions they operate within have biased roles that limit their daily choices. Moreover, these facts easily explain the ills prevalent in modern science, just as they explain related ills in many other realms of life. To blame scientists' "ways of thinking" for causing the ills of science is as silly as blaming athletes' ways of metabolizing, or actors' ways of memorizing, or workers' ways of coordinating their hands, or family members' ways of speaking for the ills of competitive sports, Hollywood culture, capitalist work, and patriarchal family life.

That said, it is also important to note that the *difference* between science and the rest of what people do is grossly misunderstood by most "anti-rationalists," in part because they generally take for their archetype either a demented, Frankenstein bio-physicist, or an average bourgeois economist who has sold out to wealth.

- First, serious scientists don't disavow intuition, hunches, guesses, experience, or any other avenues to a new idea. They use all of these, nearly all the time, just like everyone else.

- Second, serious scientists don't depend for verification entirely on logic and deduction, but instead elevate experiment—which is actual events and experience—to the determining position.

- Third, while people who pretend to be scientists, such as economists, sociologists, and psychiatrists, sometimes claim that the range of their knowledge is everything and the scope of their wisdom is without limit, serious scientists admit: (1) that the set of all things that the rules of evidence plus logic and theory can sensibly inform us about is tiny compared to the set of all things people care about, and (2) that all knowledge is contingent and may be proven false any time in the future.

Ironically, therefore, what actually distinguishes science from non-science is precisely: (1) science's eagerness to change its ideas rather than hold them as fixed dogma; (2) science's openness to simultaneously celebrating multiple conflicting explanations, at least while there is no convincing way to choose among them; (3) science's disregard for credentials, authority, or even past achievement in judging any person's claims; and (4) science's elevation of experience to the prime arbiter of disputes. In other words, real science distinguishes itself from non-science by its adherence to exactly the aims critics of science say they seek.

Finally, and perhaps most ironically, instead of buttressing racist, sexist, classist, and ecological insensitivity, employing rationality, logic, and the rules of evidence generally helps counter those distortions, though not always sufficiently to offset an overarching institutional context and therefore not always sufficiently to prevent these ills from infecting scientific practice. What is arguably racist and sexist, however, is saying that beyond different cultural values and experiences, Easterners think differently than Westerners or women think differently than men.

Effects of Anti-Rationalism

Aside from offering mistaken understandings of science and unwarranted leaps of opposition, anti-rationalism has other, more strategic problems. Here, I mention three.

First, in the struggle to improve society, activists confront big guns, big media, and big money with, essentially, our minds and bodies. Anti-rationalism says let's reject a significant portion of the former. There's an interesting strategy. Give away your chief asset before the contest even begins.

Second, there is no such thing as choosing to be systematically non-rational. That would be a kind of permanent primal scream. We can be more or less rational by trying to limit or enhance the extent that other factors override our rationality or the extent of investigation and evidence we employ, but even anti-rationalists are rational as a matter of course. Rationality is, after all, just another name for how all people think. We all express our allegiances and determine our actions partly based on our rationality and partly based on additional things like desire, fear, and habit. The fact that no one knows much about how rationality works or even about its *many* dimensions certainly doesn't preclude us from acting rationally nearly all the time. Indeed, we cannot do without either rationality, including logic and the rules of evidence, for long without disastrous results.

It follows that if dispensing with rationality was the anti-rationalist agenda, their cause would not only be unwise, but also doomed. How would they ever argue their case? However, since it is quite possible to reduce one's use of evidence and logic in certain contexts, it is not necessarily futile for anti-rationalists to urge that everyone should do this every time they disagree with what anti-rationalists believe. Indeed, while it lacks philosophical profundity, this would be a very effective plea for an anti-rationalist to make to enforce that his or her critics never utter an effective contrary sound about anything anti-rationalist might believe. While I'm not saying all anti-rationalists have this as their purpose, I am saying that anti-rationalism leads to this, more or less inexorably, and that to employ more anti-rationalism on the left would therefore be self-defeating for making the world a better place, though it might do wonders for some people's careers.

Third, once one removes evidence, deduction, and argument as our favored means for choosing among views, what's left? How should we decide what explanations to support, what policies to advocate, what tasks to undertake? The claim of science is that we should use our experience and the experiences of others, our intuitions and the intuitions of others, and even our fears and guesses and the fears and guesses of others, all mediated, however, by logic and the rules of evidence. We should assemble the whole mass of elements into "an argument" where we distinguish facts from wishes, and assess the extent to which we have a compelling or only a very tentative case. However, if we set rationality aside, instead of using logic and the rules of evidence to help sift though and verify connections and implications, we will have to rely *only* on feelings, emotions, preferences, or whims—or on obedience to some authority. Given the institutional context in which we have matured and now function, the most likely possibility is that we would wind up deciding what positions to advocate on the basis of the style or credentials of presenters. Charisma and herd mentality would replace informed judgment, and the left would turn into the right. Another wonderful strategy.

An Antidote

When a paranoid individual claims the CIA is after him, it's hard to contradict the story. Anything you say is made part of the delusion. If anti-rationalists were really irrational, the same would happen. No appeal to evidence, logic, or implication could affect the irrational person's view because he or she would just reinterpret it to fit his or her schema. But anti-rationalists are generally not irrational. They are either: (1) people who sensibly want to ratify the worth of other ways of knowing than science, but who wrongly feel they need to denigrate science to succeed; (2) people justifiably hostile to scientists and other authority figures who, however, lack a viable alternative understanding and therefore desperately welcome whatever seems to be on their side; (3) academics with delusions of philosophical grandeur; or (4) ideologues who have found a new way to silence whomever they disagree with.

In all four cases, the only response to anti-rationalism is to steadfastly employ whatever experience, reason, and evidence we can muster to explain the true origins of the ills we face and to offer a real alternative vision and strategy that might better fulfill people's hopes and desires. Along the way, however, not succumbing to rationality-baiting and being honestly respectful of anti-rationalists but also forthrightly critical of the views they espouse may also help.

— September 1992

Rationalism

Last issue I rebutted the claims of people I ungraciously called "irrational-ists." I used a variety of arguments and examples to show how their opposition to scientific thinking and "Western rationality" was ill-conceived and reaction-ary. This month, since a rejectionist broom can leave a possible void, I'm going to try to more positively define and defend "being rational," particularly for political analysis. So, what constitutes being rational?

(1) We know it can't mean being correct. Often people are rational and wrong. Often two rational people reach opposite conclusions, both of which can't be right. Being rational therefore doesn't mean always attaining the truth.

(2) We also know there are different degrees of "being rational." We are all easily rational up to a point but must exert considerably more effort to attain higher levels of precision.

(3) We know that being rational goes beyond being logical. We've all dealt with people who we considered irrational even at a moment when they were carefully obeying the rules of logic. Being logical does not alone constitute being rational.

(4) Finally, we know that being rational differs from being dogmatic. It includes recognizing the possibility of being wrong and being willing to test one's claims over and over.

A good definition of being rational has to explain the above points. The dictionary tells us that to be rational is "to draw inferences logically from facts known or assumed." As a first approximation, this is quite good. For with this as our definition, "being rational" would lead to truthful, accurate conclusions only when the "facts known or assumed" are true and sufficiently encompass-ing, and when we understand them sufficiently so we don't introduce errors while using them to logically draw inferences. As a result, with this definition of rationality the above four conditions are met.

We can certainly get wrong inferences even while being rational. For example: The things that we think are true facts might be false, leading to wrong inferences. Or we might think our facts represent all that is critical where actually additional facts negate the inferences we draw. Or we may draw inferences logically, but on the basis of a wrong understanding of some of the true facts. Likewise, with this definition, increasing degrees of "being rational" correspond to taking greater care in ascertaining relevant facts and carefully drawing logical inferences. Obviously this can increase the likelihood of our inferences being true. Also, being logical isn't sufficient to make one rational because good logic applied to incorrect or incomplete information will only accidentally yield truthful inferences. And finally, since true inferences depend on true facts and logical analyses, rational claims are testable rather than having to be accepted or rejected solely on faith. The originator and evaluator of any claim can and should test it, and, when new evidence comes to the fore, test it again.

Also with this definition, people are rational, at least to some extent, almost all the time. After all, in almost everything we do, we "draw inferences logically from facts known or assumed." Errors are common, despite the fact that people are usually at least somewhat rational, for the reasons noted above. Moreover, biases, in the form of believing misconceived facts or letting desires or fears overwhelm our capacities for logic are also common. When these biases are extreme, of course, we label the result irrational. If it's self-conscious, we also call it hypocrisy, manipulation, dishonesty, etc.

So why is the dictionary definition only a "first approximation?" Something is missing: hypotheses, which, when complex, are often called theories. When we are rational, contrary to what the dictionary definition implies, we don't always go from facts via logic to inferences. Instead, often we get the inferences ahead of time and only then try to validate them by way of facts and logic. For example, we might have a hunch, an intuition, or a guess at a hypothesis. We might use an analogy to settle on a hypothesis. Or we might be offered a hypothesis by someone else. The point is, often we first have some claim about the world—a hypothesis—and only then see if we can find a set of facts from which we can use logic to infer the truth of the claim. This is an important addition because it highlights the difference between thinking up a hypothesis or theory as the first step, and then deciding whether it is true as the second. For the first step, unlike what the dictionary definition implies, anything goes, including analogies, hunches, extrapolations, intuitions, guesses, poetic flights of fancy, brainstorming, and even random rearranging of concepts or notions. For the second step, however, the dictionary definition comes more into play as the rules of evidence and logic take precedence.

With this clarification, we can see that when we move from daily life to science the only change that occurs in our mental orientation is that our methods for removing biases and pursuing greater precision become more disciplined. Philosophers of science try to write down methods for this, but scientists rarely if ever pay attention to their efforts. Instead, scientists learn the methods of science by emulating their teachers as part of learning their craft. Still, however difficult it may be to precisely enumerate the various ways scientists check their work, we know that at the heart of the matter is the scientist's commitment to obeying "the rules of evidence" and respecting the priority of repeated experiments, ongoing experience, and careful logic. In general, the closer we come to a scientific stance the less likely we are to include false facts, leave out relevant facts, misinterpret true facts, draw illogical inferences, or let biases bend our criteria for accepting facts or making inferences.

And that's it. Unless we want to get into philosophical nit-picking, there is nothing mysterious or complex about being rational or, for that matter, scientific. It is, however, sometimes hard work.

To be rational is simply one among many capacities associated with being human. To exert rationality, at least to a degree, comes naturally. To attain a scientific standard of rationality, on the other hand, requires more discipline. Moreover, the fact that we can employ a gradation of discipline in our rationality is quite lucky since if we had to test our data for biases, cross check it for completeness, and wait for confirmation from others who undertake related experiments just to decide it was okay to cross the street upon seeing no cars coming, we would never get to the other side. On the other hand, if we could only attain the spontaneous level of rationality associated with looking both ways and then doing the right thing, we would never have attained an understanding of physics sufficient to use electricity, a knowledge of biology sufficient to discover antibiotics, a knowledge of chemistry sufficient to make various cleansers, etc.

So how much rationality, from the street-crossing level to the scientific, do we need for making political judgments?

A Case Study in Rationality

Suppose we are offered a controversial hypothesis—for example, "JFK would have ended the Vietnam War had he only lived a little longer. He was killed for this reason. Moreover, his murder has drastically altered the nature of government and life in the U.S. ever since." How do we decide whether to accept or reject it?

A lot depends on the store of relevant background information we have at our disposal. What are our available "facts known or assumed" that we can draw inferences from? If among these we have a repeatedly verified theory about social relations and the JFK hypothesis is sharply contrary to that theory, we can quickly reject it. This is like not crossing the street if we see a car coming. The problem, of course, is that however often this is a valid and efficient way to respond, if our theory is actually false for this context, our inference will be false as well and we will have misjudged the hypothesis. Worse, this dynamic can cause a well-meaning but nonetheless stultifying sectarianism in which we let a previously convincing theory (e.g., marxism or neo-classical economics) dictate our current and future actions without repeatedly assessing new evidence that our theory may be flawed.

The alternative to a reflex rejection of the JFK hypothesis solely because it flies in the face of our preferred theoretical understanding, is to re-test our theory by showing in detail a line of argument that leads from more basic "facts known or assumed" to the hypothesis's renunciation. This way we have the possibility of discovering that our theory has a problem or, alternatively, we can explain our opposition to the hypothesis in a testable way that doesn't presume agreement about broader theoretical matters. Then, instead of dogma that supporters of the hypothesis can only ignore or succumb to as "received wisdom," they encounter a careful multi-step argument whose logic and premises they can test. At that point, they can either continue the debate by carefully evaluating the argument, or they can move into sectarian mode, ignoring the argument or dismissing it by fiat, but not by way of additional evidence or logic.

It sounds pretty abstract, but in practice it's quite comprehensible and relevant, as a couple of examples might clarify.

Someone might believe the JFK hypothesis from intuition, a guess, watching Oliver Stone's movie, reading Mark Lane's book, investigating documents, etc. In contrast, Chomsky, for example, has a store of "facts known or assumed," including some relevant knowledge about the historical period as well as a broader theoretical understanding of how the government and society works that together lead him to quickly reject the JFK hypothesis as contradictory with how the real world works and with known facts about the period. For Chomsky, it may even be hard to conceive how a serious long-time student of social relations could believe the JFK claim. So what does Chomsky, or anyone in his position, do?

One option is to just ignore the claim or dismiss it out of hand. This has the virtue of being quick and trouble free and of seeming proportional to the worth of the hypothesis. But what if the hypothesis persists? Suppose many people begin to take it quite seriously. Now what?

The next option is to briefly summarize a theory of society and point out that the hypothesis is inconsistent with that repeatedly verified theory and therefore must be wrong. This is okay at the beginning of an exchange, but at a late stage it would be sectarian. It asks the adherents of the now widely held hypothesis to drop it merely because it contradicts a theory someone else, or even they, previously believed. But why should they do this? Why shouldn't they instead say, "Hold on, our new claim is true, it's your old theory that's refuted? We are open to new insights. You are obstinate and sectarian about your old ways?"

So, the third option is to offer a comprehensive argument, with detailed logic leading from testable facts through to the rejection of the hypothesis itself.

Well, if you take a look at Chomsky's article in this issue, that's what it does. It attempts to refute the JFK hypothesis in a rational way that needn't be taken on faith but can instead be evaluated by each reader. Moreover, it attempts to present a comprehensive enough argument so that either the reader will find that some of the "facts known or assumed" in the argument are actually false, or that some of the logic employed is faulty, or that the argument refutes the JFK hypothesis. In this way, Chomsky takes the debate away from a clash of unsupported dogma and moves it into a more rational context of testable evidence and inference.

Roughly, Chomsky assesses the facts that others offer to support the JFK hypothesis and shows how they are either false or misinterpreted. He then offers counter-facts, detailing where he gets them from and why they can be believed. He also considers various implications of the JFK hypothesis, for example, for what should have followed after LBJ took over, and shows how these too contradict what the JFK hypothesis entails. Likewise, he shows that JFK's overall behavior, not just regarding the war but regarding broader issues of foreign and domestic policy as well, contradict the JFK hypothesis. And so, when we finish the piece, we are left to wonder, what will advocates of the JFK thesis do next?

To their JFK hypothesis, Chomsky has countered with another:

> *Basic policy towards Indochina developed within a framework of North-South/East-West relations that Kennedy did not challenge... [it] remained constant in essentials: disentanglement from an unpopular and costly venture as soon as possible, but after victory was assured.... Tactics were modified with changing circumstances and perceptions. Changes of administration, including the Kennedy assassination, had no large-scale effect on policy, and not even any great effect on tactics, when account is taken of the objective situation and how it was perceived.*

Chomsky also offers facts substantiating his new hypothesis and simultaneously refuting the JFK hypothesis. Will the JFK theorists show that Chomsky's facts are false? Will they show that his logic is faulty? Will they simply ignore his case or proclaim it *a priori* reactionary, repeating their prior claims with no real reply to Chomsky's argument? Or will they admit that Chomsky's case is valid and drop their hypothesis? These are their four options and the four options that generally arise in each new round of a debate. The first two and the last are rational. The third is not.

Now the issue for this article isn't who's right and who's wrong. Rather it's that we can take any other controversial hypothesis and treat it similarly to how Chomsky treats the JFK hypothesis. For example, consider these hypotheses:

- In the search for a better way to organize our economy, we should incorporate markets because this is the most efficient and productive and least detrimental way to achieve orderly allocation on a large scale.

- In the effort to convey radical ideas and visions to a broad audience, we should contour our actions and language to be easily reported through mainstream print and video media.

- Leninist organization is well suited to revolutionizing life in the U.S.

- If our society is going to become less oppressive, it will primarily happen through electoral change.

- Radicals need money to win change and wealthy people have it, so radicals eager for change should center their fund-raising efforts on wealthy constituencies.

In every case different kinds of exchanges can occur. Adherents and doubters of each hypothesis can shout their preferences back and forth, with no recourse to evidence and logical inference, no one ever changing their mind, no one learning anything, etc. Indeed, even if one party to the exchange moves on to a more rational stance open to communication, it takes two to tango. There will be no progress without both sides transcending dogma.

However, just being rational isn't always enough. For example, each side could rationally argue for its position based on a preferred theory, noting that the theory sustains the claim. But now the debate goes back a step. Why should either side believe the other side's theory, be it neoclassical economics, marxism, or whatever? And we may quickly return to the shouting match.

Another possibility is that each side, guided by its own theory, presents a comprehensive argument with clearly delineated facts, assumptions, and logical inferences. Then, a real exchange is possible. This transcends dogma and a clash of rationality too succinct to evaluate. It reaches a plain of real debate over testable claims and inferences. Of course, to get this far requires hard work that is only worth undertaking when the hypothesis in question matters a lot, but at least we know which procedures augur the possibility of progress and which don't. Agreeing on that, progress ought to be possible, whether deciding our view of JFK, or markets, or working with mainstream media, or Leninist organization, or electoral politics, or fund-raising, etc.

— October 1992

PART TWO

The Present Now
Will Later Be Past:
Thinking About
The Future

Dear Robert

Robert Heilbroner is a respected professor from the New School of Social Research and the author of important studies on economic history and Marxism. In *New Perspectives Quarterly* (Fall 1989), he says, "Less than 75 years after the contest between capitalism and socialism officially began, it is over: capitalism has won." He adds, for the first time in his life, "the tumultuous changes taking place in the Soviet Union, China, and Eastern Europe have given us the clearest possible proof that capitalism organizes the material affairs of humankind more satisfactorily than socialism." And though Heilbroner hasn't proclaimed an "end to history," he does say "we are finally coming to grips with the end of the economic century. From now on, the main problems will not be economic, but cultural and political."

You say socialist aims are moral but impractical? Capitalist economy is the apogee of innovation? Exploitation is yesterday's concern? I beg to differ. From Seattle to Sarasota and from Dallas to Detroit "everything is broken."

Leipzig's East German economy can't enrich Leipzig's elites or its downtrodden. Is capitalism better because in Chicago the elites get richer and the downtrodden get nothing?

Budapest's bureaucrats fall like dominos. Is capitalism better because Washington's power brokers leave office only to go to jail, or become CEOs?

In Berlin and Prague citizens are demonstrating in the streets. Is capitalism better because residents of New York and Dallas prefer to watch TV?

How do any of the tumultuous events in Eastern Europe censure socialism?

Soviets, Chinese, and Eastern Europeans all call themselves "socialist." Henry Kissinger calls them "socialist." The *New York Times* calls them "socialist." Nearly all Western Marxists call them "socialist." Folks on the street, East and West, call them "socialist." So doesn't the recent chaos mean socialism is dying, as Heilbroner claims?

No, socialism has not yet been born, so how could it possibly be dying? People fleeing East Germany have never experienced socialism. They can't be rejecting it. Whatever we call them—I choose "coordinatorism"—the economies of the Soviet Union, China, and Eastern Europe eliminate private ownership of the means of production and incorporate markets and/or central planning to organize allocation. A few people give orders. Many people carry them out. Coordinatorism's ruling class monopolizes decision-making, higher education, and material perks *above* the heads of traditional workers. This is the system about which a Soviet economist, Nikolai Shemelev, wrote recently,

> *Massive apathy, indifference, theft, and disrespect for honest labor together with aggressive envy toward those who earn more—even by honest methods—have led to the virtual physical degradation of a significant part of the people as a result of alcoholism and idleness. There is a lack of belief in the officially announced objectives and purposes, in the very possibility of a more rational organization of social and economic life...*

Aside from the fact that this sounds like downtown Detroit, Shemelev's indictment tells us nothing about genuine socialism and about humanity in general. It tells us only "what all schoolchildren learn / That those to whom evil is done / Do evil in return." (W. H. Auden)

In real socialism—which doesn't yet exist—participatory self-management will organize economic allocation so socialist workplaces will employ equitable, democratic councils and working people will collectively administer their own productive lives, economic allocation, and social investment. No ruling class will dominate workers' days and expropriate their energies. Not having evil done to them, workers will not do evil to others, nor will they wallow in "alcohol or idleness."

If any of you believe that in Leningrad working people have until now socialistically controlled their machine-tool assembly lines, decided their Lada (car) designs, and determined who gets to eat the wheat they grow or be warmed by the coal they mine, then the current crises will leave you feeling that people are creatures of such decrepit design that an economy organized on the basis of institutional competition and control is the only antidote to intrinsic human sloth. But this conclusion does not follow from the facts. (1) The economies now failing have never had socialist organization. (2) Heilbroner aside, their failure neither condemns socialism nor elevates capitalism.

Following the fine and sober book by Hungarians George Konrad and Ivan Szelenyi, *The Intellectuals on the Road to Class Power* (Harcourt, Brace, Jovanovich), we can transcend the U.S. government, the Soviet government, the *New York Times,* and most Western Marxists, to see that in the Eastern bloc, as in the West, intellectuals' earnings substantially exceed worker's earnings. White-collar people live in larger and more comfortable dwellings in more pleasant neighborhoods. They get quicker permission to settle in the cities, to live in subsidized housing with superior services, and to travel. They live relatively close to their places of work while a good part of the working class must commute from ill-serviced villages. Children of the intelligentsia

attend better schools and attain university-level degrees in higher proportion.
Only intellectuals and their dependents gain entry to special hospitals providing outstanding care for state and party officials. Even the cafeterias of
institutions employing mostly intellectuals offer better and more varied meals
than factory canteens. More important, Konrad and Szelenyi also tell us,

> For all his [sic] alleged 'leading role,' [the worker in these economies]
> has just as little say in the high- or low-level decisions of his enterprise
> as the worker in a capitalist plant. He has no voice in deciding whether
> operations will be expanded or cut back, what will be produced, what
> kind of equipment he will use and what direction (if any) technical
> development will take, whether he will work for piece rates or receive
> an hourly wage, how performance will be measured and production
> norms calculated, how workers' wages will evolve relative to the prof-
> itability of the enterprise, or how the authority structure of the plant,
> from managing director to shop foreman, will operate.

Workers get what they can the same way in the East as in the West, by
demanding and sometimes winning it.

Capitalism and coordinatorism are different systems having different
strengths and weaknesses. But in both capitalism *and* coordinatorism "labor is
external to the worker. Workers do not affirm themselves in their work. They
do not feel content but unhappy." Work does not "freely develop workers'
physical and mental energies" but "mortifies their body and ruins their minds."
Workers "only feel themselves outside their work, and in their work feel
outside themselves." They are "at home when they are not working and when
they are working they are not at home." "Workers' labor is therefore not
voluntary but coerced; it is forced labor." Finally, it is "not the satisfaction of
a need; it is merely a means to satisfy needs external to it." (Karl Marx)

Perhaps the biggest difference between East Germany and East New Jersey
is that there coercion and fear induce cynicism to diminish class struggle, while
here media manipulation induces cynicism to diminish class struggle. Choosing between TV and truncheons, Heilbroner tells us, is the human condition.
Having malls with miles of aisles for those who can pay while the poor dine
out of dumpsters decides Heilbroner for the "tube" over "truncheons."

So who benefits from work in coordinator economies if not the workers?
Konrad and Szelenyi don't hedge: "The Communist parties, after coming to
power, quickly dissolved or transformed every organization in which only
workers participated, from workers' councils, factory committees, and trade
unions, to workers' singing societies, theatrical groups, and sports clubs...."
From this Konrad and Szelenyi deduce that Bolshevism "offered the intellectuals a program for freeing themselves of the duty of representing particular
interests once power had been secured, and it used particular interests simply
as a means of acquiring power." They conclude that:

With the expropriation of the expropriators—that is, with the transfer of the right to dispose over the surplus product from landlords and capitalists to intellectuals in power, or to worker cadres whose political positions and functions made intellectuals of them—and with the destruction of the immediate producers' organs of management and control, the Bolsheviks traced the outlines of a new rational-redistributive system [that I have been calling 'coordinatorism'].

The myth of "Soviet socialism" and the power of its tanks have periodically crushed working people's aspirations to develop new economic visions. Now, with the *seeming* collapse of coordinatorism, sensible people like Heilbroner suggest taking socialism permanently off the human agenda. He wants to cement the cage of capitalism around us for all time. Is this political maturity?

You may hear me, but you don't agree. My words imply that even the Bolshevik revolution wasn't socialist, and this claim, you say, shows that I'm grasping at straws, unwilling to release my dreams of economic liberation when cornered by Heilbroner's deduction of capitalism's conquest.

My central argument is this: The choices for developed economic institutions are threefold, not twofold. The weakness of coordinatorism—now moving from a central planning to a market emphasis—doesn't imply capitalism is the only remaining choice. In coordinatorism central planning ensures that workers obey orders (as in the Soviet Union), or that markets elevate technocratic accounting while subordinating workers to coordinator intellectuals and managers (as in Hungary). Weighing its plusses and minuses coordinatorism stinks, yes. But socialism is still a desirable alternative. Here's why.

Coordinatorism distributes productive responsibilities so some people do primarily conceptual, administrative, and creative tasks (the coordinators), while others do primarily rote and delegated tasks (the workers), with the former ruling the latter. Socialism will distribute productive responsibilities so that everyone has a balanced mix of tasks and opportunities conveying a fair measure of intellectual and rote, conceptual and executionary labor, with all workers prepared to play a proportionate role in determining events.

Even if coordinatorism in Eastern Europe, China, and the Soviet Union entirely collapses, this would indicate nothing about socialism other than that we still ought to give it a try. Karl Marx said about desirable economic production:

In the individual expression of my own life I would have brought about the immediate expression of your life, and so in my individual activity I would have directly confirmed and realized my authentic nature, my human, communal nature. Our productions would be as many mirrors from which our natures would shine forth. This relation would be mutual: What applies to me would also apply to you. My labor would be the free expression and hence the enjoyment of life.

This sentiment is socialist. It rejects regimented central planning and competitive markets.

Leon Trotsky, a famous creator of the coordinator system said: "[One-man-management] may be correct or incorrect from the point of view of the technique of administration...." The social rule of workers over society "is expressed...not at all in the form in which individual economic enterprises are administered." That is, we can leave the usual factory hierarchy familiar to capitalism in place so long as central administrators rule "in the interests of workers." But, adds Trotsky, "It is a general rule that man will try to get out of work. Man is a lazy animal." So naturally the upper-echelon comrades must sometimes coerce workers for their own good—as in smashing workers' autonomous organizations. Finally Trotsky added:

> *I consider that if the Civil War had not plundered our economic organs of all that was strongest, most independent, most endowed with initiative, we should undoubtedly have entered the path of one-man management much sooner and much less painfully."*

In other words, Trotsky didn't gravitate toward coordinator structures out of Civil War-compelled necessity, as apologists maintain, but because he preferred it. Moreover, by "less pain" he can only mean that he thought there would have been a reduced need to kill working-class dissidents and smash autonomous workplace organizations if these had not had the chance to grow during the civil turmoil, as if that turmoil and not worker desires for liberty was the primary prod to the class-conscious opposition he crushed. These elitist sentiments defined Trotsky's agenda for society.

William Morris, who obviously had little effect on Trotsky, was an early socialist who urged:

> *What is it that makes people happy? Free and full life ... the pleasurable exercise of our energies.... I think that is happiness for all, and covers all the difference of capacity from the most energetic to the laziest. Now whatever interferes with that freedom and fullness of life, under whatever guise it may come, is an evil; is something to be got rid of as speedily as possible. It ought not to be endured by reasonable men [and women], who naturally wish to be happy.*

Lenin, in contrast, evidenced a coordinator orientation when he said: "It is absolutely essential that all authority in the factories should be concentrated in the hands of management." He followed this coordinatorist logic to its tragic conclusion noting that "any direct intervention by the trade unions in the management of enterprises must be regarded as positively harmful and imper-missible," and therefore deserving repression, overseen by him ..."Large-scale machine industry, which is the central productive source and foundation of socialism calls for absolute and strict unity of will... How can strict unity of will be ensured? By thousands subordinating their will to the will of one."

For Lenin, like Trotsky, the "will of one" could be just. In his response to dissident workers who wanted more influence of their own, Lenin said:

A producer's congress! What precisely does that mean? It is difficult to find words to describe this folly. I keep asking myself, can they be joking? Can one really take these people seriously? While production is always necessary, democracy is not. Democracy of production engenders a series of radically false ideas.

Perhaps one of the radically false ideas Lenin had in mind was that work should become "a free expression and hence the enjoyment of life." Rosa Luxemburg highlighted the essence of a truly socialist disposition in her criticism of the Bolsheviks:

Finally we saw the birth of a far more legitimate offspring of the historical process: The Russian workers' movement, which for the first time, gave expression to the real will of the popular masses. Then the leadership of the Russian revolution leapt up to balance on their shoulders, and once more appointed itself the all powerful director of history, this time in the person of his highness the Central Committee of the Social Democratic Workers Party. This skillful acrobat did not even realize that the only one capable of playing the part of director is the collective ego of the working class, which has sovereign right to make mistakes and to learn the dialectics of history by itself. Let us put it quite bluntly: The errors committed by a truly revolutionary workers' movement are historically far more fruitful than the correct decisions of the finest Central Committee.

Luxemburg also captured the difference between coordinatorist and socialist inclinations when she said:

The discipline which Lenin has in mind is driven home to the proletariat not only in the factory, but in the barracks, and by all sorts of bureaucracies, in short by the whole power machine of the centralized bourgeois state... It is an abuse of words to apply the same term 'discipline' to such unrelated concepts as the mindless reflex motions of a body with a thousand hands and a thousand legs, and the spontaneous coordination of the conscious political acts of a group of men. What can the well-ordered docility of the former have in common with the aspirations of a class struggling for its emancipation?

More recently, Noam Chomsky tells us that since the Bolshevik Revolution, "Both of the major world propaganda systems have described this destruction of socialist elements as a victory of socialism. For Western capitalism, the purpose is to defame socialism by associating it with Moscow's tyranny; for the Bolsheviks, the purpose was to gain legitimacy by appeal to the goals of authentic socialism." Chomsky also notes that "this two-pronged ideological assault, combined with other devices available to those with real power, has dealt a severe blow to libertarian socialist currents that once had considerable vitality, though the popular commitments to such ideals constantly reveal themselves in many ways."

But to rebut the "two-pronged assault" Chomsky says,

My own hopes and intuitions are that self-fulfilling and creative work is a fundamental human need, and that the pleasures of a challenge met, a work well done, the exercise of skill and craft, are real and significant, and are an essential part of a full and meaningful life. The same is true of the opportunity to understand and enjoy the achievements of others, which often go beyond what we ourselves can do, and to work constructively in cooperation with others.... The task for a modern industrial society is to achieve what is now technically realizable, namely a society which is really based on free voluntary participation of people who produce and create, live their lives freely within institutions they control, and with limited hierarchical structures, possibly none at all.

And that is the socialist point. Not merely to understand the economy. Not to change it into a new but still class-divided system. But to make it classless via a reorganization of production, consumption, and allocation that elevates social solidarity, collective self-management, and productive diversity to the highest priority.

To consign true socialist sentiments and activist program to history's ash can on the grounds that coordinator economies have finally begun to crumble under the dead weight of their own hypocrisy is a convenient non-sequitur for champions of capitalism.

Clarifying the ills of capitalism and coordinatorism and determining what a real socialism can be like so that we can then act on the insights is harder, more dangerous, and less lucrative than currying media favor with triumphal pronouncements about "the end of history" or the "victory of capitalism." But it is also honest, dignified, and for anyone who seeks true liberty, pragmatic.

In the East people are trying to attain something better than they have had. Their efforts graphically demonstrate the power of people in struggle and thus the efficacy of opposition to injustice, there and here. We should hope that they are not side-tracked by Twinkies, TV, and Toyotas.

— December 1989

Revolutions In The East

As a Czech poster put it, "the Poles took ten years, the Hungarians ten months, the East Germans ten weeks, and the Czechoslovaks only ten days" to topple regimes once viewed as unassailable. Here is an attempt to distinguish the good news from the bad, taking note of what is most surprising as well as what is not.

Evil Empires: One Down, One to Go

The best news is that imperialism and political authoritarianism have once again succumbed to human aspirations. Shortly after World War II, the Soviet Union imposed its priorities on the sovereign nations of Eastern Europe. From the perspective of over 100 million East Europeans, what has mattered most since then is that for 40 years their governments have ruled only at sufferance of the Kremlin.

There is no justification for one people dictating the social affairs of another, even *if* the institutions "exported" are benign compared with indigenous arrangements. But in this case there is no need to consider the subtleties of the adage "revolution cannot be exported" because in post-war Eastern Europe the system imposed by force was *not* progressive. (1) Political life in any positive sense ceased to exist for two generations. Instead, "politics" became resisting police states in apparent competition to see which could first hire as many informers as informed upon. (2) The effect of "socialist realism" on East European culture was little different from the effect the Vandals had on Rome. In Czechoslovakia, for example, in the aftermath of the Soviet invasion of 1968, a flourish of activity in cinema, drama, and literature was stamped out completely and replaced with "socialist realist" propaganda, mislabeled "cul-

This essay was written primarily by Robin Hahnel, and adapted by Michael Albert for publication in *Z Magazine*. It borrows from prior work by Albert and Hahnel appearing in *Socialism Today and Tomorrow*, South End Press, 1981.

ture." And, in the end, (3) the question of whether Soviet-East European trade was a rip-off or a subsidy hardly mattered since the system imposed created "zombie" economies in East Europe, just like their Soviet prototype.

We should not be deceived by the seeming ease with which one regime after another has been toppled in the past 12 months. For the past 40 years, the overwhelming unpopularity of Soviet imperialism has been demonstrated in daily passive resistance as well as periodic, heroic rebellions. The Czechoslovak, East German, and Bulgarian people benefited greatly in 1989 from the domino effect of events in Poland and Hungary. But events in Hungary reflected over 10 years of self-disciplined, painstaking changes that whittled away Soviet dominance while expanding the borders of tolerated dissent. In the case of Hungary, the changes were largely orchestrated by factions within the Communist Party, something like puppets toying with their puppet masters. The people of Poland won their freedom with a ten-year slowdown strike after one of the most impressive organizations ever to challenge an authoritarian regime, Solidarity, was physically crushed by the Polish military using the excuse, "better Polish than Russian bayonets."

Moreover, the gradualist Hungarian struggle from 1968 to 1989 was largely a reaction to the Soviet invasion of 1956. And the rise of Solidarity in 1980 had been preceded by important challenges from intellectuals and workers in 1976 and 1970. And while the Czechs benefited from the domino effect in 1989, they paid their anti-imperialist dues during the Prague Spring of 1968.

In any case, we have just witnessed an anti-imperialist victory of immense proportions. More than 100 million people who have had little or no say over their internal and external affairs for 40 years are beginning to exercise their sovereign rights. What requires explaining is why the revolutions could succeed in 1989, and why so many anti-imperialist militants in the West are having trouble rejoicing.

Of course the most self-serving and easily disprovable interpretations are offered by the gloating Western establishment and mainstream media. They see: (1) the West finally winning the Cold War due to "our" steadfast defense of freedom and liberty, and (2) the triumph of capitalism over socialism.

First, NATO intransigence and the Reagan arms buildup acted only to *delay* the end of the Cold War by giving Brezhnev and company an excuse for continued belligerence. If there was any Western contribution to ending the arms race, it was by the Western peace movement who apparently taught Mikhail Gorbachev and masses of West and East Europeans, if not their own leaders, that since in nuclear war everyone loses, anyone who can start a nuclear war is as powerful as the side with the largest arsenal.

Moreover, the Western Alliance did not send troops into Hungary in 1956, Czechoslovakia in 1968, or Poland in 1981, or break relations until the Havels of Eastern Europe were freed from jails. Official Western support for the

Eastern European opposition was always calibrated to deflect scrutiny of injustice in the West by focusing attention on injustice in the East. While Gorbachev is no "born again" anti-imperialist, it was his decision not to send tanks into Eastern Europe that facilitated the East European revolutions of 1989. Western escalation of the arms race did not force this concession. It was the cumulative moral, political, and economic costs of holding onto an empire, and the incompatibility of the Brezhnev Doctrine with the internal reforms Gorbachev seeks, that brought an end to the doctrine.

Second, the claim that the 1989 revolutions vindicate capitalism over socialism is even more absurd. The argument is a non-sequitur now, as it would have been 60 years ago if someone had claimed then that the Great Depression in the West vindicated Stalin. And the claim that the failures of the Eastern European and Soviet economies are the failure of socialism is also false. Regardless of what their rulers and detractors conspired to call them, as we will explain below, none of these economies was ever socialist.

Once it was clear that Moscow was unwilling to send tanks, the days for Communist governments in East Europe were numbered. Whether Gorbachev foresaw that this would lead not only to the demise of hard-line regimes, but of reform Communist regimes, Comecon, and the Warsaw Pact is hard to know. But the alternative of ordering military intervention to support regimes committed to perpetuating precisely what he was intent on dismantling in the Soviet Union was, apparently, even more problematic.

In any case, what is now obvious, and should have been all along, is that the Soviet puppet governments in Eastern Europe were completely dependent on external military support. When politics finally was reduced to a matter of internal forces, one side had nobody on it. The puppet Soviet regimes in Eastern Europe melted away just as fast and bloodlessly as the government in El Salvador would disappear if politics in Central America was reduced to a question of internal forces, say by our electing Jesse Jackson president of the U.S. on a Rainbow Coalition ticket.

Ethnic Revolt in the Soviet Union

But if anti-imperialists can unabashedly celebrate the death of Soviet rule over Eastern Europe, what should we make of challenges to Soviet government authority coming from Tallinn, Riga, Vilnius, Kishinyov, Baku, Alma-Ata, Dushanbe, Ashkhabad, Tashkent, Yerevan, Tbilisi, and Kiev?

The Soviet Union, according to a 1990 *National Geographic* map, is "the largest country on earth, an unwieldy federation containing a hundred ethnolinguistic groups" and almost as many movements seeking national liberation.

The Baltic Republics of Lithuania, Latvia, and Estonia were independent between the world wars but were ceded to the Soviet sphere of influence in 1939 as part of the Hitler-Stalin pact, and annexed by Stalin in 1940 along with Moldavia, which Stalin pressured Romania into ceding at the same time. Not surprisingly, nationalist and separatist sentiment is strongest here.

Most of the other republics were inherited from the old Czarist empire as a result of the February and October revolutions of 1917 and the civil war of 1918-1921, in which internal opponents, actively aided by all the Western powers including the United States, failed in their efforts to dislodge the new Bolshevik government. When the Union of Soviet Socialist Republics was created in 1922, it consisted of the Russian, Byelorussian, and Ukrainian Republics, and the Republic of Transcaucasia, which included all of what are now the Republics of Georgia, Armenia, and Azerbaijan.

On the other hand, various Central Asian nationalities fought a guerrilla war with the new Soviet regime during the 1920s. And while the Republics of Uzbekistan and Turkmenistan were added relatively quickly in 1924, the Tajiks, who speak an Iranian language and were once part of the Persian empire, were not integrated into the Soviet Union until 1929. But with the exception of the Baltic Republics, Moldavia, and Tagikistan, non-voluntary integration of minority nationalities predated the Bolsheviks. And in the important case of Azerbaijan, splitting the Azeri "community" between what is now Iran, Turkey, and the Soviet Union predates the Russian Revolution.

But this is not to say "nationality" has not always been a serious issues in the political life of the Soviet Union, nor that the legitimacy, much less the wisdom, of central government policies in this regard are unimpeachable. Quite the contrary: In large part, today's ethnic problems in the Soviet Union result from "community" policies every bit as mistaken as the "political" policy of creating a single-party state, or the "economic" policies of authoritarian management within enterprises and bureaucratic, central planning.

From the very beginning, Lenin and the Bolsheviks promised a different relation between the central government and the historically distinct communities that had been forcibly integrated into the Czarist empire. The Union of Soviet Socialist Republics was described as a voluntary union of republics with legitimate, autonomous rights, including rights of secession, guaranteed in the Constitution. But, from the beginning, the relation between Soviet rhetoric and reality in this regard was a case study in "doublespeak." The gap between rhetoric and reality widened steadily during Lenin's years and assumed Orwellian dimensions during Stalin's long reign. While rhetoric highlighted "voluntary association, autonomy, and respect for indigenous cultures," reality featured a policy more aptly labeled "cultural homogenization."

Proponents of cultural homogenization defend it as the only means of preventing genocide, racism, jingoism, ethnocentrism, pogroms, and religious persecution. The idea is that integrating historically distinct communities into a single, shared culture characterized by "scientific" rather than "primitive" modes of thought and by socialist norms and values can resolve antagonisms between the likes of Armenians and Azerbaijanis while creating communist men (and women?). Clearly the Azeri pogroms against Armenians in Nagorno-Karabakh, the retaliatory expulsions of Azeris living in Armenia, the arming of the Popular Front of Azerbaijan and the Armenian National Movement, the well-planned pogrom against Armenian residents in Baku that precipitated the Soviet Army intervention, and the recent events in Ashkhabad and Dushanbe where Moslem majorities reacted to rumors of preferential resettlement of Christian Armenian refugees in their republics, indicate that the policy has failed. When dictatorial repression disappeared, the old antagonisms proved to be sharpened, not softened, by years of cultural homogenization.

While some people argue that the failure of cultural homogenization to resolve these and other "intercommunity" hostilities *was* due to faulty implementation of a sound policy, and while others attribute it to the fundamental intractability of the human condition, a more plausible explanation is that the policy of cultural homogenization is inherently flawed and self-defeating. Moreover, it was not for lack of numerous "revisions," "corrections," and attempts to "perfect" the policy that it failed. For 70 years the central government alternated a "hard sell" and "soft sell" version of cultural homogenization—sometimes executing, arresting, or deporting nationalists and religious leaders, burning books written in non-Russian languages and non-Cyrillic alphabets, and banning symbols of cultural identification; and sometimes relaxing restrictions to the point of celebrating "quaint" local customs and "native" dances and music. But the shifts have always been tactical. The ultimate goal has always been relegating community differences to a harmless past while forging a new, common cultural identity.

The case of Sultan-Galiev is illustrative. Sultan-Galiev became a Communist in 1917 and organized the Musulman Communist Party. He fought against the White general, Kolchak, in the civil war, and received promises from central Bolshevik authorities—over opposition by local Russian leaders—that he would be permitted to establish a Musulman State at the war's conclusion. Stalin, who was in charge of national matters for the Party even in Lenin's time, later withdrew the promise and ordered the merging of the Musulman Communist Party with the local Russian Communist branch in Central Asia.

Stalin opposed what he termed "indigenous nationalism" as counterrevolutionary. Sultan-Galiev urged that policies be adopted that would preserve the progressive features of Islam. When Sultan-Galiev's protests were ignored he came to the conclusion that the Eastern proletariat (Russians) were not interested in liberating the Eastern peasants (Moslems) but in exploiting them, and he subsequently led uprisings against the Russians. Sultan-Galiev feared continuation of Russian imperialism under Bolshevik auspices and became what we, today, would call a "revolutionary nationalist." He was finally captured, tried, and expelled from the Party by Stalin in 1923.

The point is this example of the history of *Soviet* ethnic and cultural policy is unusual only in the leniency of the sentence. It sheds considerable light on hundreds of incidents that do not receive the attention afforded separatist movements in the Baltic Republics and the intercommunal strife between Azeris and Armenians in the Western media. One recent example, which happened to occur in one of Sultan-Galiev's old strongholds, illustrates glasnost in practice as well as the difficulties of reconciling community autonomy with protection of fundamental personal rights:

Moscow, Friday, Feb. 15. Thousands of people defied a ban on protests in Dushanbe, the violence torn capital of Tajikistan, to demand the resignation of the entire local Communist Party leadership, Soviet media said today. A crowd estimated at 8,000 also demanded jobs for tens of thousands of unemployed, better housing, and an end to the sale of pork, which the largely Moslem population is forbidden to eat.... The news agency said 18 people had been killed and 200 injured since the violence began Saturday night.... On Wednesday, young women on a bus were beaten up for 'breaking Moslem law,' by traveling in public without their heads covered, said Interfax, a publication of Moscow Radio.

For 70 years incidents such as this went unreported. Leaders were executed or exiled to the Gulag, and whole villages were "collectively" punished much as the Israeli Army collectively punishes whole villages active in the Intifada today. For 70 years every effort was made by Party branches, Komosol, and the "League of the Militantly Godless" to extirpate local customs, traditions, and literature, and force-feed school children dogmatic Marxism-Leninism-atheism. Nor was Stalin the only leader who meted out the hard-line version of cultural homogeneity. After Stalin died, Beria argued for relaxing the drive for cultural homogenization while Khrushchev, a political and economic would-be reformer, opposed any liberalization. In 1956 Khrushchev stressed that a period of "cultural rapprochement"—presumably what had taken place under Stalin!—should be followed by a period of "cultural amalgamation." Khrushchev hailed the Soviet Union as "a new type of ethnic community higher than the nation" and pushed polices aimed at "complete unity," "a future single worldwide culture of communist society" into which all "indigenous cultures" would be assimilated.

Is it naive to imagine that if a policy of respecting and facilitating Moslem traditions rather than denigrating and repressing them, while protecting the rights of young women who chose not to participate, had been practiced judiciously for the past 70 years, the situation would be different today?

The nub of the problem is that in either hard-sell or soft-sell form, cultural homogenization threatens historically distinct communities' self identity, predictably eliciting defensive responses to legitimate anxieties. Therefore, from the perspective of the victims, though some who pursued the policy may have had praiseworthy motivations, Marxist cultural homogenization was essentially no different than Czarist cultural imperialism. The content of the external culture that the "outsiders" attempted to impose was different under the Czar and the Bolsheviks. But the new threat to cultural identities was, if anything, greater during Soviet than Czarist rule because of the more thorough system of intrusion on personal life and the greater messianism of the new rulers.

So while Soviet government policies did not create the antagonisms between Azeris and Armenians, nor the lamentable patriarchal aspects of Central Asian Moslem communities, Soviet policy has continued to aggravate intercommunity antagonisms and undermine the legitimacy of insiders battling oppressive aspects of their community practices by threatening the very existence of minority communities. Instead, what was called for was a policy we call "intercommunalism," that is recognizing the legitimacy of historic communities, guaranteeing every community within the Soviet Union the necessary means to carry out the activities that define and perpetuate their historic identities, and limiting intervention to the protection of an individual's rights to leave a community without harassment or physical harm.

Which is not to say that the community issues that have dominated the grassroots response to Gorbachev's opening from the top, much to his dismay, will be easy to resolve. But recognizing not only the Czarist imperial legacy but also the counterproductive effects of the Soviet policy of cultural homogenization does put today's "nationalist" movements in a different light. Not only Gorbachev but most Western observers who wish glasnost and perestroika well see the nationalist movements as distractive at best, and reactionary at worst. The only sympathy afforded nationalist movements from outside seems to come from Western right-wing circles who desire dismemberment of the Soviet Union. But our interpretation implies not only that community movements for self-determination have legitimate grievances, just as political movements of relatives and friends of the victims of Stalin's political terror have legitimate grievances, but that demands for community self-determination are as much part of a new, progressive Soviet society as demands for more political democracy.

While there is no point in thinking outside critics can prescribe Soviet policy, neither should critics avoid difficult issues. So what would promoting autonomy within solidarity imply for the Soviet Union today?

The Baltic Republics should be free to secede, even though it would be foolish for them to do so. During his recent whirlwind visit to the Baltics, Gorbachev told the secession movements he did not care to dispute their rendition of the past, but that in the future the community policy he stood for and needed their help to implement would be dramatically different. He implicitly renounced past policy and promised autonomy. And he told the Baltic separatists that while independence would preserve their cultural autonomy, it would also require a degree of economic self-sufficiency that, as Gorbachev suggested, would prove inefficient, and therefore a high (and in his view unnecessary) price to pay. We are in no position to judge Gorbachev's sincerity or the likelihood that his views will prevail. Surely his arguments that the Baltic independence movements might upset reform for the rest of the Soviet Union and that pursuing independence might force him (or his replacement) to crush them have practical but no moral weight. In any case, there is more than ample historic cause—illegal annexation, mass executions and deportations of Baltic patriots, calculated Russification, not to speak of suppression of indigenous culture—to justify secession. And it may turn out that it is too late to build sufficient trust to attain autonomy within a federation. Either the past may be too bitter, or the promise of changes may lack sufficient credibility. If this proves true, as it appears it will, the Baltics should be free to secede without penalty, and extended an open hand of economic and international cooperation as well as an open invitation to re-associate later.

The Azerbaijan-Armenia problem is more complicated. In addition to demands for greater autonomy vis à vis Moscow, the two nationalities lay competing claims to particular territories, most importantly Nagorno-Karabakh. Unlike the Baltic republics, separatist sentiment was not the initial problem. Both Armenia and Azerbaijan enjoyed a very brief independence in 1918-1920, but this was only because central authority temporarily disappeared during the Russian Civil War. Independence is neither a strong nor recent experience for either nationality, and for the most part growing independence sentiment in both republics is a reaction to frustration and alleged betrayals by Moscow in adjudicating the current dispute between them.

At this point Armenians are furious at Moscow's ruling that Nagorno-Karabakh would remain part of the Azerbaijani Republic and at Moscow's failure to protect the Armenian minority in Azerbaijan from vicious pogroms. Azeris, in turn, are furious at the Soviet army occupation that was precipitated by pogroms that the Azeri's claim were largely caused by the Russian-dominated Communist Party of the Republic's alternation between procrastination and stirring up hostilities out of its political illegitimacy. Azeris are also suspicious that continued military rule under the excuse of preventing pogroms is a subterfuge for suppressing legitimate rights of self-determination.

But while there are complications and uncertainties, one of the clearest principles of intercommunalism is that majority populations cannot be permitted to brutalize captive minorities. Central government is responsible for preventing pogroms by whatever means necessary. In this case military intervention was necessary, and would have been better had it come earlier and even more decisively. But what an intercommunalist policy would do now is to separate Armenians and Azeris; place a sufficient army deterrence *between* them, rather than occupying the territory of either; give each the green light and necessary means to "celebrate" their cultural identities and run their own affairs; and remove the military buffer and permit geographic mingling only when *both* sides feel secure in doing so.

There has to be a judgment as to whether too much water has passed under the bridge. In the case of the Balkan Republics, the decision is theirs to make. In the case of the conflict between Armenian and Azeri, the decision is up to the central government. Physical separation implies hardships for the populations involved and economic costs for the rest of the country, but escalating pogroms by increasingly well-armed populaces would be far more destructive and costly. It should be pointed out that continuation of military rule in Azerbaijan is not the same as a military buffer between the provinces. And failure to carry out full, mutual repatriation of minorities that are endangered on both sides means the tinderbox simply awaits a new spark.

In sum, if the cultural policy we call "intercommunalism" had been practiced since 1917, rather than deceit and cultural homogenization, prospects for avoiding secession and the need to physically separate rival communities as well as hopes for building a geographically heterogeneous federation of autonomous cultures with solidaristic relations would be far better. But intercommunalism would be no policy guide at all if it required a perfect history, since it is needed precisely because the historic relations between communities have been far from ideal. Intercommunalist principles are more or less clear: (1) protecting of minority communities and minorities within communities by whatever means necessary, (2) encouraging cultural diversity, (3) alleviating anxieties of extinction by guaranteeing all communities material means to reproduce and develop their cultural identities, (4) freeing non-members to criticize practices they deem oppressive, but (5) prohibiting external intervention in the internal affairs of communities except to guarantee that members of any community are free to leave without intimidation. How to apply the principles in actual circumstances, and the facts surrounding particular situations, will often be far less clear, particularly for outsiders.

Glasnost Yes

Glasnost began as simply the cessation of repeating lies that nobody believed anyway and the lifting of various taboos. Then it became Soviet citizens discovering their real history and the publication of non-authors and rehabilitation of non-persons. This led to increasing freedom of thought and expression, followed by party and Soviet elections that were not necessarily "fair" but were at least contested with the possibility of embarrassing surprises for establishment candidates. Recently the Central Committee voted to rewrite Article 6 of the constitution that guarantees the Communist Party a leading role in Soviet society, and Gorbachev has reversed his position against other parties being legalized. In local elections this winter, candidates from a host of parties and groups from the entire political spectrum are competing. And it is likely that formal as well as de facto legalization will be extended to parties that espouse non-Bolshevik solutions in the near future. What all this amounts to is that under the label of glasnost, the Soviet Union is joining what Marxists have traditionally referred to as the "bourgeois democratic revolution." In less condescending terms, the Soviet Union is poised to step out of the political dark ages into the *relative* sunlight of representative democracy—70 years and tens of millions of lives too late.

All this is a significant improvement over the authoritarian, bureaucratic suppression of political life that began in the first year after the October Revolution, became firmly entrenched in the aftermath of the civil war during Lenin's time, was carried to insane extremes by Stalin's quarter-century of barbarous rule, and was institutionalized by Brezhnev for another 20 years after Khrushchev's sneak preview of glasnost was canceled at the insistence of his "corporate" sponsors.

The February revolution that toppled the Czar was carried out by a broad coalition of political parties including "bourgeois republican" parties like the Cadets, peasant-based parties demanding land reform like the Social Revolutionaries, urban and rural anarchists, and Marxists of both Menshevik and Bolshevik persuasion. The legal political spectrum shrank to Left Social Revolutionaries, anarchists, and Bolsheviks as a result of the October Revolution. By the outbreak of the civil war the only legal party was the Bolsheviks. Whether or not this was avoidable, and whom, if anyone, should be blamed, is irrelevant to the fact that political life had shriveled greatly even before the civil war. Except in the remarkable case of Nicaragua, where the Sandinista ruling party permitted its sworn enemies unprecedented political rights, civil wars are notorious for shrinking political liberties, and the Russian civil war was no exception. But after the civil war ended and the Bolsheviks had established political authority over virtually all of what had been the Czarist empire, Lenin's response to popular demands for legalizing non-Bolshevik, socialist parties, and demands for new elections to the Soviets so they could again become real governments, rather than the rubber stamp governments of the civil-war period, was to send a military expedition to Krondstat to silence the outcries. At the same time internal factions within the Bolshevik Party were banned and Lenin's theory of political vanguardism and democratic centralism was expanded into a comprehensive theory of a single-party state. Political debate within the Bolshevik Party continued after Lenin's death and through the mid-1920s, but by 1929 all factions had been eliminated except for Joseph Stalin's.

In the next quarter-century, political centralism reached a level of insanity difficult to comprehend. According to Andrei Sakharov, not only did 10 to 15 million people perish from torture, execution, hunger, or disease in the notorious Gulag, but between 1936 and 1939 more than 1.2 million Party members, half of the total membership, were arrested—of which more than 600,000 were executed or died in camps. And this occurred even though by 1936 all non-Stalinist factions in the party had long since disappeared! According to Nikita Khrushchev's famous secret speech to the Party Central Committee in 1956, "Of the 139 members and candidates of the Party's Central Committee who were elected at the 17th Congress, 98 persons, i.e. 70 percent, were arrested and shot, mostly in 1937-38, and of 1,966 delegates to the Congress with either voting or advisory rights, 1,108 were arrested on charges of anti-revolutionary crimes."

Enough facts such as these had reached the outside world so that at least the outlines of this history was known even before Khrushchev's revelations. But then Khrushchev backed off, and Brezhnev continued to obscure the truth for another 20 years. Only with glasnost have Soviet citizens been permitted to uncover their own history. But the refusal to live up to, much less surpass, the political freedoms of the "bourgeois democratic" revolutions before and after the civil war, and the stark terror of a police state that required a penal system averaging 5 million inhabitants a year for a quarter century—10 percent of whom died each year from malnutrition, disease, executions, and suicide—is only part of the story. *Washington Post* correspondent David Remnick was on the mark when he observed:

> *Election day in the Soviet Union for the past seven decades was perhaps the most pathetic ritual of a totalitarian system. Local Communist Party leaders drew up a slate of candidates, and party 'agitators' got out the vote hoping they could fulfill their duty to guide, cajole, or march the entire adult population of the city to the ballot box for a rousing show of ideological unanimity.*

According to Valentina Sotnikova, the ideological secretary of Tula's Communist Party committee, "No one ever took the elections seriously. People were completely alienated. It was a ritual, like going to a May Day parade. It was a holiday, just something you did, an excuse for a day off."

All this has changed with the elections of 1990. Covering local election campaigns, in what he terms "a kind of Slavic Super Sunday," in March in the Russian, Byelorussian, and Ukrainian Republics, David Remnick reports the ratio of candidates to open positions in the Ukraine is more than 7 to 1, in Russia more than 6 to 1, and in Byelorussia about 3.5 to 1. And while 85 percent of the candidates for legislatures are Communist Party members, that includes members of Democratic Platform, the internal opposition faction whose program was published in *Pravda* the day before the election. And many of the other Party candidates also belong to independent opposition groups. In any case, the candidates range "from KGB officers to dissident priests, and from Russian nationalists to social democrats." The high level of interest cannot be attributed to independence sentiment since this is the Russian "heartland." Instead voters ask: "Why are our hospitals so filthy and why must we pay bribes to the nurses for things like anesthesia or an extra blanket? Why do we find more and more homeless people and addicts sleeping in the parks and the railway stations? Why is there no meat? No gasoline? Why can we see the air and not breathe it?" In fact, the biggest issue in parts of the Ukraine and Byelorussia is the Chernobyl accident and its aftermath. Sentiment ran so high in the campaign that incumbents in the Ukrainian Soviet voted to phase out the four reactors still in operation. Now debate centers on adequate cleanup programs and reparations for victims.

In any event, while there is no denying that glasnost began as a revolution from above, it has since become the heady stuff that popular revolutions are made of. Which is not to say glasnost has achieved participatory democracy, or was ever meant to. Nor does it mean the limited gains of glasnost are secure. But the notion that single-party states and "vanguard" parties governed by "democratic centralism" are politically progressive is dead. More than anything else, the East European revolutions of 1989 were a gigantic referendum rejecting what we call "political Marxism Leninism." By this we mean the view of political life, shared by all Marxist Leninists, that heralds the "dictatorship of the proletariat," political vanguardism, the single-party state, and internal democratic centralism as an *advance* over "bourgeois democracy." Instead, the Marxist-Leninist vision of political life is and always has been a recipe for disaster, whether it is espoused by members of "ruling parties" in the East or by opposition parties and sects in the West, by Stalinists or Trotskyists, by Maoists or even Guevarists.

Outlawing all but a single "vanguard" party ruled by "democratic" centralism has nothing to do with democracy except its subversion. These political institutions systematically impede participatory impulses, promote popular passivity, and breed authoritarianism, bureaucratism, and corruption. The word "democratic" in "democratic centralism" is like the word "freedom" in "freedom of enterprise." Just as "freedom of enterprise" means the absence of freedom for the majority who must work for others, "democratic centralism" means the absence of democracy for all but the Party leadership. More than anything else, and in particular more than any economic failures, it is the failure of "political Marxism-Leninism" that is the essence of the revolutions of 1989.

But before moving on from politics to economics, a note of caution. Gorbachev did not unleash glasnost to have it flower into participatory democracy. And we in the West know all too well that representative democracy can be crafted into a system that reproduces oppressive social relations, maintains unjust privileges, and subverts rather than facilitates possibilities for participatory democracy. As we watch glasnost in the Soviet Union and the evolution of political life in Eastern Europe, the critical issue is whether ordinary people are increasingly able to formulate and express their political wills, or whether information, means of expression, and choice of candidates increasingly become the exclusive province of social elites. In the Soviet Union, Gorbachev's predilection for a U.S.-style "strong" presidential system rather than a European-style parliamentary system is worrisome. The degree to which the indigenous political groups that carried out the revolutions in Eastern Europe are being replaced by imitations of traditional Western European parties as elections approach is discouraging. But perhaps most important to watch will be the transformation of the media.

The Orwellian ministry of propaganda is dead or dying, but what will replace it? Unless ordinary citizens have access to media, unless grassroots political organizations can frame issues and options, unless the ability to project opinions is organized democratically and fairly, the revolution toward democracy cannot succeed. If new elites learn from their Western counterparts how to weave an infinitely more subtle lie—if *Pravda is* replaced by the *New York Times*—the victory of "mature" and "responsible" democracy will be proclaimed and echoed between self-congratulatory media empires in the East and West—but participatory democracy will recede, and the battle for democracy will wait to be fought another day. Defining the thinkable rather than forcibly substituting lies for truth is a change in form, not substance.

Perestroika, No

Now for the worst news. Not only have the new Polish and Hungarian governments already embraced the most self-destructive kind of capitalism dependent on foreign capital, virulently laissez-faire, and accompanied by a nonsensical consensus that they are too "poor" to afford a welfare safety net; and not only are the other new governments in East Europe moving rapidly in the same direction; and not only are ideas for workers' self-management, environmental planning, protecting workers' health and safety, and consumer protection vanishing from debate throughout Eastern Europe; but *perestroika,* the movement for economic reform in the Soviet Union, began as an explicit rejection of socialist economic principles and—if present trends continue—will end in either a rationalized coordinatorism or in capitalism.

In particular, the economic program implemented on January 1 by the new Polish government could not be more disappointing, and if anything it is even worse than the draft program approved by the Council of Ministers on October 9, which states:

> *Parallel with efforts to counteract inflation the Government shall take steps leading to complete change in the economic system. This will consist of introducing the market economy institutions which have proven themselves in developed Western countries. Instrumental to that will be: (1) ownership changes, making the ownership structure similar to that in the industrially developed countries; (2) application of a full market mechanism, particularly the freedom of price-setting and elimination of rationing; (3) opening the economy to the world by introduction of convertibility of the zloty, which will allow for increasing domestic competition and permit rational specialization; (4) reform of the banking system and the rules of money-credit policy to correspond with strict banking criteria; (5) launching a capital market; and (6) establishment of a labor market.*

The anti-inflation program referred to consists of:

> *Reducing the subsidy to coal, reducing the number of subsidized foodstuffs and inputs for farm production, suspending the central budget payments to local budgets, and modification of the wage indexation rules to counteract the inflationary climb of wages; [all while] eliminating the price ceilings.*

Presumably, since the Council of Ministers predicted in the same document "initially, following introduction of these measures, there cannot but follow a rapid jump in prices and drop in the statistical index of real wages," they were not disappointed by the 70 percent inflation and the 40 percent reduction in real wages in the first 30 days of the program!

The privatization program is no less thorough.

> *Material components of state assets will be sold including housing, land and building lots, small plants, service and trade outlets, shares of the State Treasury in existing companies, productive assets from liquidated enterprises and suspended central investment projects, along with privatization of enterprises.*

But in case anyone should fear a "fire sale," the Council of Ministers assured "there will be absolute observance of the rule of public-auction form of sale." Continuing, "The Government shall apply for lifting the applicable constraints on the size of a private farm and shall review the other acts pertaining to trade in land, with a view to eliminating all the unnecessary barriers." And "the

Government will apply for elimination of constraints on the freedom of: disposition of buildings and residential premises, building housing for sale, setting rents and charges according to market rules." So it was not only would-be Polish capitalists but would-be Polish landowners and landlords as well who had reason to jockey for position at the January 1 starting line. And they damn well better position themselves well, because there was no rule limiting entrees in the great Polish January 1 sweepstakes to amateurs. Professionals were declared eligible in these Polish Olympic games: "Foreign investors will be able to purchase stock in Polish enterprises and also set up wholly foreign-owned enterprises."

We quote at length to emphasize the magnitude of the rout, and also because this account provides an all too accurate indication of what is happening in Hungary as well. Moreover, this is clearly the direction Czechoslovakia, Bulgaria, and Romania are headed, and what may lie ahead for the Soviet economy if perestroika fails. Perestroika is a strategy for moving from one form of non-capitalist and non-socialist economy to another. The strategy is remarkably farsighted, but quite risky. It could fail if: (1) essential features of the reform are blocked, and the traditional economic model is reimposed; (2) the forces unleashed by perestroika, and by the far more disruptive policy of glasnost lead to a restoration of capitalism; or (3) the popular forces unleashed lead instead to real socialism (the least likely but only desirable possibility).

Gorbachev initially presented perestroika as a revitalization of the existing Soviet economy. This posture was dictated by the major obstacle at the time: the party aparachiks and central planning bureaucrats, as well as the managers of less profitable enterprises. In combination, glasnost and perestroika directly threatened the material privileges of what Gorbachev deemed the unproductive elite who not only dominated the power structures of the old political and economic system, but had long legitimated their rule by cloaking themselves in the mantel of socialist rhetoric and concessions to workers' security. So Gorbachev's first task was to reassure his conservative opposition and make it difficult for them to rally working-class sentiment against perestroika. Now that the conservative opposition is in disarray, he talks of "revitalizing socialism" much less often. But far from "revitalizing socialism" perestroika explicitly rejects the fundamental precepts and goals of a socialist economy.

True socialism will be based on a system in which democratically organized workers and consumers participate in planning their joint economic endeavors in light of full knowledge of the social effects of their decisions. While the old Soviet system of bureaucratic, centralized planning was neither democratic, participatory, nor efficient, perestroika explicitly rejects the goal of socialist planning. In his book, *Perestroika*, published in 1987, Gorbachev wrote:

> *The reform is based on dramatically increased independence of enterprises and associations, their transition to full self-accounting and*

self-financing…. They will now be fully responsible for efficient management and the end results…. In this connection, a radical reorganization of centralized economic management is envisaged in the interests of enterprises. We will free the central management of operational functions in the running of enterprises.

Perestroika is a program of replacing bureaucratic planning with markets and competition, not with socialist planning and cooperation.

True socialism will be based on the principle, "From each according to ability, to each according to effort." A socialist economy will not view differences of luck, job placement, talent, and preparation and training undergone at social rather than personal expense as legitimate bases for differential reward. Under socialism personal sacrifice for the social interest, or effort, will be rewarded for efficiency and equity reasons until mutual trust and solidarity proves sufficient to permit distribution entirely according to need.

It is important to be clear that while sentiments for socialist distributive principles existed in the early years after the Russian Revolution, (1) socialist distributive principles were never practiced by any Bolshevik government; (2) Stalin moved exactly in the opposite direction during forced industrialization, when skilled labor was in shortest supply; and (3) it was Stalin who first coined the phrase "levelers" as an epithet aimed at his opponents, that is, at his contemporaries who dared support socialist distributive principles. So, Gorbachev, rather than correcting the "leveling mistakes of Stalin" as he puts it, is instead fully in the anti-socialist tradition of rationalizing unjust inequalities. Gorbachev writes:

Equalizing attitudes crop up from time to time even today. Some citizens understood the call for social justice as 'equalizing everyone.' But what we value most is a citizen's contribution to the affairs of the country—the talent of a writer, scientist, or any other citizen. On this point we want to be perfectly clear: socialism has nothing to do with equalizing…. Much is said about benefits and privileges for individuals and groups of individuals. We have benefits and privileges that have been established by the state, and they are granted on the basis of the quantity and quality of work.

Real socialism will also stand for every citizen's right to a socially useful job. But Gorbachev warns us "the high degree of social protection in our society…makes some people spongers," and complains that "the state has assumed concern for ensuring employment [so] even a person dismissed for laziness or a breach of labor discipline must be given another job."

But our point is not that Gorbachev is yet another Soviet leader who has betrayed socialist principles. Gorbachev says all these things because perestroika requires it. Perestroika is a process of moving from the old non-socialist system to a new nonsocialist system. Since the new system is to be based on markets rather than planning and cannot function coherently if wages are determined politically rather than competitively, perestroika means eschewing the remnants of socialist ideology that helped hold the social contract behind the old system together, but which is counterproductive in the new system and an obstacle to its birth.

The traditional form of a coordinator economy combines hierarchical relations of production with bureaucratic, central planning. The social contract that held this system together in the Soviet Union for over 60 years included job security and an ambiguous wage system that paid lip service to socialist values in exchange for workers' acquiescence in their economic disenfranchisement and toleration of official and unofficial corruption. This was the traditional coordinator economy: an economy without capitalists, but with a ruling class of planners, administrators, and other conceptual workers (or coordinators), who controlled economic decision-making with their own interests first and foremost. We can call this economy "Coordinatorism 1," a public-enterprise, state-managed, centrally planned economy.

Perestroika is a strategy for moving from Coordinatorism 1 to a slicker, more competitive "Coordinatorism 2." The new version of coordinatorism *would maintain hierarchical relations of production,* but would feature allocation determined by free markets rather than planning. It would be a public-enterprise, state-managed, market economy. But Coordinatorism 2 would require a new social contract as well. And in particular, part of the ideological underpinnings of the old social contract would be dysfunctional in Coordinatorism 2. Coordinatorism 1 could operate coherently with a system of wages and prices that were political compromises designed to both reward elites and to pacify "the masses," since production decisions under central planning need not be based on wages and prices. That is, resource allocation and production decisions in Coordinatorism 1 could be carried out independently of wages and prices, which could therefore play a purely distributive role.

But in Coordinatorism 2 wages and prices necessarily play an allocative as well as distributive role. And if wages and resource prices and costs based on them do not reflect relative productivities, the resulting economic decisions will be inefficient. Hence arises the need to forge a new social contract that abrogates employment-security and eschews economic rewards based on effort or need in favor of rewarding performance solely according to profitability.

Incidently, this explains a nonsensical argument common in the mainstream press. It is frequently mentioned that if "full cost accounting" were implemented, 40 to 50 percent of economic enterprises would go bankrupt in the Soviet Union, Poland, Hungary, etc. The implication is that these economies are total basket cases and the efficient approach is to shut down roughly half the economy. But nothing of the kind is called for. If full cost accounting *at Soviet, Polish, or Hungarian prices* were implemented in West Germany, France, or the U.S., 30 to 40 percent of our enterprises would go bankrupt as well. The key is the prices, which in the Eastern economies are still the old political compromise, distributive prices of Coordinatorism 1. Not only are the Eastern economies not anything like the basket cases that the Western media and Western businesses that are bidding on those enterprises would like us and the East Europeans to believe; but to shut down those enterprises would be the most foolhardy act to date. Just because a Polish coal mine or steel mill is not as productive as a Western counterpart does not mean it is not making a positive net social contribution. Usually, having people work, however poorly, is more efficient than not having them work at all!

If "price reform" is a prerequisite for a coherent Coordinator 2 economy, why does Gorbachev delay? The answer should be clear. The clean, technical phrase "price reform" means breaking the old social contract and establishing a new one. These are difficult political tasks requiring troublesome negotiations, especially when a significant portion of the society's elites along with a majority of the working class will lose in the exchange, at least in the short run.

The difficulty and danger have apparently been so great that even at the tremendous economic cost of having a non-economic system in the Soviet Union since 1986, Gorbachev has postponed the crucial price reform for almost five years. People don't expect the old system to stay in place but are unsure if the new system will come in. Parts of the old system remain, but only parts of the new system have been implemented. The actual economy is chaotic because there is no coherent system of incentives. When nobody knows what to expect or what they will be rewarded or punished for, people do nothing. And when people do nothing, there is economic crisis.

Contrary to popular and professional opinion, the Coordinator 1 economies were not in anything like a system-threatening economic crisis before the advent of perestroika. There was a political crisis of universally acknowledged hypocrisy in the Soviet Union. And a long overdue crisis of imperialism in Eastern Europe to which politically bankrupt puppet regimes responded in the 1970s and 1980s by trying to pacify their subjects via massive credits from the West, thereby generating a debt crisis. But the traditional coordinator economies did not generate a tailspin by normal operations. The Polish economy was in full crisis by 1989 because the Poles had been on a slowdown strike against the military government since 1981. And the Soviet economy is in crisis now because nobody has known what to do for over four years. But other than Poland, and up to 1985 in the Soviet Union, the traditional coordinator economies were plugging along more or less like they always had. What was alarming was that after decades of *outperforming* their Western counterparts, by the beginning of the 1980s their growth rates had dipped below those in the

West. And in a more qualitative vein, the most significant technological revolution since the industrial revolution appeared to be taking off in the West, but not in the East.

All this was sufficient to inject Gorbachev and his farsighted allies with a sense of desperation and urgency, leading them to initiate a preemptive strike to change from Coordinatorism 1 to Coordinatorism 2 before the relative economic decline worsened. But to interpret lower positive growth rates as if they were negative and evidence of economic crisis is deceptive. The Soviet economy was behind the U.S. economy in 1920, but less so in 1980. That explains the "luxury gap" and unflattering comparisons of any number of economic indices. Since 1985 the Soviet economy has been in crisis because it is in an in-between, Never-Never Land, and it won't come out of crisis until a coherent system takes hold.

In any case, while Coordinatorism 1 may have superficially resembled socialism in a few particular respects—some people confused bureaucratic, central planning with democratic, participatory planning—Coordinatorism 2 bears no resemblance to socialism other than in its having public ownership. Of course, the distinction between capitalism and coordinatorism is essentially the difference between a ruling class based on a monopoly of ownership of the means of production and a ruling class based on a monopoly of economic information and administrative control over the means of production. Therefore the most superficial resemblance between coordinatorism and socialism, the absence of capitalists, is unavoidable. But Coordinatorism 2 is no more an economy in which workers and consumers participate in democratically planning their joint endeavors and in which economic rewards are based on effort, or on sacrifice for the common good, than was Coordinatorism 1.

Facing the Dust Bin

Recent events in the Soviet Union and Eastern Europe have not only routed Communist aparachiks there, but a portion of the "Left" in the West as well. And this helps explain why some anti-imperialists are having a hard time celebrating the great anti-imperialist victories of 1989. Whether or not those in the West who have championed "political Marxism Leninism" choose to face the facts, the verdict is in. A billion and a half people, from the Berlin Wall to the Bering Sea, from Budapest to Beijing, after experiencing various versions of this political agenda for 40 to 70 years, have voted "nyet." The voice vote was so deafening there was no call for a show of hands.

Political parties in the West that continue to espouse these policies only guarantee their continued irrelevance. This is hardly new, since no party espousing political Marxism-Leninism has any following among what they conceive as "the masses" in any country whose citizens enjoy the limited fruits of "bourgeois democracy." While this was not always so, it was already the case before the revolutions of 1989. On the other hand, up to now Marxist-Leninist sects have been generally considered part of the "Left" in the West. That is, the "vote" within the "Left" was considerably more ambiguous than the vote of the citizenry at large in societies enjoying the limited fruits of representative democracy. Within the Western Left, Marxist Leninists' opposition to capitalist exploitation has been deemed sufficient to warrant their inclusion in broad progressive alliances. Indeed, Marxist Leninists have long portrayed themselves not only as members of the Left, but as its vanguard. To add to the confusion, the repressive apparatus of the state and the mainstream media frequently confer that status on Marxist Leninist sects by singling them out for special treatment. But this is not done because Marxist-Leninist sects are the most dangerous threats to bourgeois rule. It is done because focusing attention on them makes the best "media theater," furthering the cause of bourgeois ideological hegemony by casting sects in the roles of fifth columns for their ruling party prototypes and sponsors, which together threaten our democratic freedoms.

This is not an essay on strategy, coalition building, and alliances. And we are proposing no simple formulas. However, we do believe the most obvious lessons of the revolutions of 1989 are that political Marxism Leninism is a step backward from representative democracy and that coordinatorism and socialism are two very different things. The Western Left needs to digest and act on these lessons. Rather than a transition from bourgeois to participatory democracy, political Marxism Leninism is a rollback of the limited gains of the American and French revolutions—a step back toward the political dark ages. Rather than a transition from capitalism to socialism—meaning collective participatory rule by workers—economic Marxism Leninism is a transition from capitalism to coordinatorism, meaning rule by planners, managers, intellectual elites, and technocrats in general. Perhaps recent events can help the Left in "bourgeois democratic" societies see these matters as clearly as the populace they wish to lead.

Along with "political Marxism Leninism" the traditional version of a centrally planned coordinator economy has been routed. Whether perestroika will succeed in replacing Coordinatorism 1 in the Soviet Union with Coordinatorism 2 by constructing a market system with considerably more competitive pressures on managers, and a bigger stick of unemployment as well as larger carrots in the form of greater wage differentials for workers, is still in doubt. Much of Eastern Europe has already leapfrogged over Coordinatorism 2 into full-blown capitalist restoration. Moreover, should the next attempt at coordinator reform in the Soviet Union prove as anemic as the previous ones, it may be the last. While Coordinatorism 2 is not intrinsically inferior to capitalism on efficiency grounds and may well be better on equity grounds, it has nothing to do with socialism and is even harder to confuse with the kind of economy socialists find desirable than was Coordinatorism 1. Rather than an attempt to "revitalize socialism," perestroika was, and is, an attempt to forswear socialist objectives entirely in order to revitalize coordinatorism.

While we rejoice that more than 100 million East Europeans and more than 250 million Soviet citizens are finally beginning to be free to choose, we regret that they are surely going to make some bad choices, at least in the short run. Eastern Europe has again achieved political independence and is rapidly rejoining the capitalist world economy in its customary subordinate position. The Soviet Union, having replaced a dependent capitalist economy with a coordinator economy, failed to carry out even a "bourgeois democratic revolution" after overthrowing Czarism. Hopefully the Soviet Union is now joining the ranks of nations enjoying the limited fruits of representative democracy, and can do so without fragmenting into a dozen impoverished warring nations. But whether the Soviet Union is headed toward a slicker coordinator system of class rule, or toward capitalism, the leadership has dropped all pretense of pursuing real socialist economic goals.

Finally it is important to understand why there is also so little popular sentiment in the East for socialism. The worst of Marx's writings—known as "orthodox Marxism" to those of us who have taken the time to understand it before rejecting it, and simply as "Marxism" to more than 99 percent of the human race—have been deployed to justify and rationalize political authoritarianism and coordinator exploitation in Eastern Europe and the Soviet Union. All liberatory, non-Marxist, socialist currents in the Left were repressed entirely. How could one possibly expect the victims of this indoctrination to turn to something called "socialism," and look beyond representative democracy for the answers to their problems even if there were a clearly articulated and viable alternative to capitalism for them to consider?

Much of the Western Left has failed them by refusing to recognize the depravity of their condition and the reasons for it. All of the Western Left has failed them by proving incapable of conceptualizing, articulating, and projecting a viable socialist economic model and viable humanist cultural, political, and sexual models under conditions where the freedom to do so was far greater than for our brothers and sisters in the East. But much is changing, including the fact that those in search of humanist goals in the East will have more room to do so than ever before.

— April 1990

Cuba Sí?

In a 1962 speech titled "The Duty of the Revolutionary." Fidel Castro said,

The summary of the nightmare which torments America from one end to the other is that on this continent ... about four persons per minute die of hunger, of curable illness, or premature old age. Fifty-five hundred per day, two million per year, ten million each five years. These deaths could easily be avoided, but nevertheless they take place. Two-thirds of the Latin American population lives briefly and lives under constant threat of death. A holocaust of lives, which in 15 years has caused twice the number of deaths as World War I. Meanwhile, from Latin America a continuous torrent of money flows to the United States: some $4,000 a minute, $5 million a day, $2 billion a year, $10 billion every five years. For each thousand dollars that leaves us there remains one corpse. A thousand dollars per corpse: That is the price of what is called imperialism. A thousand dollars per death ... four deaths every minute.

In the nearly three decades since Castro's assessment, for all of Latin America except Cuba, the above statistics have improved little, or worsened. In the 1980s, income in Latin America, excluding Cuba, declined by 8 percent, according to the Inter-American Development Bank. Castro's injunction in the same speech is therefore as apropos today as then:

The duty of every revolutionary is to make the revolution. It is known that the revolution will triumph in America and throughout the world, but it is not for revolutionaries to sit in the doorways of their houses waiting for the corpse of imperialism to pass by. The role of Job doesn't suit a revolutionary. Each year that the liberation of America is speeded up will mean the lives of millions of children saved, millions of intelligences saved for culture, an infinite quantity of pain spared the people.

Little has changed regarding who and what is the principle enemy or the magnitude of the crimes that need rectification. And therefore little has changed regarding the urgency of transcending imperial and neo-colonial domination.

But what about "liberation?" Have the positive goals a revolution should strive for changed? What does Cuba's experience teach us in these respects?

Despite decades of CIA terror and economic boycott, Cuba greatly exceeds its Latin American neighbors in intellectual, cultural, health, educational, and political accomplishments. But where is Cuba headed now that Soviet-bloc support is in doubt? What will happen to their polity and economy now that the Leninist political model and central-planning economic model are being abandoned elsewhere?

No matter how you look at it, one-person-rule through a bureaucratic hierarchical party is dictatorship, even when, as in Cuba, the leader is benevolent. Castro is the hub; the Cuban Communist Party radiates the spokes. Parallel grassroots institutions including *poder popular* represent a participatory trend that has as yet failed to transcend Party manipulation.

To inaugurate the 1970s, Castro proclaimed:

> *The formulas of revolutionary process can never be administrative formulas.... Sending a man down from the top to solve a problem involving 15 or 20 thousand people is not the same thing as the problems of these 15 or 20 thousand people—problems having to do with their community—being solved by virtue of the decisions of the people, of the community, who are close to the source of the problems.... We must do away with all administrative methods and use mass methods everywhere.*

Cuba has the Leninist, hierarchical Party and the popular democratic *poder popular*. But, Castro's words notwithstanding, the former has consistently dominated the latter. Oversimplifying a complex and variegated political history, it follows that three main impediments have obstructed Castro's hope to substitute political participation for political administration:

(1) The Cuban Communist Party monopolizes *all* legitimate means of wielding political power and thereby ensures that there is only one Cuban political line, that of the Party and its leadership. The first problem is political Leninism.

(2) The omnipresence of Fidel Castro leaves little room for any popular vehicles to attain true decentralized grassroots power. The second problem is Fidelismo.

(3) The willingness of the U.S. to manipulate political differences to destroy Third World revolutions (as amply demonstrated by the recent Nicaraguan elections) justifies regimentation. The third problem facing Cuba is the not-so-benevolent Uncle Sam.

As Cuba loses its fealty to the East, as Castro faces the problem of succession, and as the corruption of the political bureaucracy increasingly alienates the Cuban populace, two possible political paths are emerging. Cuba can return to its early aspirations and exceed glasnost by moving from Leninism and dictatorship to participatory democracy premised on mass participation, or, instead, Cuba can defend authoritarianism and preserve elite privileges under the guise of "Defending the Revolution."

For all its accomplishments, the Cuban economy is far from "liberated." Planners, state bureaucrats, local managers, and technocrats monopolize decisions while workers carry out orders. In the resulting economy, a ruling coordinator class plans the efforts of workers and appropriates inflated pay, perks, and status.

Cuba's coordinator economy has given the Cuban people pride in national accomplishments, and major material gains in health care, housing, literacy, security, and overall standards of living. For these reasons the Cuban revolution is deservedly popular. But however admirable these achievements are when compared to conditions in Guatemala, El Salvador, or even Watts or the South Bronx, this does not justify applying the label "liberated" or "socialist." For that, there would have to be no ruling class, and workers would have to collectively administer their own efforts, with solidarity and equity.

However, as with politics, Cuban economic history has not followed a simple trajectory. The coordinator model has been dominant, but there has always been an alternative spirit manifested, sometimes in hope, sometimes in actual experiments, but regrettably never leading to liberated economic relations.

In 1962 and 1963, impressed with what they saw when visiting the Soviet Union, and seeing no other options, Cuba installed economic forms mimicking the traditional Soviet model. By 1964, disenchantment set in and a great debate ensued. In a letter written from Africa in 1965, summarizing the spirit of the recommendations he championed in that debate, Che Guevara wrote:

The new society in process of formation has to compete very hard with the past. This makes itself felt not only in the individual consciousness, weighted down by the residues of an education and an upbringing systematically oriented toward the isolation of the individual, but also by the very nature of this transition period, with the persistence of commodity relations. The commodity is the economic cell of capitalist society: as long as it exists its effects will make themselves felt in the organization of production and therefore in consciousness.

In the debate, Che disdained the use of "profitability," "material interest," and a "commodity mentality," arguing instead for emphasizing morality, collectivity, solidarity, and the criterion of use value in meeting human needs. He did not, however, champion nor even raise the issue of direct control by workers over their own workplaces or over economic decision-making in general.

Castro adopted a similarly humane but incomplete stance saying that:

We will never create a socialist consciousness ... with a 'dollar sign' in the minds and hearts of our men and women ... those who wish to solve problems by appealing to personal selfishness, by appealing to individualistic effort, forgetful of society, are acting in a reactionary manner, conspiring, although inspired by the best intentions in the world, against the possibilities of creating a truly socialist spirit.

Castro acknowledged that his desires to equalize incomes and forgo competition and individual incentives would be incomprehensible to some. He knew that to "learned," "experienced" economists "this would seem to go against the laws of economics."

To these economists an assertion of this type sounds like heresy, and they say that the revolution is headed for defeat. But it so happens that in this field there are two special branches. One is the branch of the 'pure' economist. But there is another science, a deeper science which is truly revolutionary science. It is the science of... confidence in human beings. If we agreed that people are incorrigible, that people are incapable of learning; if we agreed that people are incapable of developing their conscience—then we would have to say that the 'brainy' economists were right, that the Revolution would be headed for defeat and that it would be fighting the laws of economics...

Over the years the economic debate in Cuba has vacillated between two poles: competition versus solidarity, profit-maximizing versus meeting human needs, markets versus central planning, and individual incentives and inequality versus collective incentives and equality, with many swings back and forth over the years. Consider the following comments from Castro when the left pole was in ascendancy:

A financier, a pure economist, a metaphysician of revolutions would have said, 'Careful, rents shouldn't be lowered one cent. Think of it from a financial standpoint, from an economic standpoint, think of the pesos involved!' Such persons have 'dollar signs' in their heads and they want the people, also, to have 'dollar signs' in their hearts and heads! Such people would not have made even one revolutionary law. In the name of those principles they would have continued to charge the farmers interest on loans; they would have charged for medical and hospital care; they would have charged school fees; they would have charged for the boarding schools that are completely free, all in the name of a metaphysical approach to life. They would never have had the people's enthusiasm, the masses' enthusiasm which is the prime factor, the basic

factor, for a people to advance, for a people to build, for a people to be
able to develop. And that enthusiasm on the part of the people, that
support for the revolution is something that can be measured in terms
incomparably superior to the adding and subtracting of the metaphysi-
cians.

The problem has been that the left pole, which has argued for egalitarianism, solidarity, meeting needs, and collective incentives, has also argued for extreme central planning rather than decentralized, participatory planning with direct workplace democracy. And the difficulty here is not only that something valuable wasn't included on the left side of the debate, but that the positive goals the left championed—solidarity, equity, collectivity—were subverted by coordinator decision-making and central planning. When the left pole gained ascendancy the continuing lack of real participation and power on the part of workers meant that their enthusiasm and talent were *not* unleashed in the hoped for manner. Thus, after a few years of left influence over economic policy, the economy would eventually falter, and the turn back to the right—always urged by the Soviet advisers empowered by virtue of Cuba's dependence on Russian aid—would be legitimated.

In the face of perestroika, Cuba will not happily jump on the free-market bandwagon. They will prefer any alternative to resurgent commodity economics and a sellout to the West. But, what can they do instead?

One depressing and the most likely possibility is that they will stay the current course, defending coordinatorism while trying to rectify its worst abuses, all in the name of "defending the revolution." This option has three major problems. First, in the long run, it would not permit workers and consumers to collectively manage their own affairs. It would instead perpetuate coordinator rule no matter how successful the battle to limit coordinators' appropriation of material privileges. Second, in the short and medium term it would do little to elicit increased productivity and allegiance from the Cuban populace in an effort to ward off the hardships that further economic isolation will impose. And third, again in the short and medium term, it would do little to gain grassroots international support, which is the only possibility to mitigate reductions in Soviet bloc aid. The virtue, from the perspective of Cuba's elites, is that the approach would continue to defend elite privileges and would not risk introducing short-run turmoil.

The other option is for Cuba to take the current opportunity to return to the ideals of Che Guevara and an earlier Fidel Castro, coupled with new awareness of the importance of economic participation. This would mean installing a new economic system emphasizing workplace democracy, consumer councils, an end to the division between mental and manual labor, and a decentralized planning procedure in which consumer and worker councils participate directly in formulating, revising, and deciding their own activities. The problem with this option is that it risks introducing disruption and would further alienate both the Eastern and Western blocs, and, from the perspective of Cuban elites, it would certainly challenge, and eventually eliminate their privileges. On the other hand, besides being the only road to real socialism, the left approach has the virtue of elevating Cuba back into the role of the leading experiment in liberation, thereby eliciting greater allegiance, energy, and spirit at home, and substantial internationalist and leftist grassroots support throughout the world.

Every so often movements and countries face critical choices with world historic impact. When Solidarity began to succeed in Poland, it had the option of retaining its working-class composition and its emphasis on elevating workers to decision-making power via new economic institutions, or of jettisoning all that in favor of elevating intellectuals and adopting markets, competition, and profit-seeking despite their obvious inadequacies. So far, the liberating choice is in retreat.

When Jesse Jackson galvanized new energies across the United States, he and the Rainbow Coalition had the opportunity to develop lasting grassroots organizations and democratic movements, or to subordinate everything to narrow electoral priorities. So far, the liberating choice is in retreat.

Now Cuba can either adopt a siege mentality and defend bureaucracy, dictatorship, central planning, and workplace hierarchy, all originally copied from allies now abandoning them, or can develop participatory democracy and truly socialist economics consistent with revolutionary Cuba's past aspirations. With their Eastern bloc bridges largely burnt, we can only hope that Cuba will once again opt for "a revolution within the revolution."

—June 1990

Buying Dreams: Visions For A Better Future

Left activists are moved, first and foremost, by refusal to tolerate injustice. Still, a clear conception of improved social relations can help us understand injustices we oppose and visions, of more desirable futures can help sustain and orient struggles today. Well and good, but why should people activated by today's social movements go "dream shopping" in leftist stores?

Let's face it: Not a few left visions, peddled as dreams, have turned into nightmares. First, there was the vision of substituting public for private ownership and central planning for "anarchy." Then there was the vision of a single vanguard party, whose members are sworn to serve the interests of the working class, and whose organizational skills are honed through self-sacrifice in struggle, replacing the hypocrisy of bourgeois politicking. And of course there were the "dreams" of a socialist economy automatically emancipating women by integrating them into "productive" labor in the public sector, and of a single proletarian culture sweeping away bourgeois cultural hegemony and "primitive," pre-capitalist cultural residues alike.

No doubt some will remark that these dreams-turned-nightmares were the exclusive property of the "revolutionary left" and that the "social democratic left" disavowed them long ago. This is true, but the social democratic left also threw out the baby with the bath water. There is little chance of buying a nightmare in disguise from a social democrat, not merely because they disavow certain false visions, but because they peddle no dreams at all. They prefer to peddle only policies for which they claim an already existing mass audience, such as electoral reform, better child care, fair housing, and full employment. These reforms are well worth fighting for, of course, and self-styled "radical dreamers" who do not participate in these struggles or who "pull punches" and play with "secret agendas" are no radicals at all. But there's little reason to visit today's social democratic teach-ins if you're looking for dreams as well as

---

This article was written for Z by Robin Hahnel. It borrows from work we published jointly, including parts of *Liberating Theory*, South End Press, 1986

program. So have dreams become the exclusive wares of evangelists and gurus? Not necessarily.

The first thing we should admit is there is no automatic relation between the diminution of material scarcity and desirable social relations. When Marx characterized "communism" as, first and foremost, a society without scarcity, and implied all problems of social relations would be rendered obsolete by material abundance, he put leftists dangerously off guard. The ecology movement should have taught us all by now that there cannot be complete material abundance. Moreover, for mortal beings time is inherently scarce regardless of how high the pile of material goods may become. And for social beings, whose relation to material wealth beyond subsistence is largely a matter of "invidious comparison," in a just society the size of the overall pile of goods is largely irrelevant. The notion that a sufficient advance in the "forces of production" would obviate the need to carefully build social relations that nurture humanist themes was utopian. There is no "communism" that automatically follows "socialism" as the "forces of production" develop sufficiently.

The second step is to clarify the criteria by which possible political, economic, community, and kinship institutions should be judged. Here we should draw freely from the wisdom of the long historical practice of progressive movements. In broadest terms, desirable social institutions help all citizens develop and fulfill their maximum potentials. Moreover, they do this in ways that do not sacrifice the well being of some groups to advance the interests of other groups. Creativity, diversity, excellence, and efficiency do not require social hierarchies, any more than "human nature" dictates that men must be misogynists, women passive, non-whites analytically disinclined, or some people born to lead and others born to follow. Institutions in all spheres of social life should promote the goals of solidarity, variety, and collective self-management in which each person partakes in decisions in proportion to the degree she or he is affected by the outcome. We believe these goals promote human potentials, reflect lessons from progressive historical experience, and incorporate more specific goals worth pursuing such as peace, justice, freedom, equity, material well being, trust, and respect.

But to what extent can we project a more specific vision? What institutions promote rather than subvert these goals?

Participatory Democracy

The Marxist-Leninist vision for political life is a recipe for disaster. Stalinism was an extreme form, but a logical extension of Leninism. And the counterproductive experience of Marxist-Leninist political parties out of power is perfectly consistent with the systematic suppression of democratic political life carried out by Marxist-Leninist parties in power. That the *"dictatorship* of the proletariat" could ever be equated with a desirable form of political life shall always remain a stain on the political escutcheon of "the Left." And outlawing all but a single "vanguard" party ruled by the norms of "democratic" centralism has nothing to do with democracy except its subversion. These political institutions systematically impede participatory impulses, promote popular passivity—if not outright fear—and breed authoritarianism, bureaucratism, and corruption in government. What can be expected when external opposition is outlawed, and the party leadership is able to suppress and manipulate internal opposition by transferring members between branches to provide themselves a majority in every branch and cell?

But Western-style electoral "democracy" is also a far cry from participatory democracy. Highly unequal distributions of wealth stack the deck before the political card game begins. Citizens choose from "pre-selected" candidates who are effectively screened by society's power elites. But even if these problems were overcome, participatory democracy requires more than infrequently voting for a representative to carry out our political activity for us. While election of representatives is part of participatory democracy, frequent and regular referenda on important political propositions and policies, at every level of government, accompanied by a full airing of competing views, are as important, if not more important, than voting for candidates.

In any case, we should not expect political life to disappear, but to intensify in a desirable society. Politics will no longer represent a means by which privileged groups perpetuate their domination. Nor will oppressed constituencies have to battle against political norms that preserve an unjust status quo. But there should be no lack of spirited disagreement about social choice. While the goal of social diversity dictates that competing conceptions should all be implemented by their adherents whenever possible, there will be many situations when one program will have to be implemented at the expense of others. The problem of "public choice" will not disappear, and since a desirable society will kindle our participatory impulses, there is every reason to expect political debate to heat up as well.

The goals are straightforward. In Chomsky's words,

> *A truly democratic community is one in which the general public has the opportunity for meaningful and constructive participation in the formation of social policy.... A society that excludes large areas of crucial decision-making from public control, or a system of governance that merely grants the general public the opportunity to ratify decisions taken by the elite groups... hardly merits the term democracy.*

The central question is, what institutional vehicles best afford people such an opportunity? Ultimately, political controversy must be settled by democratic vote. And obviously such votes will be better informed the greater participants' access to relevant information concerning consequences. So it is also clear that groups with competing opinions must all have access to effective means of communicating their views. Democratization of political life must include democratization of the media.

Participatory democracy requires not only democratic access to the media and a plethora of single-issue political organizations, but also a pluralism of political parties with different social agendas. If we reflect briefly on the history of political life within the left, and the ultimate consequences of attempting to ban parties, factions, or any form of political organization people wish to avail themselves of, it should be clear that bans are anathema to democracy.

Intercommunalism

We will not be magically reborn in a desirable society, free of our past and unaware of our historical roots. On the contrary, historical memory, sensitivity to social process, and our understanding of history will all be enhanced during the process of reaching a desirable society. So the point is not to erase diverse cultures, nor to reduce them to a least common denominator. Instead the historical contributions of different communities should be more appreciated, and there must be greater means for their further development.

Trying to prevent the horrors of genocide, imperialism, racism, jingoism, ethnocentrism, and religious persecution by attempting to integrate distinct historical communities into one cultural "playpen" has proved almost as bad a dream as the nightmares this approach seeks to expunge. "Cultural homogenization" ignores the positive aspects of cultural differences that give people a sense of who they are and where they come from. Cultural homogenization offers few opportunities for variety and cultural self-management and proves self-defeating anyhow since it heightens exactly the community anxieties and antagonisms it seeks to overcome.

In a competitive, hostile, environment, religious, racial, ethnic, and national communities develop into sectarian camps, each concerned, first and foremost, with defending itself from real and imagined threats, if necessary waging war on others to do so. Dominant community groups rationalize their positions of privilege with myths about their own superiority and the presumed inferiority of those they oppress. Some elements within oppressed communities internalize these myths, and attempt to imitate dominant cultures. Others respond by defending the integrity of their own cultural traditions while combating the racist ideologies used to justify their oppression. But the solution lies in eliminating racist institutions, dispelling racist ideologies, and changing the environments within which historical communities relate. It does not lie in trying to obliterate the distinctions between communities.

An alternative is "intercommunalism," which emphasizes respecting and preserving the multiplicity of community forms we are blessed with by guaranteeing each sufficient material and social resources to reproduce itself. Not only does each culture possess particular wisdoms that are unique products of its historical experience, but the interaction of different cultures *can* enhance the internal characteristics of each and provide a richness no single approach could ever hope to attain—provided negative inter-community relations can be replaced by positive ones. But the key to this is eliminating the threat of cultural extinction by guaranteeing that each community shall have the means necessary to carry on their traditions.

Individuals should *choose* the cultural communities they prefer, rather than have others define their choice for them on the basis of prejudice. And while those outside a community should be free to criticize cultural practices that, in their opinion, violate humanist norms, external intervention, as opposed to criticism, should not be permitted except to guarantee that all members of every community have the right of dissent and to leave.

Most important, until a lengthy history of autonomy and solidarity has overcome suspicion and fear between communities, the choice of which community should give ground in disputes between two should be determined according to which of the two is the more powerful and therefore, realistically, least threatened. Intercommunalism will make it incumbent on the more powerful community with less reason to fear being dominated to unilaterally begin the process of de-escalation. This simple rule is obvious and reasonable, despite being seldom practiced to date.

While the goal is clear—to create an environment in which no community will feel threatened so that each will feel free to learn from and share with others—given the historical legacy of negative intercommunity relations, there is no pretense this can be achieved overnight. More so than in other areas, intercommunalist relations will have to be slowly constructed, step by step, until a different historical legacy and set of behavioral expectations are established. Nor will it always be easy to decide what constitutes the "necessary means" that communities should be guaranteed for cultural reproduction, and what development free from "unwarranted outside interference" means in particular situations.

But the intercommunalist criterion for judging different views on these matters is that every community should be guaranteed sufficient material and communication means to self-define and develop its own cultural traditions, and represent their culture to all other communities, in the context of limited aggregate means and equal right to those means for all.

Participatory Economics

What economic institutions and practices will permit people to pursue their material needs and desires efficiently and equitably while fostering collective self-management, interpersonal solidarity, and human and material diversity? The broad outlines of the answers are becoming increasingly apparent.

- Ownership of the means of production must be social, not private.

Traditional Marxism was off the mark in some respects, but the proposition that private ownership of the means of production implies exploitation and alienation is *not* one we need to reconsider. Private ownership of the means of production means exploitation and alienation.

- Organization of production and consumption must be democratic and participatory, not hierarchical.

Almost all progressives give lip-service to this proposition, but it means different things to different people. To us it means production should be managed by a council of all employees where each has equal say. But it also means the tasks of conception and execution cannot be distributed so some people always do the former and others the latter. Unless job complexes are arranged and rotation schemes developed so all do a mixture of conceptualizing, organizing, and carrying out production tasks, alienation and class hierarchies will persist. This does not mean every individual must rotate through *every* conceivable job. Nor does it mean expertise will not play an important role in decision-making, since democratic decision-making requires informed analysis even more than hierarchical decision-making. But planning and coordinating the productive efforts of the many cannot be the exclusive province of the few in a desirable economy.

- Allocation of goods and services should be achieved through a social, iterative, planning procedure in which distinct groups of producers and consumers propose and revise their own activities.

Neither free markets nor central planning promote human well-being and development. Markets misallocate resources; pit people against one another; and make social cooperation individually irrational. Far from being the liberators of socially productive energies their bourgeois champions claim them to be, markets breed socially destructive individualism. On the other hand, central planning has proved an unworthy substitute. Central planning breeds authoritarianism, apathy, and bureaucracy. The dead weight of central planning on people's creative capabilities is more than enough to justify the desperate groping for alternatives going on throughout the "existing socialist" world. But the answer does not lie in a return to markets. Nor should one hope for much from a combination of two allocative mechanisms, each fundamentally flawed.

Work and consumption collectives are perfectly capable of developing an overall economic plan, as well as carrying it out. Individual collectives, and federations of similar collectives, are capable of proposing activities and revising those activities in light of qualitative and quantitative information received from one another in a planning dialogue. Modern computer techniques are more than sufficient to provide collectives with accurate and useful information about the implications of their choices for others, and the implications of others' choices for them. And a social, iterative planning procedure in which all participants are on equal footing is capable of yielding not only fair, but efficient outcomes as well. What is truly amazing is how few "radical" economists have devoted any of their considerable talents and energies to the task of refining the procedures of democratic planning that have supposedly been the center piece of visions of a socialist economy for over a century.

- Distribution should be based on the principle: "From each according to ability, to each according to effort," until growing trust and solidarity permits distribution according to need.

It is now clear that the principle: "From each according to ability, to each according to work" was ambiguous. The increasing tendency to interpret this principle as "to each according to the market value of his or her contribution" must be rejected as a just distributive principle. Payment according to personal contribution may well be more fair than payment according to personal contribution plus the contribution of the means of production one happens to own. But there is nothing fair about payment according to personal contribution. And what may surprise many self-styled socialists even more, there is nothing efficient about payment according to personal contribution either.

Differences in contribution are due to differences in talent, preparation and training, job assignment, luck, and effort. As long as trust and solidarity are insufficient to elicit necessary productive efforts, an argument can certainly be made for rewarding effort on efficiency grounds. No doubt some would argue effort should be rewarded on equity grounds as well, and we are not inclined to quibble. But rewarding talent, preparation and training, job assignment, and luck makes no sense on either equity or efficiency grounds. Why is talent, which is the outcome of a genetic lottery, any more deserving of reward than the contributions of privately-owned means of production which is the outcome of an inheritance lottery? And since talent is not something reward can induce, there is no efficiency argument for rewarding it either. Provided preparation and training are undertaken at public expense, including compensation for any burdens beyond those born by people not receiving training, education neither deserves nor requires reward to induce people to seek it. Rewarding the occupant of a job for the contribution inherent in the job itself makes no sense on either grounds. And there is clearly no justice or efficiency in rewarding luck. Which leaves us with the conclusion that rewarding the combined outcome of talent, preparation, job assignment, luck, and effort—which nobody could reasonably argue is the same as rewarding effort alone—is patently unfair and inefficient as well.

Feminism

Kinship institutions are necessary for people to develop and fulfill their sexual and emotional needs and raise new generations of children. But present day gender relations elevate men above women and children, oppress homosexuals, and warp human sexual and emotional potentials. In other words, present day gender relations are almost universally patriarchal, and while there are differences, some of which are very important, this holds for "existing socialist" societies as well as for modern Western societies. In a humanist society we will have to eliminate oppressive definitions that are socially imposed so all can pursue their lives as they choose, whatever their sex, sexual preference, and age. There can be no non-biologically imposed sexual division of labor—men doing one kind of work and women another—nor any demarcation of individuals according to sexual preference. We need gender relations that respect the social contributions of women as well as men, and promote sexuality that is physically rich and emotionally fulfilling. New kinship forms must overcome the possessive narrowness of monogamy while allowing preservation of the "depth" that comes from lasting relationships. They must destroy the division of roles between men and women so that both sexes are free to nurture and initiate. They must give children room for self-management and learning, while providing the extra support and structure children need. But what will make this possible?

Obviously women must have reproductive freedom—the freedom to have children without fear of sterilization or economic deprivation, and the freedom *not* to have children through unhindered access to birth control and abortion. There can be no more compromising on this issue than compromising about private ownership of the means of production. Just as private ownership abrogates the rights of employees to control and direct their laboring capacities, denial of birth control and abortion abrogates the rights of women to control and manage their reproductive capacities and thereby their lives in general.

But feminist kinship relations must also ensure that child-rearing roles do not segregate tasks by sex and that there is support for traditional couples, single parents, lesbian and gay parenting, and more complex, multiple parenting arrangements. All parents must have easy access to high quality day-care, flexible work hours, and parental leave options. The point is not to absolve parents of child rearing by turning over the next generation to uncaring agencies staffed mainly by women accorded low social esteem. The idea is to elevate the status of child rearing, encourage highly personalized interaction between children and adults, and distribute responsibilities for these interactions equitably between men and women and throughout society. After all, what social task could be more important than rearing the coming generation of citizens? So what could be more irrational than patriarchal ideologies that deny those who fill this critical social role the status they merit? In a desirable society, kinship activity must not only be arranged more equitably, but the social evaluation of this activity must be corrected as well.

Feminism should also embrace a liberated vision of sexuality respectful of individual's inclinations and choices, whether homosexual, bisexual, heterosexual, monogamous, or nonmonogamous. Beyond respecting human rights, the exercise and exploration of different forms of sexuality by consenting partners provides a variety of experiences that can benefit all. In a humanist society without oppressive hierarchies, sex can be pursued solely for emotional, physical, and spiritual pleasure and development. Experimentation to these ends is not merely to be tolerated, but appreciated.

Yes, the vision is uncompromising. It is a vision of gender relations in which women are no longer subordinate, and the talents and intelligence of half the species is free at last. It is also a vision in which men are free to nurture, childhood is a time of play and increasing responsibility with opportunity for independent learning, not fear, and in which loneliness does not grip as a vice whose handle turns as each year passes. The vision is one where living is reclaimed from the realm of habit and necessity, and is seen and appreciated as an art form we are all capable of practicing and refining. But there is no pretense that all this can be achieved over night. Nor do we claim a single kind of partner-parenting institution is the best for all. While the contemporary nuclear family has proven all too compatible with patriarchal norms, a different kind of nuclear family will no doubt evolve along with a host of other kinship forms as people experiment with how to achieve the goals of feminism.

The Importance of Dreams

Things don't have to be the way they are. Human nature is not so stingy as to permit only minor variations on oppressive themes. The set of possible human worlds is not one-dimensional and limited to the way we live today. We must keep thinking and talking about more desirable visions, and keep refining what we want. And it is important to keep strategizing about how to reach our goals. There is no other way to "keep the dream alive." And if the dream dies, there is nothing.

— April 1989

Economics Interview

KATE REDMOND: Tell us, what is participatory economics?

MICHAEL ALBERT: It's a different way of organizing an economy. We have in the U.S. now a capitalist economy in which some people own corporations, markets regulate allocation, and if you look inside workplaces, you find a hierarchy in which some people do rote manual labor, some people have more skilled tasks, and a few people make decisions. That's the heart of our system of economy—private ownership of workplaces, markets, and hierarchical workplace organization—and I don't like it.

I don't like the private ownership because it leads to a few people owning and controlling almost all the wealth and therefore having tremendous power. In our economy, commentators discuss the bottom 90 percent of the population, and while that's an amazing and embarrassing concept, it's accurate. The top 10 percent, and actually just the top few percent, effectively run the whole economy. That's inequitable, unjust, and undemocratic, so we ought to be able to do better.

And I don't like the hierarchical division of work because it ensures that most people have little or no say over their labor and can't be equal to one another in the workplace or have a fair share of fulfilling as well as not-so-fulfilling tasks. There's no ethical reason and not even any compelling economic reason why some workers should enjoy better circumstances and have more fulfilling and less dangerous or boring responsibilities than others, much less more decision-making power. So, again, we ought to be able to do better.

And I don't like the market because the market forces people to be out for themselves with no social conscience. The market doesn't work unless people advance only themselves. When people who own businesses advance only themselves, they seek profit regardless of adverse effects on the ecology, regardless of adverse effects on their workers, and even regardless of adverse effects on consumers. If you are an individual worker and consumer and you advance only yourself—you ignore the well-being of the people who produce what you consume or consume what you produce, or who live in your community with you. This means you operate in isolation from others, even trying to get ahead at their expense. And markets also create inequality, foster unemployment, cause ecological disruption, embody alienation, promote personality distortion, and so on. So, again, why not try to do better?

Participatory economics is a new type of system based on different defining institutions. In participatory economics, instead of private ownership of capital, everybody equally owns the means of production. It's shared among the whole populace, so ownership generates no income, well-being, or power differences. How well off each person is, how much income and how much say in decisions each person has, is affected instead by allocation—and the way allocation is handled in participatory economics is very different from the market system we're familiar with in our society—and by workplace organization.

For participatory allocation, people develop a scenario or agenda for what is to be done. Everyone is a participant in that process. We each figure out what we want to do or consume, either individually or with our work group, and everybody proposes their view. The mesh of these proposals is refined, back and forth, in a number of rounds of give-and-take, until a comprehensive agenda is settled on. Everyone participates in this give-and-take in proportion as they are affected by the decisions under consideration, so the system is participatory and self-managing.

Likewise, the way you organize the workplace in participatory economics is also unlike what we're familiar with under capitalism. In capitalism, you take all the tasks in the workplace and combine them into jobs where each actor has numerous instances of only one kind of task. One person does a variety of janitorial tasks and is a janitor. Someone else answers the phone and does some other secretarial tasks and is a secretary. Someone else administers and is a manager. Another person determines financial policy, projects revenues, etc., and is CEO. Each job occupies a place in a hierarchical scheme.

In participatory economics, in contrast, we combine tasks into jobs so each person has a fair share of different kinds of *tasks*. It's like taking various items from a buffet to make a meal. The capitalist way is to take only one thing and call it a meal. Some get good ones, some get bad ones. The participatory way is to take a balanced serving of a variety of complementary items as a meal.

In the workplace, the thing you create is a job and the things you take from the menu are tasks. In capitalism, each worker gets at most a few very similar kinds of tasks at one level of authority, skill, empowerment, etc. In the participatory version, you instead combine a diverse selection of tasks into jobs so everybody has a fair share of the more rewarding and more onerous tasks. It's essential to do this, first because it's equitable. There's no more reason why some people should take risks and others shouldn't, why some people should give orders and others only be ordered around, than why some people should be rich and others poor. It's also essential to balance workplace circumstances because it empowers people to participate in decision-making. Instead of some of us being deadened and kept relatively ignorant by our work while others are continually refining their decision-making skills and monopolizing relevant knowledge—as in the hierarchical case—with participation and balanced jobs we all develop our potentials to participate with readiness and skill.

The difference between capitalism and participatory economics is the difference between the kind of economy that spends immense sums building missiles that sit in the ground but little to finance quality health care for all, and the kind that does the reverse. It's the difference between the kind of economy that uses schools to teach most people how to endure boredom so they'll be prepared to work obediently for other people who have had elite schooling, and the kind of economy that emphasizes developing all peoples' skills and talents so everyone will be prepared to participate and contribute in a balanced way. It's the difference between elites making all decisions, and everyone playing a fair and proportionate role, between a few people having immense power and wealth while most are barely getting by or worse, and everyone having a fair share.

So your approach eliminates specialization, decreasing efficiency?

We don't eliminate specialization so much as narrow specialists. Take the example of a hospital. We'll still have surgeons. We don't do away with surgery or with the special skills, knowledge, and talents needed to do surgery well. It's just that people who do surgery will do other things, too, so that their overall work responsibility is fair. More important, the ex-secretary and everyone else at the hospital will now also do a job that combines a variety of tasks and responsibilities in a fair mix.

But if surgeons have to spend some time doing things other than surgery, like cleaning up part of the hospital, then aren't we losing output?

Yes, if you can only have the number of people trained in doing surgery as we have now and take away some of their surgery time. But suppose we have more surgeons. Then, there's no new surgery shortage. Or, for that matter, suppose we have today's surgeons spend some of the time they devote to golf doing non-surgical work so they have their fair share of diverse types of task. Again, there's no new surgery shortage.

In our economy most people don't have their skills and capabilities developed. To keep some people at the top, capitalism intentionally under-utilizes many other peoples' talents and creativity. What participatory economics does instead is establish fairness while not wasting most people's abilities so only a few can dominate.

But how do we get there from here?

The basic rough answer is that people get together and develop an understanding of the roots of the problems in society so they are not distracted by peripheral issues. Then they begin to organize movements to deal with those problems, to win reforms and win changes, whether in their income or for more control over their job, or other gains. They build these movements until eventually they begin to make demands that are more structural. They may create new institutions as they proceed, for example, councils in workplaces and communities that start to do the kind of things they will later be responsible for in participatory economics. That's the way change has occurred throughout history, whether around this issue, economics, or around issues of race, sexuality, ecology, or whatever: partly winning reforms, partly building new relations, finally redefining basic structures. It's very difficult, especially at the outset, but once the process reaches a certain level of awareness and involvement and a certain scale of its own institutions and organizations, progress can be very rapid indeed.

Under the participatory approach, would everyone get paid the same?

Yes. The work that we do has a mix of tasks different for each person but comparable in terms of their fulfillment or onus. My work day is like yours and ours is like everyone else's, not in details, but in overall demands and rewards. So why should one person get paid more than another? The only way to earn a little more than someone else, or than you did last year, is to work extra hours. You could work some overtime, or you could work less than society's average to earn less. But essentially income would be geared to effort where effort is measured by how long you work at a job equally demanding as everyone else's. Compare that to a system in which the CEO of a corporation not only has less risky, boring, and debilitating tasks and more tasks that are intrinsically rewarding, but also earns as much as 80, 100, or even 200 of his employees. Capitalism is theft, greed, exclusion. Participatory economics is equity, solidarity, participation.

It sounds a lot like socialism. Is this socialism?

It depends on what we mean by socialism. The word has for decades been applied to the Soviet system, and participatory economics is nothing like that. I described the system we live under now, capitalism, as private ownership of capital by a small group at the top, markets, and a hierarchical workplace. The Soviet system doesn't have that small group owning the means of production. Their revolution got rid of that and replaced it with state ownership. But that was still an elite group, so that change was one elite, the capitalist class, replaced by another, the state bureaucracy. The Russian revolution also replaced the market with central planning. But that's again very different from what I want. That's where a particular group of planners decides an agenda for the whole economy. The central planners send down a set of orders to all the workplaces. All the actors in the society respond to the orders by saying whether they can fulfill them. That information goes back to the center. New orders come down. Up goes obedience. It's just a very authoritarian, hierarchical system. And finally, the Soviet workplace was organized just like Ford Motor Company or other U.S. workplaces. They would be hard to distinguish, except by level of technology. The internal structures of the Soviet workplace and the U.S. workplace were otherwise quite alike. So no, the system that I'm proposing is not that.

But, of course, that's also not what socialism was supposed to be. The reason why the Soviet system was called socialist was twofold. The Soviet elite called it socialism so they could be legitimated by the label. Who could rebel against the system if it was already the best one conceivable? The U.S. elite called the Soviet system socialism, in contrast, so socialism would be delegitimated by the identification. If the Soviet Union was socialist, what sensible citizen of the U.S. could want to oppose capitalism? So if socialism means the Soviet system, what we've been talking about has nothing to do with socialism. On the other hand, if socialism means people controlling their own lives and economy with equity, diversity, participation, and self-management, then you could call the system I'm proposing socialist.

Let's talk a little more about markets. You want the abolition of the market...

That's exactly right. I'm an abolitionist regarding markets. Obviously, it's not a popular position right now, when there is a general conception that markets are somehow the panacea for everything. But I think that's a giant con job.

By a market we don't mean just the places where you go and purchase things. We mean a system where producers offer things, consumers purchase things, prices mediate between the two, and a balance comes by way of pressures associated with supply and demand. But market competition requires that everybody be greedy. It produces the opposite of solidarity and empathy. Nice guys finish last is actually true. Markets not only don't reward caring about others, they make it impossible for people to take into account the conditions of others. When we buy a compact disc, we don't think about the condition of the workers that produced the disc. We have no information that would let us do that. It isn't even an option. And the same goes in reverse. At work, we don't think about the people who are going to consume the product we're completing. I try to get ahead and so do you, and we all do it without regard for the impact on others.

Markets also misvalue things. They undervalue the worth of products that have positive public impact. So they undervalue public goods like parks or public education or public health care and ecological balance. Conversely, markets overvalue things that have private good effects but public bad effects. So they overvalue a car which pollutes and hurts the public but helps the person who individually buys it. So with markets you get a very skewed development. Markets bend the direction of the economy to emphasize narrow individualism and reduce sociality.

Also, markets foster a class division between people who make decisions and people who don't, and this is not only not fair, but the conflicts that arise between managers and workers, experts and clients, limit productivity, as does the under utilization of many peoples' talents.

I could go on, but all in all, markets lead toward privatization, inequality, and ecological decay and away from social concern, equity, and ecological balance. They under-utilize capacities and waste talents. They serve certain elites very well and are therefore defended by those elites who tell us that markets are wonderful. But it's a con job. And you only have to look around to see it. But the massive propaganda about markets is overwhelming, and people sometimes succumb.

What if the marketplace were taken out of the political realm? If there was still competition, which the U.S. seems so hooked on as a motivator, and yet economics was not dictated by different political mechanisms that drive it.

Most of those driving mechanisms are economic. The government certainly participates in economics and can make outcomes worse or better, but the basic features I've been talking about are due only to the economic attributes I emphasized: private ownership of capital, markets, and hierarchical workplace organization.

But let's consider competition itself for a minute. Suppose you're organizing a running race and for whatever reason, you want to motivate the fastest times. One way you can organize your race is to offer prize money and give most of it to the winner, and a little less for second and third place, and that's it. Then we'll get the best race times.

But look how this really works. Imagine that one person is really fast and can win the race relatively easily. Does she have an incentive to run as fast as she can? Not at all. Instead, you've given her an incentive to run just fast enough to win and no faster. And what about the people who are going to come in fourth, fifth, eighth, or twentieth? They have no incentive whatsoever. As soon as they see they're out of the money, as far as competitive incentive is concerned, they might as well walk over the finish line. But suppose we say we're going to reward everybody in line with their previous efforts. If you run as well as you've done in the past, we'll give you this baseline amount. If you do better, we'll give you more of a payoff in proportion to the improvement. So if you work harder, and your effort is greater, you'll get more. We're not going to give more to whomever finishes first just for winning. We're going to give more for doing better than you've done before. In this scenario, the overall speed of the whole assembly of people in the race is going to be greater than in the usual approach. Each runner has an incentive to go as fast as she can, regardless of how fast anyone else goes.

In fact, simple-minded competition is not so efficient after all. It is good for the few who win, but it isn't good for the overall productivity of the whole group. Does rewarding those at the top tremendously and those below barely at all elicit production? Well, yes, you can have a society with industry and output that functions that way. Especially if you're willing to use military power throughout the rest of the world to rip off riches to make up for inefficiencies. But could we do much better? Yes. It's just that in my way of doing better, you have to have equity, and the people at the top are much more concerned to prevent equity than to maximize productivity.

What's the scale you're looking at?

You can have a participatory economy in a small country or a large one. Participatory economies can have many differences depending on cultures, levels of development, and so on. It would be different in different places, but you can have it at any scale ... but I think maybe you're referring to what's the scale of the institutions within the economy. Do we break down large firms and communities...

And are these communities self-sufficient?

What you are perhaps leading toward is that there is a fourth alternative to the market, central planning, and participatory economics. We could get rid of allocation entirely. Have collective ownership, no hierarchy, and small self-sufficient communities where there is face-to-face economics in which you don't have people in point A producing stuff that's consumed far away at points B and C, so you don't have an elaborate allocation system at all. This is a solution. But it's a solution that gives away, I think, a great amount of development and economies of scale. On the one hand, I don't think a good economy is one in which you don't have hospitals, in which you don't have computers, in which you don't have cellos, and in which you don't have telephones. On the other, I also don't think a good economy is one in which you have to have 40,000 plants to manufacture each product—from toothpicks to pencils to bicycles to heart-lung machines—so every community can have them without having to get them from any great distance away. This immense duplication of effort and workplaces is not even the most ecologically wise way to create things. There is too much redundancy and waste of resources.

So my answer is that the scale you choose for communities and the degree to which you choose small industries versus larger ones is a social decision.

You weigh off the gains of decentralization versus the gains of economies of scale. What's nice is that in participatory economics this is a decision you can make and implement, self-consciously, with full debate, and with room for correction as you learn more. But in capitalism and the Soviet system alike, there is a drive toward centralization and a drive toward large-scale units regardless of their bad effects and way past the point that centralization and large scale make sense. So I think the scale will be smaller and more decentralized in a participatory economy. But not so small or so decentralized that there is waste or loss of valuable capabilities.

Going further into the details, is there room for things like insurance companies, the media? What role would media play?

There are no insurance companies. There are no banks. No IRS. No Wall Street. Many institutions we're familiar with are gone, or at least don't exist in anything resembling the form they now take. There's no advertising as we know it because you only want to let people know about things, not trick them into buying stuff that's inferior or that they don't really need or won't benefit from. There's no redundancies of products in the sense that we know it. No real-estate firms, brokerage houses, surveillance and control systems, as we know them. And obviously there's no military production in the sense that we know it. The savings associated with all this that could be put to social good are immense. And the reason these things don't exist is they just don't have any role. You don't need insurance when your income is guaranteed, when health care is guaranteed, when housing is guaranteed. You don't need banks when you're not doing private investments and you don't have to use banks for mortgages and the like. Participatory economics doesn't have those institutions. No welfare system. No unemployment bureaucracies. It has new institutions, though, associated with the allocation procedures we talked about earlier.

But, of course, media still exists. Media is communication and it's crucially important in any society. A critical problem with our own society today is the kind of media we have. The media is, like every other economic institution, controlled by a relative few who have certain interests and make sure that the media comply with those interests. And radio stations like this, as a result, are very important. Community radio is very important. Alternative print media is very important. It's very hard for these efforts to become large, however, in a society like ours, but they are nonetheless an important outlet.

In a good society media is important because you can't have democracy, participation, and self-management, unless you have access to information. It doesn't make any sense to have a right to make a decision about something if you don't have the information you need. Suppose there's going to be a first-in-a-long-time election in a Central America country where the U.S. is involved in an-ongoing struggles. If you look behind the mainstream news, you discover that before one of those initial "free elections," the U.S. and its local client regimes destroy the local labor unions, disrupt the religious community groups, close down local independent radio stations and newspapers, and eliminate the means for people to get together to develop a position and share ideas about agenda. Then they have a "free election" to choose between candidates that Washington finds acceptable. Like in U.S. elections, there is no real discussion of program or issues, but just a couple of interchangeable people competing for an office. Once you get rid of the possibility of real serious public grappling with ideas and possibilities, then you can have a "free" election, because nothing is at stake. So in participatory economics, since participation and freedom are taken seriously, of course there will be media operated according to the equitable, balanced, and participatory norms of the economy as a whole.

One of my concerns is always the accessibility of these ideas to the folks who need them most. People who are struggling day-to-day with survival and who have the least to lose and most to gain from the system changing. How are you putting this out in a popular fashion?

Just as you see here, coming on a radio show like this and trying to get the ideas across. I have a hard time, though. There is never enough time to really do justice to alternative ways of thinking and organizing on a single show or even at a conference. And, also, I don't know whether I'm as clear as I could be. It's particularly difficult to get information to struggling folks, because you can't do it by way of *Time* magazine. You can't do it by way of NBC. So we instead try to develop our own media and our own outreach. We're doing it at Z. And we're trying to expand into other means of reaching out as well. You're doing it in community radio. Other periodicals like *Dollars & Sense, In These Times, Monthly Review, Radical America,* and the *Progressive* are doing it in print, and so on. Of course, a free press isn't particularly relevant if the only people who have access to it and control over it are the rich. Then it's a rich press. Or a press for the rich. And we have to try to overcome that as part of the process of developing movements and winning change.

— November 1992

Participatory Economics

According to most economists, the activities of separate groups of producers and consumers can be coordinated by markets or by authoritarian planning—but there is no "third way." Those who call for planning by producers and consumers themselves only delude themselves and others. Economic pundits claim it is impossible to democratically plan a complex modern economy. Alec Nove threw down the gauntlet in no uncertain terms in *The Economics of Feasible Socialism* (London: George Allen and Unwin, 1983):

> *I feel increasingly ill-disposed towards those who ... substitute for hard thinking an image of a world in which there would be no economic problems at all (or where any problems that might arise would be handled smoothly by the associated producers...). In a complex industrial economy the interrelation between its parts can be based in principle either on freely chosen negotiated contracts [i.e., markets], or on a system of binding instructions from planning offices [i.e., central planning.] There is no third way.*

We disagree. The truth is that socialism as originally conceived has never been tried, but not because it is impossible. Council communists, syndicalists, anarchists, and guild socialists fell short of spelling out a coherent, theoretical model explaining how such a system could work. Our predecessors frequently provided stirring comparisons of the advantages of a libertarian, nonmarket, socialist alternative compared to capitalism and authoritarian planning. But all too often they failed to respond to difficult questions about how necessary decisions would be made, why their procedures would yield a coherent plan, or why the outcome would be efficient.

In two recent books we set out to rectify this intellectual deficiency by demonstrating that a non-hierarchical, egalitarian economy in which workers' and consumers' councils coordinate their joint endeavors themselves—consciously, democratically, equitably, and efficiently—was, indeed, possible. In

---

The above essay was written jointly with Robin Hahnel.

The Political Economy of Participatory Economics (Princeton University Press, 1991), hereafter *Participatory Economics*, we presented a theoretical model of participatory planning and carried out a rigorous welfare-theoretic analysis of its properties. In *Looking Forward: Participatory Economics for the Twenty First Century* (South End Press, 1991), we examined the intricacies of participatory decision-making in a variety of realistic settings, described day-to-day behavior, and treated a number of practical issues conveniently ignored by theoretical models.

The most common argument against the participatory economic system—based on democratic workers and consumers councils, remuneration according to effort, balanced job complexes, and participatory planning—have heretofore been to insist that it is impossible. But recently the focus of criticism has changed. Recent critics have not challenged the technical feasibility of our model. None has argued that our planning procedure is incoherent, or incapable of yielding a feasible plan under assumptions traditionally granted other theoretical models. None has claimed that "participatory planning" as we spell it out would fail to generate reasonable estimates of social costs and benefits, even though there is no private ownership of productive resources and no market. Nobody has argued that we erred in concluding there are incentives for consumers to use relatively less costly goods and place socially responsible limits on their overall consumption requests in our system. None has challenged our conclusion that enterprises would have to make efficient use of resources and inputs they receive under the procedures of participatory planning. Instead of the old argument that such an economy is impossible, critics have turned to challenging the desirability of such a system. In other words, to all intents and purposes critics have dropped the claim that a non-hierarchical, egalitarian, libertarian, nonmarket economy is impossible, and begun to argue instead that it is not the kind of economy they and others would want to live in.

Objections to a Participatory Economy

There are too many meetings: First, we offer Pat Devine's response to this objection to his version of democratic planning:

> *In modern societies, a large and possibly increasing proportion of overall social time is already spent on administration, on negotiation, on organizing and running systems and people. This is partly due to the growing complexity of economic and social life and the tendency for people to seek more conscious control over their lives as material, educational and cultural standards rise. However, in existing societies*

much of this activity is also concerned with commercial rivalry and the management of the social conflict and consequences of alienation that stem from exploitation, oppression, inequality and subalternity. One recent estimate has suggested that as much as half the GNP of advanced Western countries may now be accounted for by transaction costs arising from increasing division of labor and the growth of alienation associated with it [D. North, "Transaction Costs, Institutions, and Economic History," in the Journal of Institutional and Theoretical Economics, 1984].

Thus, as Pat Devine points out in *Democracy and Economic Planning* (Boulder, Col: Westview Press):

There is no a priori reason to suppose that the aggregate time devoted to running a self-governing society ... would be greater than the time devoted to the administration of people and things in existing societies. However, aggregate time would be differently composed, differently focused and, of course, differently distributed among people.

Second, we quote from David Levy's review of *Looking Forward* in *Dollars & Sense* (November 1991):

Within manufacturing firms we find echelons of managers and staff whose job it is to try to forecast demand and supply. Indeed, only a small fraction of workers directly produce goods and services. The existing system requires millions of government employees, many of whom are in jobs created precisely because the market system provides massive incentives to engage in fraud, theft, environmental destruction, and abuse of workers' health and safety. And even during our 'leisure time' we must fill in tax forms and pay bill. Critics of Looking Forward's complex planning process should examine the management of a large corporation. Large corporations are already planned economies; some have economies larger than those of small countries. These firms supplant the market for thousands of intermediate products. They coordinate vast amounts of information and intricate flows of goods and materials.

In sum, "meeting time" is far from zero in existing economies. But for a participatory economy we can break the issue down into meeting time in workers' councils, meeting time in consumers' councils, meeting time in federations, and meeting time in participatory planning.

Conception, coordination, and decision-making is part of the organization of production under any system. Under hierarchical organizations of production, relatively few employees spend most, if not all, of their time thinking and meeting, and most employees simply do as they're told. So it is true, most people would spend more time in workplace meetings in a participatory economy than a hierarchical one. But this is because most people are excluded from workplace decision-making under capitalism and authoritarian planning. It does not necessarily mean the total amount of time spent on thinking and meeting rather than doing would be greater in a participatory workplace. And while it might be that democratic decision-making requires more "meeting time" than autocratic decision-making, it should also be the case that less time is required to enforce democratic decisions than autocratic ones. It should also have been clear from our discussion of participatory workplaces in chapters two and seven of *Looking Forward* that meeting time is part of the normal work day, just as it is for managers and supervisors in existing economies, not an extra burden and infringement on their leisure.

Regarding the organization of consumption, we plead guilty to suggesting that these decisions be arrived at with more social interaction than in market economies. In our view, one of the great failures of market systems is that they do not provide a suitable vehicle through which people can express and coordinate their consumption desires. It is through a layered network of consumer federations that we propose overcoming alienation in public choice combined with isolated expression of individual choice that characterizes market systems. Whether this will take more time than the present organization of consumption depends on a number of trade-offs.

Presently economic and political elites dominate local, state, and national public choice. For the most part they operate free from restraint by the majority, but periodically time-consuming campaigns are mounted by popular organizations to rectify matters when they get grossly out of hand. In a participatory economy, people would vote directly on matters of public choice. But that doesn't require a great deal of time, or mean attending meetings. Expert testimony and differing opinions would be aired through a democratic media. Individuals with strong feelings on particular issues would presumably participate in such forms, but others would be free to pay as much or as little attention to these debates as they wished.

We also believe the amount of time and travel devoted to consumption decision-making in our model would be less than in market economies. Consumer federations could operate exhibits for people to visit before placing orders for goods that would be delivered directly to neighborhood outlets. And serious R&D units attached to consumer federations would not only provide better information about consumption options but a real vehicle for translating consumer desires into product innovation. While the prospect of proposing and revising consumption proposals within neighborhood councils might appear to require significant meeting time, we tried to explain in chapter four of *Looking Forward* why, with the aid of computer terminals and rather simple software packages, this needn't take more time than it takes people currently to prepare their tax returns and pay their bills. In any case, nobody would have to attend meetings or discuss their neighbors' opinions regarding consumption requests if they chose not to; the existence of greater opportunities for efficient social interaction prior to registering consumption preferences could be utilized or ignored as individuals chose; and time necessary for consumption decision- making would be treated like time necessary for production decision-making—as part of one's obligations in a participatory economy, not part of one's leisure time.

But how much meeting time is required by participatory planning? Contrary to critics' presumptions, we did not propose a model of democratic planning in which people, or their elected representatives, meet face-to-face to discuss and negotiate how to coordinate their activities. Instead we proposed a procedure in which individuals and councils submit proposals for their own activities, receive new information including new indicative prices, and submit revised proposals. Nor did we suggest meetings of constituents to define feasible options to be voted on. Instead we proposed that after a number of iterations had defined the major contours of the plan, the professional staffs of iteration facilitation boards would define a few feasible plans within those contours for constituents to vote on without ever meeting and debating with one another at all. Finally, we did not propose face-to-face meetings where different groups would plead their cases for consumption or production proposals that did not meet normal quantitative standards. Instead, we proposed that councils submit qualitative information as part of their proposals so that higher-level federations could grant exceptions should they choose to. Moreover, the procedure for disapproving proposals is a simple yes-or-no vote of federation members rather than a rancorous meeting.

But while we do not think the criticism of "too many meetings" is warranted, we do not want to be misleading. Informed, democratic decision-making *is* different than autocratic decision-making. And conscious, equitable coordination of the social division of labor *is* different than the impersonal law of supply and demand. We obviously think the former, in each case, is far preferable to the latter. But this is not to say we do not understand this requires, almost by definition, more meaningful social intercourse.

The system is too intrusive: In "A Roundtable on Participatory Economics," in *Z* (July/August 1991), Nancy Folbre referred to this problem as "tyranny of the busy-body" and "dictatorship of the sociable." In a class one of us taught, the issue came to be known as "the kinky underwear problem." Nancy Folbre also cautioned of the potential inefficiency of groups dominated by the sentiment, "Let's not piss anybody off." David Levy observed that while *Looking Forward* reminded him in some respects of Ursula LeGuin's novel, *The Dispossessed*, readers should be warned that LeGuin's subtitle was "An Ambiguous Utopia" because "reliance on social pressure rather than material incentives create a lack of initiative, claustrophobic conformity, and intrusiveness." In comradely private communication, Tom Weisskopf cautioned against "sacrificing too much individuality, specialization, diversity, and freedom of choice." What is the source of these misgivings, and how do we respond?

For us it is important to distinguish between misgivings that any and all participatory processes may be "too intrusive" and the criticism that some of our specific measures are more socially intrusive than need be. First, let us reiterate features of our model designed to protect the citizenry from tyrannical busy-bodies. Beside being free to move from one neighborhood to another, consumption proposals justified by one's effort rating cannot be vetoed. While there is nothing but a motion to close debate to prevent a busy-body from carrying on about someone else's consumption request, it is difficult to understand why people would choose to waste their time listening to views that had no practical consequence. Individuals can also make anonymous consumption requests if they do not wish their neighbors to know the particulars of their consumption habits. In workers' councils, balancing job complexes for empowerment should alleviate one important cause of differential influence over decision-making. Rotating assignments to committees also alleviates monopolization of authority. On the other hand we stopped short of calling for balancing "consumption" complexes for empowerment, and refused to endorse forcing people to attend or remain at meetings longer than they found useful. An apt analogy is the saying, "You can lead a horse to water, but you can't make it drink." We had every intention of leading people to participate, but no doubt, some will drink more deeply from the well of participation than others, and those who do will probably influence decisions disproportionately. Even so, those who are more sociable would have a difficult time benefiting materially from their efforts, and the anti-social should suffer no material penalty. In any case, better dictatorship of the sociable with no material privileges than dictatorship of the propertied, dictatorship of the bureaucrats and party members, or dictatorship of the better-educated.

We also fail to understand why our proposal is not seen as thoroughly libertarian. People are free to apply to live and work wherever they wish. People can ask for whatever consumption goods and services they desire and distribute their consumption over their lives however they see fit. People can apply to whatever educational and training programs they want. And any individual or group of individuals can start a new living unit, consumer council, or worker council with fewer "barriers" to overcome than in any traditional model. The only restriction is that the burdens and benefits of the division of labor be equitable. That is why people are not free to consume more than their sacrifice warrants. And that is why people are not free to work at job complexes that are more desirable or empowering than others enjoy. It may be that some chafe under these restrictions, or find them excessive. We certainly never suggested they be forced on a citizenry against their will. We simply believe the logic of justice requires these restrictions on "individual freedom," just as the logic of justice places restrictions on the freedom to profit from private ownership of productive property. As citizens in a participatory economy we would argue and vote for these restrictions until convinced otherwise.

The system misfocuses priorities: Pat Devine criticizes our model for overly concentrating on popular participation in small and local decisions at the expense of larger social issues. In private communication Peter Dorman put the issue somewhat differently: "Since democracy is not easy or costless to practice, we should economize on its use."

Obviously, we would be unhappy with a model that diverted people's participatory energies from more important issues to more trivial ones. And in retrospect, we can see how our exposition could lead people to conclude we attach too little importance to long-term development and investment decisions. In *Participatory Economics* we were anxious to demonstrate that participatory planning was more likely to achieve allocative efficiency than traditional alternatives. Accordingly, we concentrated on a static model without resorting to the typical artifice of pretending the conclusions apply to many time periods as well. In *Looking Forward* we wanted to explain what a participatory economy would "feel like" to ordinary citizens. So we mostly discussed day-to-day production and consumption concerns and how they would be handled.

But our intent was that the procedures of participatory planning should also be used to formulate long-run plans. Once again the options are: (1) relegate long-run planning to the vagaries of the market place, (2) entrust long-run planning to a political and technical elite, or (3) permit councils and federations of workers and consumers to propose, revise, and reconcile the different components of the long-run plan.

There is an extensive and compelling literature to the effect that *laissez-faire* market systems are *least* appropriate for long-run development decisions. Indeed, traditional socialist critics of capitalism such as Maurice Dobb and Paul Sweezy were most convincing when arguing the theoretical advantages of planning over markets to achieve growth and development. Even the terribly flawed Soviet version of planning demonstrated important advantages over market economies in this regard. Moreover, every historical case of successful development by a "late comer" has been an example of the efficacy of planning rather than laissez faire, ideological claims to the contrary notwithstanding.

Rejecting the vagaries of the marketplace, if the political and technocratic elite is not chosen democratically, the dangers and disadvantages are obvious. But even if those who are entrusted to conceive and negotiate the long-term plan are chosen democratically, as they are, for example, in Pat Devine's vision of "negotiated coordination," there would be less room for popular participation than under the procedures of participatory planning. Since we agree with Devine that choosing between transforming coal mining so as to dramatically improve health and safety, replacing highway travel with a high-speed rail system, or transforming agriculture to conform to ecological norms—not all of which can be done at once—has an important impact on people's lives, we are anxious that popular participation be maximized in these matters.

So, as always, the issue comes down to how can ordinary people become best involved in a particular kind of decision-making? In our view, the federation of coal miners, the federation of rail workers, the federation of automobile makers, the federation of agricultural workers, and the transportation, food, and environment departments of the national federation of consumers should all play a prominent role in formulating, analyzing, and comparing the above alternatives. In our view, even regarding major, long-term choices, people participate best in areas closest to their personal concerns, and participatory planning is designed to take advantage of this. This is not to deny that everyone would vote on major alternatives. Nor do we deny there is an important role for expertise. But besides the professional staffs of iteration facilitation boards, professionals in R&D units working directly for the above federation would play an active role in defining long-term options. And with the aid of relatively accurate indications of social costs and benefits, we believe workers and consumers through their councils and federations can play a prominent role in long-term planning just as they can in annual planning and managing their own work and consumption.

The system provides insufficient incentives: Our model of a participatory economy is designed to maximize the motivating potential of non-material incentives. There is some reason to hope jobs designed by workers will be more enjoyable than ones designed by capitalists or coordinators. There is every reason to believe people will be more willing to carry out tasks they themselves proposed and agreed to than assignments handed them by superiors. There is also every reason to believe people will be more willing to perform unpleasant duties conscientiously when they know the distribution of those duties as well as the rewards for people's efforts are equitable.

But all this is not to say there are no material incentives in our model. As we explained [in previous chapters], one's efforts will be rated by one's peers who have every interest in seeing that those they work with work up to their potentials. Moreover, one's effort ratings in work will affect one's consumption rights.

It is true we do not recommend paying more to those with more education and training since we believe it would be inequitable to do so. But that does not mean people would not seek to enhance their productivity. First of all, the cost of education and training would be born publicly, not privately. So there are no material disincentives to pursuing education and training. Secondly, since a participatory economy is not an "acquisitive" society, respect, esteem, and social recognition would be based largely on "social serviceability" which is enhanced precisely by developing one's most socially useful potentials through education and training.

The same logic applies to innovation. We do not support rewarding those who succeed in discovering productive innovations with vastly greater consumption rights than others who make equivalent personal sacrifices in work. Instead we recommend emphasizing direct social recognition of outstanding achievements for a variety of reasons. First, successful innovation is often the outcome of cumulative human creativity for which a single individual is rarely entirely responsible. Furthermore, an individual's contribution is often the product of genius and luck as much as diligence, persistence, and personal sacrifice, all of which implies that recognizing innovation through social esteem rather than material reward is superior on ethical grounds. Second, we are not convinced that social incentives will prove less powerful than material ones. It should be recognized that no economy ever has or could pay innovators the full social value of their innovations, which means that if material compensation is the only reward, innovation will be under-stimulated in any case. Moreover, too often material reward is merely a symbol, or imperfect substitute, for what is truly desired, social esteem. How else can one explain why those who already have more wealth than they can consume continue to strive to accumulate more? In any case, these are our opinions. Actual policy in a participatory economy would be settled democratically in light of results.

Nor do we see why critics believe there would be insufficient incentives for enterprises to seek and implement innovations, unless they measure a participatory economy against a mythical and misleading image of capitalism. Sometimes it is presumed that innovating capitalist enterprises capture the full benefits of their successes, while it is also assumed that innovations spread instantaneously to all enterprises in an industry. When made explicit it is obvious these assumptions are contradictory. Yet only if both assumptions hold can one conclude that capitalism provides maximum material stimulus to innovation *and* achieves technological efficiency throughout the economy. In reality innovative capitalist enterprises temporarily capture "super profits" (in Marxist terms) or "technological rents" (in neoclassical terms) which are competed away more or less rapidly depending on a host of circumstances. Which means that in reality there is a trade-off in capitalist economies between stimulus to innovation and the efficient use of innovation, or a trade-off between dynamic and static efficiency.

In a participatory economy, workers have a "material incentive," if you will, to implement innovations that improve the quality of their work life. This means they have an incentive to implement changes that increase the social benefits of the outputs they produce, or reduce the social costs of the inputs they consume, since anything that increases an enterprise's social benefit to social cost ratio will allow the workers to win approval for their proposal with less effort or sacrifice on their part. But just as in capitalism, adjustments will render any advantage they achieve temporary. As the innovation spreads to other enterprises, as indicative prices change, and as work complexes are re-balanced across enterprises and industries, the full social benefits of their innovation will be both realized and spread to all workers and consumers.

The faster the adjustments are made, the more efficient and equitable the outcome. On the other hand, the more rapid the adjustments, the less the "material incentive" to innovate and the greater the incentive to "ride for free" on others' innovations. While this is no different than under capitalism, a participatory economy enjoys important advantages. Most important, direct recognition of "social serviceability" is a more powerful incentive in a participatory economy, which reduces the magnitude of the trade-off. Second, a participatory economy is better suited to allocating resources efficiently to R&D because research and development is largely a public good that is predictably under-supplied in market economies but would not be in a participatory economy. Third, the only effective mechanism for providing material incentives for innovating enterprises in capitalism is to slow their spread, at the expense of efficiency. This is true because the transaction costs of registering patents and negotiating licenses from patent holders are very high. But while we would recommend it only as a last resort, the transaction costs of delaying the recalibration of work complexes for innovative work places, or even granting extra consumption allowances for a period of time would not be high in a participatory economy.

In general, we find much of what parades as scientific opinion about incentives plagued by unwarranted assumptions. We are neither as pessimistic about the motivational power of non-material incentives in an appropriate environment as many of our fellow radicals have become. Nor do we see any inappropriate obstacles to the deployment of material incentives in a participatory economy should its members decide they are warranted. In the end we are quite comfortable with the very traditional socialist view that a mixture of material and social incentives would be necessary during the process of creating an equitable and humane economy. But that social progress hinges, in part, on the diminishing reliance on material incentives.

Conclusion

The issue is simple:

- Do we want to try and measure the value of each person's contribution to social production and allow individuals to withdraw from social production accordingly? Or do we want to base any differences in consumption rights on differences in personal sacrifices made in producing the goods and services? In other words, do we want an economy that implements the maxim "to each according to the value of his or her personal contribution" or an economy that obeys the maxim "to each according to his or her effort?"

- Do we want a few to conceive and coordinate the work of the many? Or do we want everyone to have the opportunity to participate in economic decision-making to the degree they are affected by the outcome? In other words, do we want to continue to organize work hierarchically, or do we want job complexes balanced for empowerment?

- Do we want a structure for expressing preferences that is biased in favor of individual consumption over social consumption? Or do we want to it to be as easy to register preferences for social as individual consumption? In other words, do we want markets or nested federations of consumer councils?

- Do we want economic decisions to be determined by competition between groups pitted against one another for their well being and survival? Or do we want to plan our joint endeavors democratically, equitably, and efficiently? In other words, do we want to abdicate economic decision making to the market place or do we want to embrace the possibility of participatory planning?

—January 1992

PART THREE

Like Goliath,
They'll Be Conquered:
Thinking About Change

Resurrect The R-Word

Revolution to many means chaos, violence, and death. Disagree? Me too. But should we resurrect the R-word?

Economics

Consider this: eight million unemployed, 35 million poor, 20 million "hungry," 400,000 homeless, a third of government expenditures financing militarism. IBM controls 80 percent in computers; GE and Westinghouse control 85 percent in heavy electrical equipment; Boeing and McDonnell Douglas control 80 percent in aircraft; 10 out of 14,500 banks own 34 percent of all assets. Workers sell their ability to produce and as a reward suffer subordination, lies, chicanery, and manipulation. Ambulance-chasing is a profitable professional pastime. Commodity fetishism is the only respected way of life.

Scoring high on the "I own" meter requires accumulating and debauching without a care. Not capitalists' genes, but the institutional byways they traverse exterminate their human sentiments. To argue that capitalists will freely forsake economic violence is utopian. Capitalism will *never* give us fine schools, good health care, equitable incomes, solidarity between workers, people before profit, and an environment suitable for human habitation.

Fairness, humane investment, and social self-management require collective public ownership, decentralized participatory planning, and jobs incorporating comparable access to information, responsibility, and skilled work.

We have economic violence. We want economic liberty. The difference is transformative. We need the R-word.

Kinship

Over recent decades, feminists have taught that women and men are equal; gender is social; and girls and boys, mothers and fathers, aunts and uncles, daters and datees, top and bottom, are not anatomic roles but historically contingent outcomes. We are what we do, and we can do other than what *Playboy,* Hollywood, or the "guys" advise.

A woman is raped every 6 minutes, upward of 45 percent of all women suffer rape or attempted rape at least once in a lifetime, 92 percent of all women suffer sexual assault or harassment at some time, and 4 out of 5 murdered women die at the hands of male killers, one-third to one-half of whom are their spouses. Women earn about 69 percent for comparable work, but most women can't get comparable work (in 1986, 62 percent of all women who were working had jobs in occupations that were at least 70 percent female), and women get top pay for modeling, acting, turning game-show cards, homemaking for the rich, and street-walking in Manhattan. As of 1979, women did four times as much housework as men and still took most responsibility for child-rearing. U.S. teenage pregnancy is highest in the developed world while the multi-billion-dollar U.S. pornography industry evidences mind-staggering manufactured sexist perversion. Child-rearing and education relegate to young women the freedom to be "feminine" and to young men the freedom to be "manly." Billion dollar diets mutilate millions of human psyches and hundreds of thousands of human bodies. Tens of millions of men and women suffer indignity, brutality, and even death for their homosexual preferences, and the elderly suffer isolated poverty while productive tasks they could do go undone.

Macho doesn't presuppose male genes. It is not inscribed in their DNA that women should be objectified and battered. Kinship violence stems not from genes gone bad, but from fragmented families, pseudo-sexuality, reductive education, competitive courting, and sexist economics, politics, and culture.

To transcend gender violence we need sex-blind roles; support for single, coupled, and multi-parenting arrangements; and easy access to high-quality daycare, flexible work hours, and parental-leave options. To extend gender peace we need freedom for children to develop views with their peers and without excessive adult supervision. For gender liberation we need retirement guided by personal inclination not age; liberated sexuality respecting all choices and inclinations; and norms of courting, child-rearing, and work, free from gender bias—in short, a transformation replacing this country's patriarchy with gender equality and sexual freedom. The R-word fits again.

Culture

The ethnic, racial, and religious ways we find to understand ourselves and our place in society help define our lives.

Slavery, apartheid, separate but equal, racism, ethnocentrism, colonialism, and religious bigotry are all systems in which one community subordinates another or two communities wage endless conflict that deadens the cultural prospects and the souls and bodies of all concerned. "Walk on water, walk on a leaf / Hardest of all is to walk on grief."

In the U.S., some blacks and Hispanics earn big salaries and high status as comedians and athletes, reinforcing acceptable images, while Native Americans don't earn big bucks at all. Sixty percent of all blacks, 53 percent of all Hispanics, 48 percent of all Asians, but only 27 percent of all whites live in deteriorating central cities. The median family income for Hispanics is roughly half that for whites with blacks down another 10 percent. Black infant mortality nearly doubles that for whites. Criminal prosecution, allocation of educational resources, and mass media images all communicate that nonwhite communities are inferior. These differences subjugate whole peoples denying their cultures and their potentials for developing and fulfilling themselves.

The U.S. is far from being a compendium of diverse communities, each free to develop in harmony with others, each respecting and learning from the different cultural answers others offer, each protecting the rights of all. Collapsing all cultures into the norms of the dominant few via "integration" is no solution. Instead, resurrect the R-word.

Politics

U.S. politics features media-reinforced apathy, bribes, scams, repression, aid to dictators, regressive taxation, choices between candidate clones, wars, and no accountability. Real democracy features self-management, plebiscites, honest information, informed public debate, maximum accountability, and no possibility for accruing excessive power.

Transition from spectator politics to participatory politics requires new political forms. We need institutional means to develop new viewpoints, debate them, refine them, fight for them, and enact them. Information and power are key. We lack both. We need both. Repeated Watergates, Irangates, and popular resistance campaigns that redress grievances may forestall dictatorship but they will not create new institutions able to propel informed participation. Bring back the R-word.

The Planet and the Ecosphere

Nations fight nations, torture and war ravage the human legacy, hunger runs rampant. Nuclear and chemical wastes infect, air pollution congests, the seed-base depletes, Three Mile Islands fester, forests diminish. Neither the world as a social system nor the world as an ecosphere can withstand much more. Without international equity and new means for care-taking the earth, all will go to hell in a turbocart. In a dirty world, the R-word is *not* a dirty word.

Sensible Debate

Embarrassment on hearing the R-word conveys that liberated human history is impossible. Equating the R-word with "blood-lust" accepts that struggle for change can yield only minimal gains or, if we get too ambitious, worse than what we already have. To debate the propriety of "revolution" reflects timidity about truth. We must no longer debate the R-word as if humanity may after all be able to flourish within the dictates of capitalism, patriarchy, racism, and authoritarianism. But a host of related issues do warrant debate.

What characteristics would desirable economic, kinship, cultural, political, international, and ecological goals have? How do we win immediate reforms while strengthening our ability to fight for long-run aims? What kind of organization, ideology, and tactics do we need to reach our goals? Since attention to economics, gender, culture, politics, world relations, and ecology yields contrasting socialist, feminist, nationalist, anarchist, anti-interventionist, and ecological agendas, how can a new movement retain the integrity and autonomy of each, while realizing solidarity among them all?

Debating these and related questions while consciousness-raising, demonstrating, and organizing isn't "utopian" but is instead the only comprehensive approach to social change.

To win a new world, even to significantly improve this one, we must know what we want. To journey from here to there, we need to know where "there" is. What is a participatory economy and what steps can attain it? What is a feminist kinship sphere, a culturally intercommunal community sphere, and a participatory political sphere? In each case, what steps can take us from what we have to what we want? In face of the horrors we all know so well, it does not evidence maturity, pragmatism, or wisdom to dismiss revolutionary desires as strange. It evidences ignorance, defeatism, or even lack of humanity. Don't whisper the R-word.

To seek complete freedom does not require adopting arrogant postures that alienate potential allies, but it does require sober yet comprehensive desire, and careful yet unrelenting critique. Liberalism's half-way programs and tempered rhetoric strengthen the two greatest obstacles to justice in the U.S.: the popular views that you can't beat City Hall and that even if you do beat the bastards, it won't mean much because the new bosses will be as bad as the old ones. Isn't it obvious that the left won't arouse hope and deserve commitment until its morality, tone, and spirit transcend Band-Aid bureaucratic fixes?

We can't win what we won't even name. We can't orient today's reforms to furthering tomorrow's victories if we refuse to define what tomorrow's victories need to be. Blind strategy is no strategy at all. Resistance is good. But to get to liberation, in speaking, writing, thought, and action—resurrect the R word.

—May 1988

Shut It Down

George Bush, the White House, the Pentagon, the House, the Senate, the *New York Times*, the *Washington Post*, ABC, NBC, CBS, the mainstream national media, corporate capital, patriarchs, and racists have together unleashed a rain of destruction on the people of Iraq, and, before it's over, perhaps on people throughout the Middle East. Of course they have brought economic hardship and therefore widespread death to the disadvantaged throughout the world all along. Peace and prosperity for the rich, war and deprivation for the poor. Business as usual.

Admit the ugly truth. Bush, the White House, the Congress, and the mass media do not care about the lives of U.S. troops except insofar as loss of their lives might fuel resistance and thereby thwart war aims.

They do not calculate for one micro-second the human suffering their policies unleash on the people of Iraq, except insofar as that travail might provoke further resistance in the U.S.

They do not respect national sovereignty or they would have opposed Iraq's war against Iran instead of supporting it, opposed Israel's violations of Lebanon's sovereignty instead of supporting it, opposed Turkey's violations of Cyprus instead of supporting it, opposed Indonesia's genocidal assaults on East Timor instead of providing aid. National self-determination obviously means nothing to those who invaded Grenada and Panama and mined Nicaragua's harbors in open defiance of international law.

They do not care about democracy or removing a violent, oppressive dictator or they would not have supported Hussein before August 2, just as they would not have supported Pinochet, Somoza, Marcos, the Shah of Iran, and Noriega, and just as they would not now be trying desperately to replace Violeta Chamoro with a someone better able to reconstitute death squads to stamp out the legacy of Sandinismo. Murderousness and an aversion to justice are the *best* credentials for obtaining U.S. support. Murderers like Hussein fall out of favor with the U.S. only when they disobey "our" will.

They do not care about preventing the spread of weapons of mass destruction or they wouldn't produce them, wouldn't use them, and wouldn't obstruct all international efforts, including in the Middle East, to eliminate them.

They only care about enlarging their own power and wealth, and about that, there are no buts allowed.

The money going to war could go to ending hunger. Bush doesn't care. Stephen Solarz doesn't care. For that matter, not more than a handful of Congresspeople care.

"Don't be silly," they would say if they had the courage to speak openly, "If we didn't use the wealth in war we certainly wouldn't use it to eliminate hunger. That would aid the poor. That would shorten the 'stick' we use to get the poor to do our bidding. It would reduce our relative advantage. It would be worse than war." These are the people we're dealing with. This is not rhetoric. Understand these truths and while each new affront will nauseate you, it will not sidetrack your activism.

Capitalism is theft. It is also brutality, corruption, lying, cheating, killing, all coupled to an almost infinite capacity for egoism. NBC worries about a terrorist attack somewhere in the U.S., perhaps in some subway train or office building. Meanwhile the U.S. Air Force rains terror on a whole country. Capitalism is hypocrisy. It is not "surgical war" but "surgical morality" that applies whenever, wherever, and however the U.S. wants, which means never when moral accounting would interfere with the interests of U.S. elites. Don't let capitalism destroy your will to resist. Shut it down.

Patriarchy is male domination. And it is also repression of human sentiment to preserve gender hierarchy. It is macho posturing built on violence against women and engendering a military mindset that celebrates destruction, enjoys obliterating defenseless opponents, and identifies courage with mindless obedience to anyone wearing more metal and ribbons on their chest. Don't let patriarchy destroy your will to resist. Shut it down.

Racism is mental and physical lynching with rules, words, money, culture, law, and clubs. And it is also elevation of self over others culminating in a nationalist crescendo that consigns people to a subhuman status to justify destroying them to save them. Don't let racism destroy your will to resist. Shut it down.

The state is the armed might of a society hell-bent on domination. Bush is a surgeon who will calmly remove beating hearts, sunder healthy limbs, and sacrifice working minds. He will limit carnage only to diminish dissent. We can end his violence. Don't let the power of the state deter your will to resist. Shut it down.

The mass media is a product of capitalism, sexism, and racism, subject to oversight by the state. The government has put restraints on the media's access to the battlefield, driving them away from the sights and sounds of war because reporters who smell fame in the throes of battle may let their hunger for Pulitzer Prizes interfere with their skill at obscuring truth. But here at home no such restraint is required. For the most part the media knows it is not their place to report on hundreds of thousands of antiwar demonstrators shutting down bridges, occupying post offices, stopping traffic, marching, teaching, setting up peace and justice centers. But since they must admit something is going on, their role is to pan in on a few vigils, some scenes of hippie protesters mulling about, and a barrage of interviews with relatives of soldiers supporting the war juxtaposed with frequent shots of Young Americans for Freedom counter-demonstrating. This is the media's role. Subservience. Don't let the mass media destroy your will to resist. Shut it down.

Don't direct your anger at a young woman just out of high school going to the Middle East to fight. Support her by bringing her home alive and unscarred by the experience of killing, wounding, and maiming her fellow human beings. Be angry at her role, imposed by oppressive institutions. Don't direct your anger at a construction worker or mail carrier who wears a flag and shouts for victory. For the institutions that produced these misguided sentiments, feel anger, yes. For the person, feel a commitment to communicate, to organize.

However, for anyone who has enjoyed relative luxury, who has had the benefit of substantial education, who has enjoyed the relative freedom of a well paying and secure job, and who nonetheless mouths idiotic, racist, jingoist bullshit, feel righteous anger. And let it show.

And for the folks who claim moral outrage and opposition but go on litigating, prescribing, bossing, and teaching as usual, feel anger. These people have no excuse not to give their resources, time, money, and energy to stop this war. They have freedom from oversight and financial want as well as access to the truth. They have the opportunity to act with near impunity. To say they are against the war and do nothing is the worst kind of hypocrisy.

Finally, the Congresspeople, like Ted and Joe Kennedy, who voted against the war and 48 hours later voted to "support the President," deserve a special place in Hell. The only behavior sicker than their's comes from financiers whose reaction to war is the same as their reaction to all of human life—wondering what will be the effect on their stocks, bonds, and currencies.

As I write, just days after the U.S. attack on Iraq began, people are demonstrating all across the country. Actions range from teach-ins to vigils, marches, civil disobedience, and blocking traffic, to taking over buildings and institutions. Participants come from every imaginable constituency.

While Bush and Co. cannot and will not hear our analyses or moral pleas, they do hear the threat of increasing and diversifying opposition. Though our opposition was not enough to prevent war from starting, it can prevent the war's enlargement, prevent nuclear assault, end the war, curtail the further militarization of our society, and win conversion. We must talk, organize, teach-in, rally, march, sit-in, occupy, and disrupt targets ranging from federal buildings and recruitment centers, to radio and TV stations, ROTC offices and research facilities, dilapidated drug rehabilitation centers, rape crisis centers, soup kitchens, and housing agencies, and to the White House. Shut down what should not be permitted, and fund what we need.

The Berlin Wall was taken down by massive movements and then by average folks wielding crowbars. Next target: The Pentagon. Shut it down.

Hussein is a thug but the Iraqi people are as innocent as civilians in any war. That their deaths should not be in vain, that the deaths of citizens in the Third World suffering economic calamity should not be in vain, and that the deaths of U.S. GIs should not be in vain, we have to end the war and go on to end militarism.

It can be done. And we must do it. It will not be easy or quick. But the alternative is too deadly to permit. Shut it down.

—February 1991

After The "Turkey Shoot"

Antiwar activists weren't cluster bombed or physically beaten. But we are depressed, and with ample reason.

- 100,000, perhaps 200,000 or more, Iraqis died in a "Turkey Shoot" inappropriately called a "war."

A *New York Times* photo showed thousands of cars burned on the road from Kuwait to Basra. The caption read "Vehicles caught in bombing while retreating." In this picture diligent readers could see the charred, mangled, unmentioned corpses only with the aid of a powerful magnifying glass, but bombardiers had a better view. In a *Washington Post* interview a pilot complained that the Air Force was unable to reload cluster bombs fast enough to kill all the retreating "targets." Tie a yellow ribbon for that pilot, please.

For military wisdom, the *Boston Globe* quotes an officer surveying charred teenage bodies at ground level. The soldier is chagrined, but comfortingly deduces that for the U.S. to have had so few casualties and the Iraqis so many there must have been "divine intervention" on the side of "good versus evil." He never considers the slightly more plausible conclusion that this "war" was one of the most wanton, cowardly massacres in modern military history. Will the troops now busy bulldozing bodies into mass graves tell all after returning to the "mother of all fatherlands," or will ticker-tape parades replace honesty as therapy? Tie another yellow ribbon, please. Perhaps the U.S. construction giant, Bechtel, ought to paint a big yellow sign in the rubble, "The Real Great Satan Was At Work Here."

It is little comfort that fewer U.S. troops died of war-inflicted wounds than might have died in street violence had they all spent the same six months living in a ghetto in any major U.S. city. Over 40 Iraqi divisions decimated, the entire infrastructure of Iraq destroyed, much of Kuwait bombed to dust, ecological chaos, and about 100 "allied" battlefield casualties. As cleanup (mostly body removal) reveals that Iraq had no battlefield-available chemical weapons, no massive impenetrable fortifications, and few fortifications of any kind at all, could it be any clearer that the entire media discussion of Iraq's "military might" was a disgusting charade to fool the American public? Should the world try Hussein for war crimes? Sure, along with Bush, Baker, and the CEOs of CBS, ABC, NBC, CNN, the *New York Times,* and the *Washington Post.*

- A Goebbels-like mass-media campaign successfully manipulated public opinion.

Rampant flag-waving patriotism—derived from intense alienation turned to collective euphoria over winning—was sustained more by ignorance than malevolence. But this offers little solace for movement activists whose main responsibility is uncovering truth and raising consciousness.

Yes, a post-war poll showed that less than a third of respondents were aware that Israel was occupying land in the Middle East, that only 3 percent were aware of Syria's occupation of Lebanon, that just 15 percent could identify the Intifada, and only 14 percent knew that the U.S. had been almost alone in the UN in rejecting a political settlement between Israel and the Palestinians, and that, in contrast, 81 percent knew all about the Patriot missile and 80 percent knew Saddam Hussein had gassed the Kurds.

Yes, before the war 75 percent of the U.S. public favored negotiations. And yes, if everyone had known that the hypothetical negotiation scenario proposed by pollers was actually what Saddam Hussein was repeatedly asking for, 99 percent would have favored peace.

So, yes, the public wasn't consciously for barbarism. Instead, in a corrupt, uncaring, and decaying society, once the leadership chose barbarism, people wanted so badly for their country to be on the side of right that they didn't assess whether their morals were consistent with U.S. policy. But this lack of conscious malevolence is no reason to exult. After all, similar ignorance and mob psychology sustained the nazification of Germany.

- Bush took a big step toward establishing a mercenary future for the U.S.

U.S. elites went to war (1) to control Middle East oil as an international economic lever; (2) to ensure that Middle East oil profits prop up our banks and now our construction industry ("we destroyed the country to rebuild it"); and (3) to establish that we are a gun for hire which will mercilessly repress any Third World country trying to establish the slightest control over their own destiny, regardless of whether they undertake these actions from a right-wing or left-wing stance. Bush has traveled far toward implementing this vision and that is truly depressing.

But, still deeper, I think many activists are wondering, why am I doing what I do? Why am I radical, dissident, pacifist, feminist, anti-racist, green, gay rights, anti-capitalist? Why do I uncover every disgusting nook and cranny of oppression and brutality instead of doing what gives me most pleasure? Is this sensible? Is it hopeful? Doesn't some of the rampant depression now sweeping activist communities stem from a fear that winning is impossible and we may be wasting our lives?

I don't think people who feel this way will be dissuaded by calls urging, "Don't mourn, organize." We did organize. And it galvanized tremendous opposition. And it wasn't enough.

Could We Have Done More?

In any complex undertaking it is always possible things could have been done better. Instead of having two coalitions confusing people and dividing resources, we could have had one that was clear, principled, and eloquent. More of the opposition could have avoided accepting turf defined by the administration and media—"do we or don't we support the troops?"—and focused on the fact that U.S. Gulf policy was criminal and the war unjust. Everyone could have worked just a little harder, demonstrations could have been a little better planned, speakers a little better prepared, and leadership a little more willing to incorporate new ideas and energies.

But, given the outpouring of antiwar activity across the country, these criticisms are minor. The truth is, given our starting point on August 2, our antiwar effort was about as good as we could have hoped for. As a curb on war-making, episodic organizing is dead.

Crises come and go. During crises attention is aroused, energies grow, and activism naturally increases. By saying "episodic organizing is dead," I don't mean future crises won't spur increased activism. And I don't mean that the logic of raising the social cost of hated policies by education, demonstrations, and disobedience is mistaken. Nor do I mean that it's bad for people who were previously uninvolved to be roused for the first time to undertake critical initiatives during a crisis. But if there is not an *ongoing* infrastructure of grassroots and national movement institutions, the growth in energy that occurs with the onset of each new crisis will never be well captured, long retained, nor curb each new crisis before it explodes. Therefore, building a lasting, systemically-focused movement must become priority number one for long-term activists.

The U.S. state and its agencies have learned the lessons of struggle taught by the 1960s and have modified their behavior and that of the media accordingly. That transformation, coupled with the exit of the Soviets as a serious international force, has left a new organizing context. When war threatens, if antiwar movements organize from scratch, then by the time they attain an organizational capability to begin to wipe away media/government lies and confusions, the war is over. Media madness drowns out antiwar arguments until ticker-tape victory parades crowd antiwar demonstrations off the streets.

But what if instead we had started opposition on August 2 not from scratch but with well-established capabilities? Imagine, for example, as one of many lost past possibilities, that Jesse Jackson's Rainbow campaigns over the past decade had been primarily movement-building efforts with an electoral component as just one aspect. Imagine that, as many urged at the time, when Jackson and the Rainbow apparatus traveled all over the nation their chief priority was to help establish grass-roots organizations, provide resources and skills, and build local structures that could later fight for local agendas.

Imagine also that after the elections, instead of gutting what could have been a community-based, institutionally sound, multi-issue, multi-tactic Rainbow in favor of a narrowly defined, electoral machine, the Rainbow leadership had further democratized the Rainbow, developed new chapters, and steadily improved their means of national communication and education.

Suppose also that over the same years we had done more to develop alternative media, applying more resources to the most economical and effective approaches at our disposal. And suppose, too, that in the 1980s we had reached the obvious conclusion that we needed both the "autonomy" of movements and organizations clearly focused around particular oppressions— racism, battering, AIDS, housing, income distribution, foreign policy, schools, health care, conversion, etc.—and also an overarching alliance of all these in which a regular exchange of views *and* material aid and energies was natural. And suppose we achieved a considerable degree of this "autonomy coupled with solidarity" through the Rainbow or some other union of all these movements.

Finally, suppose that after the Vietnam War (the contra war, Grenada, Panama, etc.), instead of moving on to other crises and leaving the field clear for mainstreamers to define the history and meaning of our past experience, we had done a better job of educating the public about exactly what had occurred and why, better preparing people to understand future events not as aberrations or errors, but as logical outgrowths of elite-serving national policy.

In this scenario, on August 2, there would have been thousands of local peace and justice groups, all with well-developed organizing skills, ties to their communities, and ties to one another. There would also have been a representative organization to coordinate their crisis efforts, disseminate written resources for grassroots organizing, provide speakers for teach-ins, set dates for demonstrations, and even raise money to help sustain local work.

And there would have been many more independent radio stations as well as far more visible radical print media able to provide mutual support, analysis, and aid.

Even if there weren't yet workplace, neighborhood, and union branches of this peace and justice movement, which would certainly be a necessary step on the way to lasting structural transformation, this level of activist infrastructure, political sophistication, and mutual support, would have been enough to allow a movement around the Gulf crisis beginning its work on August 2 to force a negotiated rather than a military settlement.

Moreover, since less than all this won't do, whether you see yourself as a revolutionary out to replace patriarchy with feminism, racism with intercommunalism, authoritarianism with democracy, and capitalism with participatory economics, or as a reformer intent only on attaining more justice within the system, you have a clear agenda. Yes, the revolutionary has to provide long-term vision while the reformer doesn't. But for short-term aims, both need to build a multi-focus, multi-constituency, grass roots-based, nationally organized, institutionally strong opposition. Avoiding this to deal only with crises never made much sense. Now, to avoid it makes no sense at all.

There are two reasons to be radical, green, pacifist, feminist, gay rights advocate, antiracist, and/or anti-capitalist. (1) Because it is right. (2) Because it is right and can succeed. The first reason can sustain a relatively small movement undertaking endless episodic organizing that rarely if ever wins anything. The second reason can sustain a powerful movement that educates the public and organizes lasting institutions and thereby wins reform after reform on the road to a transformed society. To begin to make the second reason real and thereby turn back the current tide of depression, those who have the energy and endurance to accept the challenge must make the above hypothetical scenario a future reality.

—*April 1991*

At The Breaking Point?

In Black, Latin, and Native American communities, police repression, homelessness, hunger, unemployment, disease, and constant TV reminders of unattainable comfort crush hope. Drug dealing, theft, alcoholism, and omnipresent gang hostility shatter dignified daily life. Toy guns are out. Real guns are in. The price of rebelling is being beaten, jailed, or shot. The price of obeying is starving plus being beaten, jailed, or shot.

Elites refuse to improve dismal services, provide minimal housing, redress rotten schooling, or raise the minimum wage. Yet they still need minority community members as service and assembly workers and as preferred consumers of the liquor, cigarettes, and other deadly garbage they market.

So mainstream leaders confront a perennial problem: How can they maintain U.S. minority communities marginally above a genocidal standard and yet simultaneously "induce" them to "appreciatively" fill society's most subordinate roles? Examining budget allotments and public rhetoric confirms what analyzing history predicts. Elites favor repression to subdue minority opposition and to further isolate minority poverty from "polite society." How can rich people trickle down aid to "less capable" white folks when Black and Latin slaves are not in their proper place, out of sight and mind, except to exploit?

U.S. minorities once again face steady decline unless they force their oppressors to change policies. But the Catch-22 is that when minority communities rebel, elites cheerfully reply with more repression. And once the fast bullets fly, only domestic white opposition—certainly not elite remorse or international outrage—will contain the damage.

The U.S. now has (1) politically formally equal, (2) geographically semi-separate, and (3) economically harshly unequal relations between whites and people of color. South Africa has (1) politically extremely unequal, (2) geographically fully separate, and (3) economically grossly unequal relations between the same communities.

As South Africa attempts to leave apartheid and the U.S. gradually approaches it, the two countries may meet in the middle. In both South Africa and the U.S., the potential for positive change depends on resistance by the most oppressed. But to succeed, anti-apartheid resistance in South Africa must inspire international outrage that limits white violence, while anti-racist resistance in the U.S. must inspire domestic white support that limits Wall Street and White House violence.

U.S. Black, Latin, and Native American communities are at the breaking point. They may pursue random riots that raise social costs but also weaken minority neighborhoods and "justify" military repression. Or they may create their own "Intifadas" that raise social costs while also strengthening minority neighborhoods and delegitimating military repression. In either case, U.S. Black, Latin, and Native American communities will need white support.

If white opposition to racist repression doesn't increase, the Reagan years will have been a mild prelude to far worse. The U.S. will be a militarily dominant, economically besieged country. It will have corrupt, hypocritical politics emphasizing cults of personality. It will suffer growing sexual violence. Culturally it will have unfettered racism and jingoistic nationalism. "Amerika" has always seemed an ultra-extremist epithet, but our imminent future, similar to Germany's past, could give this ugly re-spelling real meaning.

On the other hand, if there is growing white support for steadily increasing Black, Latin, and Native American resistance, the plight of society's most oppressed communities could improve and set off a new decade of radical opposition. The U.S. civil rights movement turned back the worst ravages of racism and birthed the "1960s." A new movement of U.S. Intifadas could reverse racism and unleash a comprehensive radicalism in the 1990s.

Doesn't it follow that along with their other priorities, progressives should oppose homelessness, unemployment, poverty, police repression, and consumer exploitation in U.S. third world communities? And shouldn't we try to identify, understand, and uproot racist ideology in white communities?

Who? Among media institutions, at least progressive periodicals like the *Nation,* the *Progressive, Mother Jones,* and *In These Times*; independent progressive radio stations throughout the country like WBAI in New York and Pacifica in California; and local newspapers like the *LA Weekly* and New York's *Village Voice.* Among activist organizations, at least the Rainbow Coalition, SANE, CISPES, NOW, DSA, the AFSC, NCIPA, ACTUP, Food First, ecology movements like the Greens, Left Greens, and Greenpeace, and labor organizations from rank-and-file caucuses through national unions....

With what focus? Well, how about five simple points:

Over three million homeless people wander our backstreets eating out of garbage cans and sleeping under newspaper blankets in bedrooms shared with alley-rats. Isn't it obvious that the homeless and their supporters need to force corporations, hotels, motels, and the government to right this wrong.

(1) We should undertake massive civil disobedience and occupations of vacant buildings, offices, and hotels demanding housing reform.

Over 7 million people between the ages of 22 and 59 have annual incomes under $4,000. Nearly 11 percent of all families are poor. The Census Bureau estimates it would cost $33 billion to bring these people above the poverty line—which, according to *Forbes Magazine*, is less than the net worth of Donald Trump and his 14 richest penthouse peers. High unemployment constantly threatens workers with dismissal, homelessness, and poverty, thus limiting their ability to win pay raises and improve their work conditions. Full employment insures workers against being fired and thereby strengthens their hand to fight for better pay and conditions. Clearly winning full employment will be a great advance for justice in the U.S.

(2) We should initiate a full-employment campaign, including calls for a national "equality and justice day" followed by equality and justice month, leading to increasingly militant local regional and national workplace and neighborhood actions.

Cocaine, heroin, and crack together murder a few thousand people yearly. Cigarettes and liquor together murder nearly half-a-million people and debilitate tens of millions more. Preying on ignorance and depression with hard drugs is grotesquely inhumane. Isn't the same true for preying on ignorance and depression with liquor and cigarettes? Cigarette and liquor advertisers are drug dealers. To physically impede manipulative advertising of addictive drugs will positively renew society and particularly its most oppressed citizens.

(3) We should undertake a militant campaign of grassroots resistance against liquor and cigarette companies' efforts to addict poor and particularly third world communities, including demanding an end of debilitating manipulative advertising and a reallocation of hundreds of millions of addictive liquor and cigarette advertising dollars to supporting public education and medical programs.

Junk-bond kings earn as much as $200 million a year. Teachers earn as little as $15,000 a year. A few suburban schools feature clean classrooms, well-stocked labs, good texts, and grassy playing fields. Most urban schools feature lead paint, metal detectors, few texts, and concrete playgrounds. Some youngsters enjoy libraries. Others dodge knives and learn hate. Since lack of education denies the right to fulfill human capacities, attempting to redress low educational standards while developing popular alternatives fosters equity.

(4) We should initiate a campaign to massively redistribute educational resources to shore up inner-city schools, including establishing free alternative schools.

To suffer preventable disease in a society that spends hundreds of billions of dollars funneling money to rich industrialists via weapons expenditures is obscene. To go without medical attention because a hospital is overburdened or unwilling to admit the poor, or for lack of a doctor willing to treat the poor, or for lack of insurance or income to pay fees, is obscene. Everyone in the medical profession should actively protest the U.S. health system not because medical practitioners don't earn enough—though orderlies, technicians, and nurses should protest this too—but because patients are dying. The public should scorn doctoring for dollars, hospitaling for profit, and governing without giving a damn about most people's health. If demonstrations disrupt wealthy people's hospitals and clinics and expose greedy medical administrators and doctors as promoters of disease, change will come.

(5) We should undertake a campaign for a national health plan, including attacking anti-health policies of hospitals, insurers, and the government.

Regarding all these priorities, I am talking about disarmament groups, women's organizations, labor unions, anti-war groups, student groups, green groups, civil rights organizations, gay and lesbian movements, media institutions, and everyone on the left lending their energies, time, material aid, and bodies, even as they each also continue pursuing their own anti-war, feminist, ecology, and other agendas.

But should our city's ghettos explode this summer, even all this might fall short. To ensure that the white community opposes rather than supports police repression will also require public organizing to counter racist views, feelings, and behavior in ways that inform and liberate white communities.

Institutional racism is the subordination of any one cultural community relative to another. It is a condition of unequal access to means of expression, sustenance, self-definition, or self-fulfillment for a culturally defined group. It is unequal incomes, housing, schooling, jobs, education, health care, political participation, and access to media.

Racist ideology, in turn, rationalizes these inequalities by denigrating mistreated ethnic groups, religious groups, nations, or races based on differences of culture, origin, or skin color. It emphasizes descriptions of one community as superior or more humane, and of another as inferior or less humane. It says that the oppressed are lazy, ugly, stupid, gullible, impatient, and suitable for manual, dangerous, or service tasks. It says that their oppressors are industrious, beautiful, intelligent, cautious, patient, and suitable for administrative and conceptual tasks.

Only pathological people can steal from innocent victims and then admit their deeds. Only callous people can benefit when elites trample the rights of innocent victims and then admit that the trampled didn't deserve their plight.

For the rich, racism justifies exploiting people outside their cultural community much as "classism" justifies exploiting working-class members of their own race and religion.

For the poor, racism depends more on lack of knowledge and myth, but also rationalizes inequality. We want to think our advantages stem from our being better, not from our having robbed others. We want to understand our acts of anger toward others as justified by their inhumanity, rather than as a product of ours. To view our community positively and to maintain ties to racist friends and relatives, we conveniently accept that our community is superior and theirs is inferior, so that they deserve their plight.

An alternative "intercommunalist" view is that each cultural community has its own answers to cultural problems and its own cultural definitions, all of which have much to teach everyone about human capabilities and prospects.

In this view, equitable inter-community relations will exist when each community enjoys an unobstructed right to maintain and argue for its own norms and when, in disputes, institutionally weaker/smaller communities are always protected against institutionally stronger/larger ones.

The only way to move people in the U.S. from a racist to an intercommunalist perspective is to realize that people's cultural self-definitions help sustain their self-images. A successful transition must give people a positive self-image to replace the partially self-supporting racist views they need to reject. To fight racism in ways that put nearly all white working people on the defensive and that suggest that they will wind up culturally rootless, hated, and with no self-affirming way of understanding their past is self-defeating.

There is nothing new about needing to address racism. Since even before the founding of the U.S., addressing racism has been a prerequisite for developing powerful, progressive, and radical movements here. And it still is.

— May 1990

We Will Disrupt

How many young people today believe that sexism and misogyny are still virulently active in our society and will persist until basic U.S. institutions fundamentally transform? Judging from the relative lack of feminist activism, the answer seems to be very few. Do people think sexism is an ancient holdover, now so marginalized that the continuing pains women feel must be their own fault? Or do people think women suffer because of biological and not social structures? Or that small changes made 20 years ago are all that is needed for patriarchal institutions to wither away of their own accord? Or that women don't suffer? Or that it doesn't matter? I don't know the answer, but something drastic needs to be done. I never met Emma Goldman, but Madonna is no Emma Goldman.

- Rape is to sexism what lynching is to racism.

- Battering is to sexism what night riding and police violence are to racism.

- "Chick" is to sexism what "nigger" is to racism.

- Poverty, inferior work conditions, inferior education, and cultural stereotypes are to sexism what the same conditions are to racism.

Since the hardships and losses imposed by sexism still persist, shouldn't we have increasing numbers of feminist rallies, demonstrations, and media institutions? Shouldn't the agendas, budgets, and outreach of the U.S. progressive community militantly oppose sexism?

- Rape is increasing.

To be afraid when walking in public is an abominable condition. Half the population of the U.S. endures such fear during much of their lives. Why doesn't the existence and increasing rate of rape provoke militant mass movements?

Suppose some group began to attack and sexually abuse men. And suppose this practice grew until it happened once every sixteen seconds and that this group was trying to relegate men to a materially dependent, socially subordi-

- 187 -

nate position in part enforced by fear of rampant sexual attacks. Society would be outraged. There would be no business as usual until the attacks *stopped*. But, in fact, society plods merrily along even as women suffer exactly these conditions.

- Misogynist violence against women is still increasing.

Millions of women are physically beaten each year, and beyond actual instances, the threat is almost as stultifying as the occurrence. Moreover, after women suffer physical assault, they are often ignored or blamed for their own brutalization. How can it be a personal matter or biologically inevitable that millions of women are regularly battered in their own homes? What does it mean for so many people to believe that something is disgusting, and yet do little or nothing about it?

Suppose a new women's cult formed and attracted thousands of followers, and that one of their practices was to go to bars and beat up men, and that they did this to thousands of men each month. How would the media, government, unions, community groups, and populace respond to that? Would people say it was disgusting only when asked about it, and otherwise proceed with their lives as usual? We all know that militant action would persist until the man-beating was eliminated. The fact that this kind of analogy seems extreme helps indicate how gross the problem of violence against women is.

- A million or more women walk the streets homeless; many millions suffer abject poverty.

Women still earn little more than half men's wages for comparable work which work they most often can't get. Economic dependence or destitution is thus still generally a woman's lot. And even if they escape poverty, in school, at work, and at play women still suffer from genderized expectations about "female capacities." Women are allowed to succeed as models, sexual performers, and caretakers, and are sometimes highly rewarded for doing so. But is a photo of Madonna masturbating supposed to counter the vile advertising and manipulative editorial copy in the pages of even one issue of the magazine whose cover she adorns?

In short, sexism still prevails not only in the bedrooms, families, and public schools of our society, but also in our playgrounds, malls, newspapers, movies, government, courts, universities, religions, marketplace, and workplaces. It causes a hierarchy of power and material comfort that favors men over women. It proclaims heterosexuality normal and homosexuality perverse and heaps cultural and physical contempt on women and men who practice homosexuality. It establishes roles that objectify, abuse, denigrate, and deny women the rightful fulfillment of their mental and physical capacities.

In this context, shouldn't every progressive organization in the U.S. have as one part of its agenda helping to eliminate gender-related inequality and prejudice? Anti-intervention, anti-racism, pro-conversion, or anti-homelessness movements shouldn't elevate women's liberation to the same priority they give their defining causes. That would be counter-productive. But shouldn't each reassess and, if necessary, restructure their organizational dynamics, reevaluate and, if necessary, rebuild their alliances and render support for anti-sexist movements?

When I was learning about political activism and developing my own allegiances, there was a group called Bread and Roses active in Boston, where I was at the time. These women were committed to fighting *all* manifestations of sexism, personal and institutional. They were militant and angry and often saw manifestations of sexism where others tended to see only commonplace circumstances. For having these admirable traits, they were regularly called "hysterical," "kneejerk," "frigid," and "maniacal" not only by the media but by many otherwise leftist men.

I remember how Bread and Roses would confront institutions and movements: "Respect women and incorporate women at every level of leadership and participation and eliminate gender hierarchy, or we will disrupt your operations until you do." Bread and Roses confronted local radio stations, entertainment clubs, and cultural institutions, as well as groups in the New Left. They were ecumenical in choosing targets. "Women are everywhere. They are affected by everything. Therefore no institution, no project, and no person is exempt from the demand to respect women." To call "shit-work" "women's work" does not make it conceptual, adventuresome, or engaging, nor does it justify men not doing it or women doing nothing else.

To portray women in a derogatory, sexist manner was to invite unremitting criticism. To ignore women's opinions, relegate women to lowly tasks, or visually or verbally objectify women was to invite harsh censure and disruption of operations. To structure gender inequality into organizations was to invite militant critique.

Marriage was called into question as an institution. The basic structure of the family was called into question. Roles associated with dating were called into question. Macho posturing, male competitiveness, and sexual objectification were called into question. Opposition to pornography (with no accompanying censoring mindset at all) was part and parcel of opposition to anything that manipulated, maligned, or mistreated women's minds or bodies or that perpetuated male behaviors that oppressed women. Childcare was no longer seen as "women's work" and mothering and fathering were replaced with parenting. What was good in familiar male and female roles was merged to become part of women's and men's agendas; what was bad was rejected. Actions were direct and clear.

Bread and Roses was only a local organization and even in Boston its outreach was limited. It was not the only militant feminist organization in the U.S., but others like it had similarly limited resources and outreach. The National Organization for Women never became a national example of this sort of committed, militant, multi-focused women's organization. Nor has any other national women's movement achieved this. This absence may help explain why many women are once again emotionally and intellectually isolated and why many accept that the pains they suffer arise from personal inadequacy or biological inevitability rather than sexism.

At one large meeting of a regional organization planning a season of major actions for the Boston-area antiwar movement, members of Bread and Roses marched in, circled the room, came to the front, told the man then chairing the meeting to sit down, and delivered an ultimatum. "Incorporate women at every level of planning and organizing and have men do their share of boring and caretaking tasks and incorporate at least 50 percent women in the tactical leadership of all the associated demonstrations and incorporate at least half women as chairs of all the meetings and rallies, or we will not permit these efforts—which we support and want to give our energies to—to proceed."

Some people that day felt that a major antiwar planning session was no place to exert feminist pressure since opposition to the war was too important to interrupt. But the majority realized that there would be no successful opposition to the war, much less to sexism, unless women were respected and won their equal place. And the men who realized the importance and legitimacy of Bread and Roses' demands did so because they were *forced* to by Bread and Roses' actions. This kind of women's organization has been absent too long. As a result, many people have forgotten or never learned the kinds of lessons Bread and Roses taught. From thinking about these experiences and our current situation doesn't it follow that this country needs:

- a national women's media that uncompromisingly identifies sexist institutions and practices and espouses original positive programs, images, strategies, and goals;

- local and regional women's movements to pressure all kinds of institutions by threatening to disrupt their operations unless they incorporate respect for the rights and capacities of women;

- a national women's movement that is militant, aggressive, multi-focused, and sensitive to all sides of feminist concern as well as to the importance of feminists playing leading roles around matters of race, class, foreign policy, government policy, and ecological preservation.

It is not my place to tell women what they should or shouldn't be doing about sexism. But it is my place to address men and male-dominated institutions. Just as whites need to deal with racism, men need to deal with sexism. We ought to make known our desire to support a reawakened militant feminism. Even more important, we should compel the still male-dominated institutions we operate in to restructure themselves to incorporate at least an equal share of women's leadership and to offer both material and organizational support for national and local women's organizing.

Whatever other impediments have obstructed the emergence of militant feminist movement on a national scale, surely the biggest has been the continuing intransigence and outright sexism of men. This needs attention— now.

—July 1990

Convert To What?

The Cold War is dead. What should the world do with the hundreds of billions of dollars of yearly military spending this will release? Why not improve agriculture, redistribute income, expand health care, eliminate unemployment, create housing, and improve schooling? Though we'd still have to decide how much to spend in the Third versus the First World, most people would welcome using the "peace dividend" to improve the lot of suffering humanity.

But Wall Street and the White House disagree. They prefer that new expenditures preserve existing disparities of resources, opportunities, and power. Corporate elites have the goods and want to keep them. Political leaders seek changes that will not rock the boats they captain.

Of course U.S. military, capitalists, and bureaucrats will fight hard to maintain bloated war production. But the rest of the U.S. political and economic elite understand that the end of the Cold War reduces their ability to scare voters into endlessly supporting military production. They need a new scam, but they also want to preserve their class, race, and gender advantages without even a hiccup of interruption.

Without pressure from below, politicians' desires to preserve ruling hierarchies will keep them from using the "peace dividend" to eradicate homelessness, reduce unemployment, or build better schools and hospitals for those who now get the worst of each. Indeed, it will prohibit doing anything that will make society's worse-off: (1) relatively wealthier compared with elites, and (2) relatively better prepared to demand more of society's output for themselves. It isn't that innovative politicians won't promise to improve people's lives with better budgets. They will. But unless they are forced, they won't stick to their constituency-rousing rhetoric. Changes they actually pursue will always be system enforcing, not system threatening.

For example, suppose that to spend some of the peace dividend humanely, decision-makers enforced a full-employment act. As society's worst-off benefited, employer's threats to displace rebellious workers down the economic ladder would lose some force. At each rung of the workplace hierarchy, workers would feel stronger. Strikes would be less risky. To lose would require moving on, not becoming unemployed and suffering miserably. In short, for workers, increased unemployment means putting up with worsening conditions, speed-up, and pay cuts to avoid losing their jobs—but full employment means employers have to worry about pushing their workers too hard and causing them to strike or quit. Fighting for full employment is fighting for power and wealth.

The same "one wins, one loses" logic explains the underlying corporate problem with increased welfare benefits, less-expensive health care, and low-income housing. Any general improvements in workers' living conditions increases their strength vis-a-vis their employers and therefore increases the amount of society's product that workers will win away from employers as higher wages, shorter hours, and better conditions. The current struggle over how to spend the "peace dividend" incorporates this same confrontation.

(1) The Cold War was a nearly perfect vehicle for scaring the public into accepting endless military production to keep profits high without upsetting class relations.

(2) Everyone perceives that the Cold War is gone and soon forgotten.

(3) Everyone realizes there is a "peace dividend" to spend.

(4) The "peace dividend" policy that would win a public referendum is using war monies to improve people's lives.

(5) To make poor people wealthier would mean elites losing many advantages.

So what will happen?

(1) Military-industrial bureaucrats and capitalists will fight a rear-guard battle to preserve their system. They will manipulate their own workers' fears of unemployment, communities' fears of losing military bases, military industry's fears of losing contracts, and politicians' fears of losing votes and donations. They will urge the existence of continuing military threats and the need to be prepared to meet them. They will benefit from any military turmoil that may occur in the near term, and the longevity of their resistance to change may even depend on a spate of international military conflicts affecting U.S. interests—the Middle East being the "best prospect" by far.

(2) More far-seeing political and corporate elites will fight for new capitalist-defending boondoggles to replace Cold War military spending. They will argue for retooling factories and reimbursing and retraining affected workers to prevent them from opposing

change. They will promote the long-term economic gains of their preferred schemes for new capitalist-supporting production.

(3) Most liberals and many progressives will jump on this anti-military but still pro-capitalist bandwagon, happy to at least reduce the war machine.

(4) Other progressives and all radicals will hold out to fight for humane, capitalist-opposing, and worker-determined production.

Who wins will depend on a fight for the "hearts and minds" of the U.S. public. Capitalists and their allies will lie, manipulate, intimidate, and coerce. Anti-capitalists and their allies will tell the truth, address people's real interests, and use alternative media, person-to-person outreach, demonstrations, civil disobedience, etc.

This battle could span the 1990s. Military bureaucrats and defense-industry defenders will hang on longer than many people think. They have a world of war-makers/profiteers ready to create crises conducive to their arguments for maintaining bloated defense spending. Ultimately, however, they will lose. But who will win?

If more far-seeing capitalists and their liberal political allies win, it will mean a further entrenchment of elites, elite institutions, and elite-serving mythology, as well as a redeployment of vast resources without, however, a concomitant improvement in most people's lives.

If radicals win it will mean an enlargement of anti-capitalist movements and institutions, an expansion of the public's political consciousness, an increase in worker participation in economic decision-making, and a redeployment of vast resources with a concomitant improvement in the immediate life circumstances and in the short- and long-term bargaining power of workers.

It follows that fighting over how to spend the "peace dividend" is really fighting over two directions for society: (1) further solidifying elite rule and associated injustices; or (2) improving peoples' lives and developing forces that can revolutionize future economic and social life.

Can we predict the battle lines of this struggle more precisely? Well, the military-industrial diehards will argue that we still need a military deterrence because a new threat might arise and we don't want to reduce our ability to respond. Radicals, in contrast, will argue that we must spend the "peace dividend" (or even the "peace principal") on housing, schooling, infrastructure, and attaining full employment, and that we can only ensure this by incorporating workers centrally into decision-making about new investments. But what about liberals who need a new focus to sustain huge expenditures that the public will support even against its own real interests? What will fit this description?

Space travel is one possible focus. Building rockets, space stations, and all the accompanying paraphernalia won't improve the lot of society's poor, and it is high-tech and expensive. The economy is fueled, profits are made, hierarchies are preserved—but what is the rationale? How do elites get the public to urge that society's wealth should be spent on colonizing Mars while conditions deteriorate in Milwaukee? It would be a desperate PR campaign to convince people that this must be done for the sake of science or adventure. Convincing people that we need to escape a dying planet is too implausible, even for Madison Avenue. After all, the only targets of space colonization are dead planets. So while we can expect a campaign to expand space travel, we can also predict that it will not consume much of the "peace dividend."

"Drug wars" is an alternative focus that has the considerable advantage of helping elites maintain the capacity to intervene militarily throughout the world. But how much can you spend doing battle with a crime cartel located in Colombia or Peru? Any military expenditure to deal solely with Third World countries runs into the problem that, unlike the arms race with the Soviet Union, there is no way to even claim the other side can keep up. There is no remotely creditable competition. Worse, as public relations increases people's worries about drugs, a growing desire to reduce drug demand may promote the idea that a direct attack on poverty and homelessness might be a better drug war strategy than international interdiction.

"Computer wars" against the Japanese would be a perfect focus, except it entails having the government meddle in a growing private sector of the economy. Moreover, computer production is at the hub of most other modern industries, which means computer wars would risk abrogating the market dynamic in a good part of the economy. Also, there is the chance that a major increase in the availability and capacity of computers could be ideologically or materially destabilizing. Perhaps the approach could work economically, but given current ideological preferences and the risks involved, it is not likely to be tried as a first resort.

In contrast to the above options, "disease wars" seems to have impressive future potential. Scare the hell out of people with an array of real and imaginary medical threats ranging from AIDS and cancer to designer diseases produced by bio-tech errors, evil terrorists, or mutant mosquitoes. Spend huge sums on research institutes, medical-emergency ships, and curative research. The scare factor has enough element of truth to work nicely. The occasional medical breakthrough can be priced high enough so only elites benefit. And "disease wars" definitely has a high-tech, push-the-economy-forward potential. The only thing missing is the spiral-of-danger dynamic that exists with the arms race, where each gain fosters need for still another gain. Instead, with a "disease wars" approach, as cures for existing diseases are found, producing new diseases to battle against has a definite down side. After all, the rich get sick too. Remember, far-sighted capitalists are looking to replace a material/ideological, arms-spending rationale that lasted nearly a half century.

So we come to what may prove to be the best solution for elites to try: "ecology wars." Turn the Pentagon and the whole damn military machine into an ecology machine. Gear it up to do research into new technological fixes, into what's happening in the skies and seas, and into which countries are disobeying ecology laws. Then spend money to find ecology law-breakers and coerce and punish them. This is really a winner. The death of the Earth beneath an ocean of circulating poisons is a danger well worth worrying about. The fear factor is fine. And "ecology wars" has precisely the right escalation dynamic. If ecology warriors create a new technological fix, industries need only develop a new production technique spewing new garbage to put the ecology warriors back at square one. Finally, the dynamic is as militarily sound as "drug wars," because you can use ecological crimes as easily as drug crimes to rationalize military intervention. Likewise, the public-relations problem disappears. Liberals can attack military bureaucrats and defense industry conservatives as out-of-date self-seekers. They can promote their ecological conversion agenda as consistent with the most pressing human need of the age, the need to survive planetary despoilment. They can even co-opt progressives pushing for conversion (while carefully rejecting calls for worker decision-making power), and ecological activists pushing for a safe environment (while rejecting anti-capitalist content). Via "ecology wars," therefore, at least a part of two potentially important political movements could be co-opted, the economy could be preserved, the worst ravages of ecological decay could be fought, and no elite hierarchies need be disturbed. "Ecology wars" may be even better than the Cold War.

Arguing for such an approach in a major article in the *Boston Globe,* Roger Martin says about the fear factor: "Ask the people of London or Jersey City whether they would rather live under Russian rule, or under 10 feet of water (due to rising seas), or a sky transformed into a microwave cooker (from chlorofluorocarbons) ... and there is no doubt of the answer." For high-tech effectivity, Martin celebrates the need for fleets of research vessels, arrays of satellites, advanced intelligence forces, sophisticated punitive weapons, etc. Concerning interventionism, he gives three examples of military enforcement of ecology laws—interventions in Brazil, Iraq, and Zambia—and he argues that no one could sensibly oppose law enforcement aimed at saving the planet, no matter how interventionist the resulting actions might be. "For 40 years we have—sincerely if absurdly—claimed to prefer full-scale nuclear war to the political system of Budapest or Leningrad. How much more seriously, then, should we take the threat to the very life of our planet? What considerations of sovereignty or human rights could be worth more than keeping the planet itself alive and viable? Even life under Hitler and Stalin is infinitely preferable to no life at all." In short, elites can so scare people with tales of ecological woe—even more than with tales of Stalin—that people can be manipulated into favoring any extreme in the name of planetary safety. Though he is too forthright for a large public following, Martin knows how to pitch his case to elites. In private, with capitalists and politicians, he will have many listeners.

So, what's the upshot? Certainly the end of the Cold War and the desperation of some elite figures for an alternative to military industrial production provides a political opening for the left. The public is increasingly receptive to the truth about military expenditures. Everyone knows the economy needs a fix. Red-baiting is passe. This is a context begging for activism. However, the situation also poses a real danger. The temptation of making progress by allying with "open-minded" corporate and congressional figures might cause pragmatic leftists to temper their anti-capitalist pitch. They might even emphasize only the anti-military element, perhaps even highlighting the need to get the economy operating effectively again. But if the conversion movement follows this path, its efforts will only help capitalists construct new means to preserve inequality. Just as replacing morphine addiction with heroin addiction or heroin addiction with cocaine addiction or cocaine addiction with crack addiction didn't solve addiction problems, replacing the military-industrial complex with an ecological-industrial complex won't solve industrial problems. Only a movement that understands the underlying class issues will have a chance to win real gains.

To escape co-optation, conversion activists must reveal not only bureaucratic and geopolitical but also capitalist causes of military and other waste spending. It must oppose ruling-class projects and advance working-class alternatives. It must attract a coalition of supporters that spans constituencies, communities, and agendas, and it must compromise neither content or tactics. If the conversion movement attains these aims it could conceivably defeat not only the reactionary war machine but also pro-capitalist liberalism.

— September 1990

Jackson Vs. Technocracy

What should we make of the fact that so many progressives think Jesse Jackson is too ambitious and too willing to preach rather than teach? First, working for Jackson isn't the same as saying he is the second coming of Malcolm X, Emma Goldman, and Che Guevara. Jackson is imperfect. Big surprise.

Second, what other candidate has discussed the class, race, gender, and political factors causing contemporary oppressions? As president, a Babbitt or a Simon would achieve less than a quack applying Band-Aids to cancers. However pleasant Simon and the other simpletons might seem, the rich bastards who buy and sell these opportunists prefer that they enlarge income inequality, nourish the Cold War, promote Third World interventions, impede social justice, and despoil the ecology. The result: in the U.S. the homeless must subsist on food from garbage cans eaten with cats and rats as dinner partners. Abroad: far worse. Does anyone think Lee Iacocca cares?

Perhaps when leftists were worried about Reagan's rule, there was a plausible argument for aiding decrepit liberals. But with Reagan not only brain-dead but almost off the public stage, it is time to get back to basics. Okay, you say, so we shouldn't support a stretch limo point-man like the Duke. Why should we support Jackson, and how much?

To answer, we must recognize that Jesse Jackson's politics and position derive from decades of civil rights, antiwar, gay rights, feminist, labor, and populist movement activism. True, he was not hand-picked by a fair ballot of all members of any mass movement. True, members of these movements have preferences Jackson doesn't meet. True, the electoral process provides an inhospitable haven for seekers of social change and tends to warp them to its image. But because of Jackson's roots, the constituencies he serves, the hopes he arouses, and especially his links to activism, in 1988 the Jackson campaign has a potential to expand consciousness, promote alliances, and alter institutions. Hell, it is already doing it.

Moreover, though the importance of Jackson's campaign for galvanizing the Black community is substantial, the campaign's power extends farther. The poor whites Jackson addresses have many class insights but lack clear consciousness about racism, the Cold War, sexism, and capitalism. By aligning a part of white working-class America with people of color and challenging everyone in the coalition to develop deeper understanding, Jackson can help reverse these problems and wreak radical havoc with the political status quo.

Jesse Jackson is not an electoral Dr. Huxtable. The Reverend doesn't cross over by leaving his culture behind. Whites want Jackson to out-think, not out-joke, other candidates. Jackson's campaign can align a true rainbow electorate against racism, foreign intervention, sexism, homophobia, and multinational greed. Ambitious? Absolutely.

So when supposed radicals say they would like to support the Rainbow but dislike its candidate, they ought to be told that no one is asking them to love Jesse Jackson nor electoral politics. We merely want them to see that increased success for Jackson's campaign can enhance the security and fulfillment of people all over the world precisely because Jackson's campaign threatens the system the Tweedle-Dum & Tweedle-Dee candidates legitimate. Indeed, if Nicaraguans, Salvadorans, Guatemalans, Black South Africans, South Korean workers, Filipino peasants, or any others who will be most affected by the election's outcome could vote, does anyone think they would weigh Jackson's purported personality flaws against his progressive policies for more than a millisecond? For that matter, if the media communicated honestly regarding likely outcomes from a Gore or a Jackson presidency, does anybody think the focus of concern inside the U.S. would long remain bedroom banter?

Challenging Jesse Jackson

Adviser one, an old-line DSA member, tells Jackson, "Obviously, you must oppose the contras, but your method must be to argue that supporting the contras hurts 'U.S. interests.' Wear your patriotism openly. Don't get moralistic. Talk realpolitik."

Adviser two, a radical economics professor, smoothly tells Jackson, "When you propose anti-poverty programs, you must show how your policies are 'good economics.' To be taken seriously, highlight technical efficiency."

Adviser three, an aspiring campaign official, intones, "Yes, of course, but keep it all compartmentalized. It's fine to attend gay rallies and antiwar marches and to address farmers, but it will only lose support to mention gay issues to farmers, or economic issues to gays."

Finally, adviser four, a Rainbow Coalition grassroots activist, wonders, "Since we want humane international policies that always benefit recipients, why not say so? Since we want economic efficiency only to facilitate humane ends, why not put the ends first? Since we support comprehensive Rainbow politics, shouldn't we speak about AIDS to farmers, about farm foreclosures to gays, and about anti-interventionism to both?"

Even if Jackson's campaign would propose the same policies whichever adviser wins, their differences mark the difference between "okay" and "historic" for his campaign. For if Jackson's rhetoric promotes "U.S. interests" and "efficient economics," then by their implicit assumptions, debates about what does and what doesn't fulfill "U.S. interests" or what does and what doesn't attain "economic efficiency" will only ratify reality-as-it-now-is. On TV, McNeils, McLaughlins, and McSnoozles will nit-pick about the extent to which this or that policy can attain pre-established, system-supporting ends. In boardrooms, corporate CEOs and elite politicians will celebrate that the campaign's logic ratifies status quo goals. In yuppie clubs, Ivy League academics may even break out the coke and party since their credentialed opinion still matters most. Throughout suburbia, listening to the familiar "national interests" and "economic efficiency" sub-text, lawyers may be a little less horrified by Jackson's Black power and doctors a little less prone to want to amputate his head. But downtown, the rest of us who might have been moved to political passion by a focus on meaningful goals will only become bored.

Of course, if Jackson instead heeds adviser four, choosing to emphasize goals that benefit underclasses everywhere while fostering evaluation of the ethics of programs rather then merely their technical merits, yuppies may scream that the campaign is too moralistic. However, the rest of us will become incorporated into the heart of the debate, where we belong.

Indeed, to stimulate profound passions, Jackson should not only highlight ethics and goals, align with activists at every opportunity, and strive for solidarity among diverse constituencies, he should also criticize this society's monopolization of expertise. For example, he might militantly attack the arrogance of those who close off higher education by gutting lower education. He could denounce news coverage not only of the campaign, but of world and domestic events and show what an alternative would be like. He might address the dearth of public education and skills training for adults. He could propose plans for democratizing schooling and for democratically re-conceptualizing access to new technologies and information. He could elevate not only having a fair income, but also having a balanced set of work-day responsibilities and opportunities as valid aims for economic policy. In short, Jackson ought to address what the rest of us don't like about lawyers, doctors, managers, engineers, and bureaucrats. He ought to propose changes to undo the overly hierarchical centralization of specialized knowledge, to reduce the undue authority and wealth accorded it, and to reduce the pressures that cause people who have expertise to act so high-and-mighty.

If Jackson were to eloquently set such a context for his policies—celebrating knowledge but attacking its monopolization, celebrating intellectual work but attacking the fact that so few are permitted to do it—wouldn't the farmers and industrial workers who are beginning to respect Jackson surface their class antagonism toward their immediate bosses and caretakers? If so, not only would this highlight an important class struggle, wouldn't it also advance the trust factor of Jackson's campaign, reduce the credibility of his media detractors, and make every proposal he offers more powerfully felt? Media hostility would intensify, perhaps inhibiting short-term convention vote-snatching, but those who hear Jackson's message first-hand or via honest reporting would be more deeply moved and provide a far more motivated constituency.

In recent history, the only major public figures to address role-related tensions between professionals, managers, intellectuals, and the rest of us have been Nixon and Agnew seeking to arouse hatred for innovative ideas, not for unjust social divisions. Why leave the attack on intellectual bigotry to right-wing bigots? And why try to balance ethical consistency against sucking up to Gail Sheehy, much less NBC? Better to embrace morality and speak the unadorned truth to media lies. And anyhow, who knows how many honest intellectuals and journalists will emerge from the pressures of their competitive surroundings to actively support such an unusual effort.

In short, to decide the degree of aid and energy to provide for Jackson, progressives ought to ask: To what degree does the Jackson campaign focus on peace, disarmament, ending apartheid, withdrawing support from tyrants and redistributing international and domestic resources and opportunities, versus only buying into "Cold War" and "U.S. interests" rhetoric? To what extent does it elevate the enlightened moral opinions of black, brown, red, and white working-class communities, versus appealing to the monopolized expertise of well-placed experts? To what extent is each constituency Jackson addresses challenged to add compassion for AIDS victims and respect for gays to hostility to racism and sexism and anger about foreclosures and unemployment? To what extent does the Jackson campaign incorporate the otherwise disenfranchised into goal-determination, while relegating experts to providing advice but never consent? To what extent does the Jackson campaign ratify activism, recognizing that progressive elected officials, including even a President Jackson, can only deliver on their promises if militant movements prod their vision and propel their programs?

Jackson needs to coerce media respect by amassing unprecedented grass-roots support and by simultaneously reaching out to media progressives, lending to however many of them will accept it a helping hand in their uphill struggles to deliver honest news and serious analysis. But under no circumstances should Jackson try to seduce the media or academia by playing to elite prejudices, whatever his advisers may suggest.

Let's face facts. It was on the shoals of trying to win over myopic experts by being single-issue that the Freeze withered away, fumbling massive national concern about the dangers of war. It was by substituting starring on the seven o'clock news in photogenic pre-arranged dinner-jacket civil disobedience for creating sustained community-based opposition that the early anti-apartheid movement temporarily dissipated its own potentials. And it was (and is) in pursuit of media respectability that countless social-democratic electoral campaigns sacrifice worker participation and grassroots excitement to coordinator administration. A simple rule emerges: Political excitement and integrity dissipate proportionately to efforts to coax a blessing from mainstream media and academics.

Perhaps the most overlooked insight about the left in the U.S. is not that it has suffered from racism, sexism, homophobia, and nationalism—which it certainly has—but that in the last few decades, though there have been numerous national movements rooted in Black culture, women's culture, Latin culture, Native American culture, and gay culture, there have been none rooted in white working-class culture. Whether we are talking about struggles around contracts for particular industries, or around issues like unemployment, foreign policy, investment, or ecology, as local insurgencies have enlarged, all those that could have elevated white working-class values, aims, culture, and leadership before a national audience have instead been taken over by or catered to professionals.

Part of the problem is the difficulty of seeing that comprehensive politics and pro-worker culture and goals can eventually transcend the anger they arouse in "experts" and media. But part of it is also that too many Freeze strategists, too many disarmament funders, too many union bureaucrats, too many democratic socialists, and too many campaign officials are themselves ignorant of or even disdainful of working-class culture and wish themselves and their projects to be media-beloved, even at the expense of truth and political integrity. That Bruce Springsteen, a rock-'n'-roll singer-songwriter, is the nearest thing to a white leader speaking to a mass white working-class audience in a respectful but challenging way and, in turn, expressing and advocating their sentiments publicly is a staggering truth, which we ignore at our peril.

In addition to doing better than other candidates on critically important gender, sex, culture, and political issues, the Jackson campaign can also do better on class. Let's push hard to help ensure that it does.

— February 1988

What Should Jackson Want?

The Democratic National Convention promises either confrontation or false solidarity. If Jackson seeks serious gains, he will be rejected by the Party, but revered by the people. If he seeks crumbs, the media will celebrate, but the people will lose another champion. Either way, this article is for the liberals, and Jessie too.

Immediate Relief

Basic demands can't succeed until movements *force* institutional change. Jackson should demand that particular agencies advance specific projects, and that the Democratic Party seek support for these agencies from the new president, cabinet, and Congress. If the Party accepts, Jackson should give his all. If the Party balks, Jackson should walk.

Drugs: Previous drug programs have nearly always camouflaged beefing up police and militaries. Jackson should jettison his past drug rhetoric and demand an executive agency mandated to attack criminal organizations, penalize banks laundering drug money, disband government agencies facilitating drug-running, and offer comprehensive rehabilitation and education.

But as with other regulatory agencies, any commission trying to de-drug organized crime, banks, the DEA, and the CIA will encounter immense obstacles. To build public pressure, the drug commission should first reveal how drugs, crime, and profit entwine. On the road to developing strength to counter Chase Manhattan, the commission *might* first generate support for legalization since this would at least change the profiteers from dictators and criminals to Marlboro and Seagrams. (Possible chair: Ralph Nader.)

Housing: If a party refuses to house its constituents, its constituents should refuse to support the Party. Given sufficient courage to buck traditional interests, homelessness could be easily ended. How? Refurbish abandoned buildings and give them to the homeless for rents pegged to income while giving modest recompense to former owners.

Since reaction against the precedent that private property should give way to justice would certainly impede enforcement, as with the drug case, the new housing agency should first build public support regarding obstacles to be overcome and programs to be enacted. (Possible co-chairs: Mel King and Chester Hartman.)

Arms and foreign policy: Jackson says seek diplomacy, not coercion. Buy development, not destruction. Two priority packages suggest themselves.

First, Jackson should demand a steady yearly reduction in the military budget, a steady yearly mutual U.S. and Soviet reduction in troop deployment, a steady yearly mutual nuclear warhead reduction, and a total freeze on research, testing, and deployment of nuclear weapons. The new executive agency (chaired by Ron Dellums) should be empowered to develop public support for the plan, and to negotiate it with Congress and the Soviets.

Second, Jackson should demand a statement of human rights that any country seeking military aid or alliance with the U.S. must meet, and a statement of workers' rights that any country in which U.S. firms hope to operate must meet. Regardless of ideology, if a country meets human and workers' rights conditions, military aid and business relations are allowed. If a country rejects the conditions, military aid and business relations are forbidden. (Possible co-chairs of the human and workers' rights committee: Leah Wise and William Winpisinger.)

Again, obstacles to implementation would be immense. U.S. military aid and business investment already flows more or less proportionately to human-rights violations—but the more the violations, the more the involvement. Government supports business and business is best where human rights are nil, so unions can't fight back, individuals can't fight back, wages can become subhuman, and profits can soar. Clearly, all major institutions of U.S. capitalism will oppose human and workers' rights enforcement. If the conditions prerequisite to establishing relations were really humane, the U.S. would not even be able to do business with itself.

As a result, as with the other new agencies, this one too should be empowered to publicize its efforts with the intent of developing popular movements to overcome obstacles. Initial efforts could push for withdrawal of military aid to El Salvador, withdrawal of economic assistance and business dealings with South Africa, indemnities and establishment of relations with Nicaragua, and removal of our military bases from the Philippines and Cuba.

Full employment has been rhetoric too long. The Rainbow should present a Jobs Bill based on previous efforts, but adapted to current conditions and Jackson's demand should include provision for an executive committee to pursue the Bill, including a chairperson. (Perhaps Karen Nussbaum.)

Arguments for full employment are obvious: increased well-being for the newly employed, increased productivity from a larger workforce, reduced power for owners in disputes with workers who do not have to worry about long-term unemployment. On the other hand, since capitalist opposition will be intense, this commission too should make public all obstacles to develop public awareness and organizational might in favor of full employment.

Finally, though Jackson has not put quite as much emphasis on other issues as those noted above, he should also demand commissions on AIDS, the ERA, agribusiness, affirmative action, education, etc. Goals could be a massive allocation of funds for treatment, education, and research about AIDS; passing the ERA; policing agribusiness, re. the health of the public and the survival of small farmers; renewal of affirmative action across society; rededication to providing educational resources for all constituencies, etc.

Political Empowerment

When Jackson rolls through Iowa, Maine, Mississippi, Michigan, and California, what emerges? Hope, momentum, and energy, but not enough consciousness and organization. Instead of getting separate constituencies to each support the candidate, the campaign needs to help those constituencies understand each other's priorities so that they can form lasting alliances.

Rather than settling for local workers pulling Jesse's lever in an isolated booth and then going home alone, more effort must go to promoting a grassroots redefinition of union solidarity. When Jackson elicits white working-class excitement, it is important not for each succeeding primary Tuesday, but for what it might mean about fighting racism, reclaiming class militancy, and forming new alliances over the long haul.

The speech Jackson needs to give most often is the one that says that the enemy is racism, sexism, homophobia, and profit-seeking, and that spells out how to organize because justice is the people's to win, not Jesse's or anyone else's to give. Jackson and other Rainbow organizers should travel the land again, more patiently and slowly, without the media glare, with infinitely less fanfare and expense, to talk with smaller audiences about how to build organizations for the long-haul.

But this is process. Are there also immediate reforms that can help empower Jackson's constituency?

Democracy requires full participation by all those who wish to vote. Similarly, for democracy to be meaningful, candidates should not have advantages due to their own wealth or that of their supporters. Jackson should demand full electoral democratization, including simplified registration, no purging of electoral rolls, and easy late registration and registration by mail; as well as an end to rich peoples' politics via establishing ample free TV and media access for all qualifying candidates.

Electoral democracy also requires information disseminated by other than corporate elites. Freedom of the press is useless without many presses. Freedom of speech is useless without many voices. Those with the biggest presses and the loudest stations have a responsibility to enrich media offerings. How? Tax the big and mainstream to subsidize the small and dissident. Jackson ought to demand legislated subsidization of alternative media funded through taxes on large-scale mainstream media.

Other arenas also present opportunities. For example, since many humane efforts would benefit from easier funding, Jackson should demand 100 percent tax credits for donations of $100 or less to non-profit organizations, up to $1,000 per person. Simultaneously, the definition of a tax-exempt organization ought to be simplified to include any organization that has a stringent and modest cap on employee incomes and that either reinvests or gives away all surpluses. Likewise, Jackson should demand non-profit mailing rate reductions inversely proportion to organization size.

Finally, suggesting the next FBI director (Charles Garry), CIA director (Daniel Ellsberg), and Attorney General (Eleanor Holmes Norton) can't hurt.

Hope

We the people cannot advance without mountains of hope. But the grassroots hope Jackson's campaign unleashed will not grow if Jackson receives a key to the executive washroom or a host of hamburger franchises in exchange for "maturely" delivering an army of voters and campaign workers. Yet Jackson's "selling short" isn't the real problem because the primary issue isn't the price, but the procedure.

Imagine Jackson receiving status and a powerful position, jobs for his organizational staff, and platform rhetoric for posterity, all as tokens of satisfaction at his becoming just another "insider." With Jackson as Booker T. Washington extolling how the system works if you just try hard enough, hope will dissipate. The moment of potential victory will become part of the past.

But patronage bestowed in the knowledge that the gains have been won and that their receipt will propel new demands can enhance hope. With Jackson as Martin Luther King, Jr. or Malcolm X winning grudging gains, hope will grow. The moment of potential victory will become a project of continuing uplift.

Hope will not be nourished by Bert Lance, Jimmy Carter, or Michael Dukakis becoming bosom buddies with Jesse Jackson. Can anyone who remembers Vietnam, knows El Salvador, and daily sees or suffers homelessness believe that these fellows are suddenly becoming champions of the poor and dispossessed, suddenly taking the side of workers, women, gays, blacks, and Latinos, suddenly forsaking empire for justice? Lance, Carter, Dukakis, and their pay masters haven't switched sides and they won't. Joining the Party without changing it will destroy hope. Changing the Party without succumbing to it will build hope. The respect Jackson should seek from Party elites is for the power of his constituency.

Jackson shouldn't run for vice president unless he can do it as a tribune for the people rather than a rubber stamp for a presidential puppet. Run with a people's program or don't run at all. Tell the Democrats: Win with the people, and their desires, or lose without them.

And so arises the tough question, the one designed to ensure fealty: What if Bush wins?

How hard to fight Bush is the Democrats' choice, not Jackson's, and if they would rather lose than pursue justice it should be they and not Jackson who comes away dishonored.

Dukakis as president with a dilapidated Rainbow offers less hope than Bush as president with a well-organized Rainbow propelling a people's agenda. Whether we are talking about the welfare of the homeless in New York, small farmers in the midwest, peasants in Latin America, or blacks in South Africa, what counts most is not who is president, but what is the state of the country and the movement for peace and justice.

Is all this just a prescription for grasping defeat from the jaws of victory? I don't believe it. I think the most Jackson will get without being clear that he will walk if his demands are not met will be a few worthless platform planks, some minor appointments, some breakable promises on spending, and perhaps cursory input on a few low-level cabinet selections—the equivalent of a few hamburger franchises. What he will get with the threat, he ought to find out.

But won't that guarantee Bush's victory. Why? The Democrats can choose to win with Jackson's support or to risk losing without it. The choice of Bush or not is theirs, not Jackson's.

But won't this approach leave Jackson loved by a few isolated leftists, reviled in the press, and disdained by those who fear Bush? The press will go berserk, yes. But if Jackson takes a positive program to the people and argues that Democrats only deserve support when they support that program, he will rebuild credibility and make his future campaigns far more informed, organized, and hopeful.

The goal shouldn't be a black president, but a people's black president. Stay the course, Jesse, stay the course. The final victory will be infinitely sweeter.

—June 1988

What Rainbow, Where?

While atmospheric rainbows have clear cause and definition, the political Rainbow doesn't. Who knows just what it is? What it seeks to do? How it arrives at its aims? Who is a member and who isn't?

Opposed Priorities

In the Rainbow, these opposed priorities have emerged:

- The Rainbow should primarily promote Jackson's next candidacy. It should enhance the campaign to best advance general empowerment.

- The Rainbow should politicize, organize, and win victories for the oppressed. It should promote grassroots activism to best advance general empowerment.

In one view, grassroots activism should only augment electoral emphasis. In the other view, electoralism should only augment grassroots activism.

If a Rainbower thinks Jesse Jackson is unswervingly committed to winning victories for the oppressed, that electoral politics is the central political arena, and that having too broad a definition invites confusion or elevates political purism, she or he will elevate Jackson's electoral priorities.

On the other hand, if a Rainbower worries that Jackson may not retain or may have already lost his radical priorities, or feels that though electoral politics are important, they may not be most important, or prefers a flexible definition, she or he will elevate local organization and activism.

The Rainbow debate about structure is over whether the Rainbow should emphasize internal democracy or try to accurately represent all the citizens the Rainbow fights for. Some Rainbowers claim that relying on one-member, one-vote democracy will also best ensure fair influence by wide constituencies. Other Rainbowers reply that a one-member one-vote approach would under-represent large external constituencies like the unemployed or workers.

The proposed bottom-up approach is that local Rainbow chapters would autonomously determine their own activities so that, along with a few collective choices about national priorities, the sum of their separate choices would also set the national agenda. Within chapters there would be one-person one-vote. Among chapters, there would be one-chapter one-vote. This approach would deliver democracy for members and ward off authoritarianism.

Opponents of bottom-up organization say that it will invite drawn-out meetings in which those with the greatest endurance always win their way. They propose a more top-down formulation. A national governing body would set a comprehensive national program that locals would largely implement. A central board would make most of the decisions and its members would exert influence more or less proportionately as they represent the desires of large constituencies. Nationally, having a large constituency would justify having many votes; having a small constituency would warrant having only a few or no votes. Within chapters, there would be little to vote about, but for what there was, the rule would be one-member one-vote.

Summarizing, bottom-uppers emphasize that local Rainbow autonomy and chapter rule will empower all members, fulfill democratic principles, and guard against authoritarianism. The bottom-upper argument relies on the claim that those in touch with large constituencies should be able to convince membership majorities to vote their way, and that vesting too much authority in too few hands now will ensure that those hands will never willingly relinquish their power later.

Top-downers reply that to allow relatively small groups of local Rainbow activists to determine an agenda affecting vast constituencies would substitute formal democracy for the few for real democracy for the many. The top-downer argument relies on the claim that at least until the Rainbow has a much wider base of active members who have enough political experience to participate effectively, it will be more democratic to rely on a national board composed of folks who have the most enduring and respectful ties to large constituencies.

Next, the top-downers suggest that the bottom-uppers go out and organize their own constituencies. The bottom-uppers reply, "How can we fight to democratize U.S. politics while hierarchicalizing Rainbow politics?" And the debate proceeds.

Questions about who should and who should not be a Rainbow member center around the degree of political agreement or active involvement that should be required. Is it sufficient just to want to belong? Must one also support a comprehensive program? Does one have to be active? Is the best plan to have as wide a membership as possible with a vast range of political beliefs and with people becoming more radical via their experiences in the Rainbow? Or is it better to have a narrower membership with fewer political differences and with people already pretty radical upon entering the Rainbow?

Finally, current debate about program centers on two issues: Should Rainbow chapters engage in civil disobedience that might help local constituencies even as it also impinges on national electoral plans? And should local chapters set programmatic goals that fit their local priorities but clash with national Rainbow aims—or vice versa?

For example, suppose the national Rainbow desires to cultivate relations with local politicians who might take Jackson's side in 1992, while a local chapter wants to demonstrate against one of these politicians for reasons of his or her poor stance on local housing concerns. Which aim takes precedence?

A Word About Process

In realpolitic, debates always involve people with their own prior experiences and current agendas, so that it is always difficult to keep on the substantive questions and off the personal motivations that might be subverting *other* people's judgments.

One natural response is to keep quiet about personal fears, thinking that the less public airing these get the less they will interfere. But when personal and motivational concerns don't get aired enough to be resolved, they expand to dominate private conversation. They often even crowd out serious analysis. If this were to happen in the Rainbow, as in so many other cases over the years, it would be a horrible loss since the Rainbow is too important to have its agenda determined by unresolved personal tensions.

Like most folks, I am relatively ignorant about the inner workings of high-level Rainbow debates. Nonetheless, I suspect that two opposed but rarely voiced fears are now doing considerable damage there. So correct me if I'm out of bounds, but don't a sizable number of folks in the Rainbow feel something akin to one of these two opposed worries:

- There are a lot of opportunist political self-seekers in here using the Rainbow to enhance their own electoral power or bureaucratic status with little concern for the Rainbow's broader priorities. These self-seekers want top-down organization, a solely electoral program, and nearly unrestricted membership. All those positions must be opposed to prevent the professional politicians and bureaucrats from hijacking the Rainbow for opportunist ends.

- There are a bunch of energetic leftists in here who have been trying for ages to piece together a radical movement and who now see the Rainbow as fulfilling that dream. They didn't bring masses to the Rainbow, Jesse did, and their desires to gain power in the Rainbow contradict the Rainbow's logic and history. They support non-electoral activism, bottom-up structure, and a restricted membership, but they don't offer any serious strategy for gaining power. We should oppose their positions to prevent zealous leftists from hijacking the Rainbow for sectarian ends.

Both views are partly correct because it is true that everyone—including politicians and left activists—develops opinions based on their personal experiences and desires. Of course their upcoming elections, or job security, or political influence in their own organizations affects people's calculations. But so do empathy with the positions of others and a capacity to assess situations according to overarching principles. So everyone in the Rainbow grappling with what it should be and how it should operate brings to the table a mix of their own experiences and needs, and their understanding of broader principles, and of the effects that their choices may have on other people's circumstances.

Of course, if professional politicians, left activists, or anyone else bends entirely toward using *only* their own experiences and needs, they will tend toward selfish opportunism and fail to contribute to collective efforts. On the other hand, if politicians or activists bend entirely toward empathy and/or abstraction, they will forgo the rich insights that stem from personal experience and probably diminish their views to near uselessness. Mediating must go on.

Now, everyone knows that in the heat of debate it is easiest (if often incorrect) to say that those we agree with have struck a good balance while those we disagree with are out of whack and therefore opportunist or self-seeking or overly academic but certainly not sensible. Though sometimes people are out of whack, the best operational policy always seems to be to first assume that everyone is trying to strike a good personal balance so that differences come from real disagreements that need honest evaluation.

Out-of-whackers (whether of the overly selfish or the overly abstract pie-in-the-sky variety) can and should be confronted, but constructively and only when the evidence of their culpability is overwhelming. And note: In an organization of folks as humane and concerned as Rainbowers have demonstrated themselves to be, "overwhelming evidence" is great indeed.

The upshot is that without a lot of provocation we all ought to keep political debates largely on the issues and the implications of opposed choices, not on the debater's motives. But at the same time, in a context outside the actual debate of the issues, people should freely voice their fears and motivational concerns and discuss and try to resolve them. Otherwise there will be no trust, and sooner or later, no organization.

One Person's Preferences for the Rainbow

It wouldn't be cricket to write about all this and then avoid taking a position. So here's my tentative opinion, rendered, as it were, from the outside.

I would like the Rainbow to define itself as an overarching umbrella organization that seeks to raise political consciousness in its membership and throughout the country, to pressure positive reforms for the poor and oppressed, and to win structural changes that strengthen the disempowered via electoral victories, the transformation of existing institutions, and the grassroots construction of new institutions. If supporting Jesse Jackson on the road to 1992 fulfills these aims, then along with other actions, that too should become and remain a central part of the program. But however likely that is, it should not be decided *a priori*. I do not think people should define any organization other than a fan club or an election committee in terms of one individual's aims, even Jesse Jackson's, or in terms of a specific single election, even for president in 1992. While there is obviously a place for a Jackson election committee, such a committee should be much smaller and more tightly organized than the Rainbow.

To those who say the Rainbow should define itself as pro-Jackson because that will advance the broader aims we all support, I say: Fine, since you favor the broader aims anyhow, let's take those as our priority and let that translate into support for Jackson in proportion as he continues to play a positive role. He's human and there is no point deciding in advance what he will or will not choose to do.

To those who say that broad aims invite confusion, I reply that you must mean that broad aims invite consideration of options that wouldn't be considered by a campaign committee or a fan club, and that certainly seems right and proper to me.

I like parts of both sides of the organizational argument. Direct local democracy is critical for chapters regarding their own campaigns. Moreover local chapters and also movements and organizations with a long history of activism (for example, unions or the gay-rights movement) must retain autonomy over their own efforts within a broad rubric of national Rainbow principles. On the other hand, letting a chapter of 10 or 20 or 100 people have as much say, in some sense, as organized labor, or as the unemployed, or as the homeless, or battered women, is not optimal in an umbrella organization like the Rainbow. So, it seems compromise is in order.

First, establish some national norms generally applicable to Rainbow activities. For example, a norm I would support would be no violence permitted, and one I think I would oppose would be no public criticism or demonstration against elected Rainbow members by other Rainbow members and no supporting one Rainbow candidate against another in the same election permitted.

Second, let local chapters and member organizations have autonomy over their own programs within limits set by agreed-upon national norms.

Third, let a national steering committee whose members are elected from member organizations and movements as well as from chapters and who exert influence in national meetings in proportion to the strength of their constituencies, set national policy.

Regarding its membership, let the Rainbow welcome movements, organizations, and individuals who are moving left and who do not hold views so contrary to those of the organization as to create severe contradictions. Membership should require strong agreement with at least some parts of a broad progressive program that is much like the best of what Jackson has often rhetorically espoused.

You wouldn't have to be strongly pro-abortion to be in the Rainbow. You wouldn't have to be an active gay rights activist. And you wouldn't have to be a strong anti-imperialist. But you would have to have strong agreement with at least a significant portion of the Rainbow platform and an openness to respecting and debating the rest, even if you disagreed with parts. The idea is that the Rainbow would be a place where political education and debate proceeds, and where people moving left can be respected and learn and be learned from without having to already agree to every program plank of every constituent movement and organization in the coalition.

Finally, I do worry about where Jesse Jackson is headed. He undoubtedly exists in a context of immense pressures. His life is continually on the line. Some people constantly laud him and offer little serious critique while others ceaselessly attack irrationally. The media mindlessly mucks about. The proper way to help Jackson is not to give him carte blanche. He must be accountable like everyone else—indeed, because he is a politician, more than most.

It will be too bad if Jesse Jackson decides that winning the presidency is paramount and that winning requires catering to mainstream politicians, the media, and clergy over and above pursuing a clear radical agenda including the use of what he calls "street heat."

Too bad, because first, winning the presidency not only isn't everything, it is nothing in the absence of an informed and empowered electorate; and second, because even electorally Jackson's long suit is the people, not the professionals, and he will gain power with the latter only insofar as he strengthens his relations with the former.

—February 1989

Can We Win?

I Live in Massachusetts and voters here just chose John Silber as their Democratic candidate for governor. This is supposed to send an angry message to incumbents, but the same super-liberal Massachusetts voters are also showing only marginal concern about the massive U.S. invasion of the Middle East, raging homelessness, decaying schools, dangerous streets, and disappearing jobs. Moreover, these voters have listened to Leftists try to "raise their consciousness" for over a quarter century. We need to face facts. Usually Democrats are corporate pimps disguised as public-spirited diplomats. John Silber is a fascist disguised as a bigot. To support him expresses dissent?

To succeed, the Left needs huge numbers of people to think and act radically. Twenty-five years ago my generation of Leftists began telling the truth about social problems and people thought we were out of our minds. At that time, most students and community folks believed lawyers were honest; General Motors beneficent; workers well rewarded; the government just; women housewives and mothers; and Blacks, Indians, Asians, and Latinos less than human.

Twenty-five years ago we highlighted the causes of human suffering and our message made people say we were crazy. The Vietnam war was to bring freedom to Asia, not wealth to ruling elites, they said. The U.S. never, ever, killed innocent people. Campus teach-ins on the Vietnam War were raucous because students disagreed with what "Chomsky," "Dellinger," or "Zinn" said. But gradually it became obvious that if we could convince people of what was going on and why, they would be transformed. So the Left offered more facts, images, and testimony that revealed the systemic causes of problems and began to convince people who then joined demonstrations and created more teach-ins, discussions, leaflets, and articles that convinced still more people. And the movement grew.

(1) Why can't we recruit people as effectively today?

(2) Where did the past recruits disappear to, and how can the Left retain people more permanently in the future?

Today, we still emphasize facts, images, and testimony about injustice, but our revelations have minimal impact. No one gets upset when we report corporate crimes and administrative horrors. At campus teach-ins most attenders, and there are often many, seem to calmly accept what "Chomsky," "Stockwell," or "Ehrenreich" says. Other than silly apparatchiks and cultural SWAT teams, no one calls us crazy. But while average folks often accept our analyses, they do little about it.

So why did revelation recruit people to action then, while it doesn't now?

Usually people say cynicism is the reason and leave it at that. But I think we need a deeper answer. Perhaps in the past 25 years, the Left has done one job so well that now most people no longer believe doctors, lawyers, capitalists, politicians, or even corporations and the government are dedicated to making life better. Perhaps people no longer find Left revelations so surprising. Perhaps Leftists are more surprised when something venal is discovered than are ordinary people.

If people already know everything is rotten, repeatedly reporting injustices misses the point. If people think things can never get much better, naturally they resist radical recruitment regardless of the facts about oppressions. Believing things can't get better, people want to enjoy available pleasures and avoid dwelling on the unpleasant. Not wanting to feel guilty about this choice, they don't want to be constantly reminded of society's ills. To admit the systemic roots of injustice and to feel a desire to change them, and even to hear arguments on these matters, people first need to see how it is possible to beat Washington and Wall Street and that empowering, egalitarian institutions are possible—exactly what Left organizing largely leaves out.

I am not saying everyone can give a major speech on the intricacies of capitalism, or enumerate the causes of violence against women, or explain racial income inequalities, or itemize all U.S.-sponsored third world barbarism. Nor am I saying everyone holds even a fraction of this in the forefront of their minds. I am only suggesting that maybe everyone knows these types of things exist, but tries not to dwell on it since to do so while believing that fighting for change can't work and better institutions are impossible is painful and useless. Is there any evidence for my claims that people already know how bad things are?

Recently I went to see the Hollywood movie *Air America*. In this movie, with major stars Mel Gibson and Robert Downey Jr., the CIA uses its private air force, Air America, to assist drug dealing out of Laos to raise money to finance the Indochina war. The Senate is composed of ineffectual, self-seeking yahoos. The president supports drug-running to (a) American GIs in South Vietnam and (b) citizens in the streets of major U.S. cities like New York.

In contrast to hostile reviewers, I suspect that nearly everybody who sees *Air America* finds it entirely plausible. No one not in the employ of the *New*

York Times or some Ivy League political science department walks out outraged that U.S. largesse should be so lied about. No public demonstrations call
the film blasphemous. In the 1950s, and even the mid- and late 1960s, this film
would have created bedlam. Mel Gibson would have been as reviled as Jane
Fonda's trip to Hanoi was. *Air America* says the U.S. government pushes drugs
and is arguably the main author of today's U.S. drug-addiction problem, and
viewers take it for granted.

Or consider the contemporary best-selling thriller novel. These books nearly
universally address international intrigue, including government, military, and
corporate machinations. But with the exception of Neanderthals like Tom
Clancy, today's best-selling thriller writers often imbue the CIA and U.S.
political and corporate leaders with the most disgusting personalities and have
them undertake the most vile behavior, all with obviously systemic causes.
And though readers occasionally question this or that plot device, they never
question the negative portrayals of elites and elite institutions. These writers
would have been labeled "Reds" 25 years ago. Now their graphic depictions
of injustice are common sense backdrop for intricate plots.

Likewise, I don't hear a hue and cry over pocketbook mystery novels,
though in many instances they portray urban, class, gender, and racial conditions and behavior as every bit as oppressive as anything the Left claims.

And finally, consider the October issue of the very prestigious, MIT-asso-
ciated *Technology Review,* a magazine primarily for engineers, scientists, and
the science-watching public. Gar Alperovitz's cover story details the case he
made a quarter-century ago, that the U.S. bombed Hiroshima and Nagasaki not
to end the war with Japan, but to make a geopolitical point to the world. We
killed nearly a quarter-million citizens as an exclamation point, and, arguably,
to research the bombs' effects. Thousands will at least skim this article, but I
predict that only a few academic hustlers and corporate cronies will challenge
its veracity, much less excoriate its "calumnies against our country." Yet 25
years ago most readers would have been horrified at the mainstream publication of such "lies." After all, this article claims that the single most destructive
military events ever undertaken were U.S.-sponsored for non-military, self-
serving reasons.

Tell people that U.S. cows are fed grain instead of grass to make them
tenderer and therefore more profitable, and they will believe you. Explain that
if the same grain were instead sent abroad, it would eliminate world hunger,
and they will find this too quite plausible. When they hear it, it will come as
no great surprise, that is, that tens of millions of people die each year to fatten
corporate meat profits. But instead of dwelling on this disgusting data, people
will soon turn the conversation to something more relevant like the weather,
or what's playing at the movies, or sports. These are things they can do
something about.

The upshot of all this is that to do good recruiting, Leftists not only need to continue revealing systemic oppression and explaining its causes, we also need to present alternative visions and describing possible short- and long-term strategies for attaining them. But once we get people to recognize the systemic roots of social problems and to want to organize and demonstrate for change, how come they drift back to passivity so quickly?

On this score, 1960s efforts weren't much more successful than those since. Again, we need to face facts. We are miserable at creating lasting commitment that preserves its activist edge. Many factors influence people who become activist and drift away, but a few seem central.

- The left is no fun.

I'm not joking! Once people realize that change is not an overnight affair they inevitably come face-to-face with the prospect of having only Left friends and Left things to do for years on end. For most, this is not an appealing thought. It isn't that the Left doesn't know how to party. It is that by virtue of its beliefs the Left has a hard time getting pleasure out of most things society offers as entertainment. Movies are too violent. Sports are too commercial. Nice places to go are too full of yuppies. Everything is too classist, racist, and sexist. All this might be OK if the Left created alternative ways to recreate, celebrate, or just relax, but we don't. And because we are often on edge, critical, or being criticized, these absences take a great toll. Why trust that a permanently morose and maudlin Left will create a better future?

- The left infights.

Leftists rarely support one another. We compete for who is righter, who is better, which institution deserves more support. Ideas are personal property, almost like capital. You can tell who will be at a conference just by knowing the sponsors. Everyone finds fault with everyone else, with or without justification. We seek differences not commonalities. And what solidarity there is is often ridiculous. Consider this recent example. At Z we just received invitations to put paid ads in *ITT*'s fourteenth anniversary issue and *Socialist Review*'s twentieth. Each of the invitations indicates that coughing up some ad money is the supportive thing to do. Rubbish! For each periodical to put an ad in every other periodical's yearly anniversary issue saying how much it appreciates the other's work is supposed to be a big act of solidarity. But your supportive sentiments appear, please notice, in the periodical that you are complimenting, not in your own where they might do some good. It's like kid's birthday parties. The money merely goes round and round. As one obvious alternative, how about using one's *own* pages to boost other magazines? For *ITT* and *Socialist Review* to last as long as they have is a fantastic accomplishment. Take it from me, I know. But the way for me to show real solidarity is to tell you, Z's readers, about their achievement and to urge you to give their periodicals a try. The same projects we periodically editorially compliment and direct Z's readers too, and that we run free ads for, regularly turn around and say nothing about our existence, fail to invite us to their conferences, etc. And this is endemic. It isn't just because we're ornery. The whole periodical dynamic and most Left institutional relations are a little like high school. There are in- and out-groups and some occasional shuffling, and on the side everyone fundraises in private. Sensible people who don't have fanatical staying power generally decide the whole thing is pathetic and then leave. And they are right. The whole thing is pathetic.

- The left is isolated.

The Left is supposed to talk to the most pressing needs and heartfelt aspirations of all of society's oppressed. But partly because the Left is depressed from rarely having fun, and partly because it's cynical from infighting, and partly because its culture is some kind of amalgam of politically-correct macho coupled with academic posturing, the Left is isolated from the rest of the U.S. It is hard to organize people you hate, and often the Left seems to hate everybody and everything. Or, at least it comes off that way.

- The left is confused.

How about this for a series of Left advisories. (1) Democrats are hypocrites and scum; Vote Democratic. (2) Mainstream media nearly always lie to serve vested interests; Curry favor with mainstream media to reach a wider audience. (3) Socialism is the way to go and the Soviet Union is socialist; The Soviet Union is a disgusting mess. (4) It is crucial to fight racism; Our organization has a lily-white culture and focus. (5) It is grotesque for one nation to oppress another and people's liberation struggles deserve militant support; Don't mention the Palestinians. (6) Hierarchical production relations deny worker's control; Maintain hierarchical work relations to keep your institution strong and respected. (7) Overthrowing capitalism is central to human progress; Don't mention class or capitalism publicly. (8) You can't motivate people without vision and win without strategy; We have no vision or strategy, but don't take time to read or debate. (9) Homophobia, racism, homelessness, poverty, imperialism, and sexism are all disgusting; Don't say a word or take a stand much less invest resources regarding more than one primary issue. (10) We need solidarity; Drop what you are doing and join our group. (11) Revolution is the only solution; Never say "revolution" in public.

OK. People may disagree about all the above. But to have John Silber win the Massachusetts Democratic gubernatorial nomination by 9 points while getting nearly 470,000 votes in what is supposedly the most liberal state in the U.S. says we are failing and we need to find the reasons why and correct them.

Analytically we have to demystify U.S. geopolitical and economic motives and explain a viable alternative.

Strategically, we have to recognize that Democrats no less than Republicans defend elite control and respond only to pressure, not argument. Thus, we have to dissociate from Democrats and influence them not by kissing ass, but by raising the social costs of advocating oppressive policies.

Tactically, we have to realize that media coverage will vary directly with either (1) the extent we sell out our principles, or (2) the extent we become strong enough so that we cannot be ignored. To not sell out our principles, we cannot curtail our movement's political and organizational development on grounds of not alienating NBC, ABC, CBS, the *Washington Post,* or the *New York Times.*

Moreover, if we want to build a Left that lasts past this one crisis, we will have to develop Left culture, Left ways of having fun, Left supportiveness, and Left solidarity. We will have to respect the whole array of concerns of constituencies we need to incorporate, not only in the targets we protest, but in our own organizations and behavior as well.

To do the whole peace-and-justice thing and get it wrong again because a few leaders want to retain ties to respectable Democrats, or bask in a media spotlight, or push hierarchies, or ignore vision or strategy, or focus on only one issue, would be disastrous. Let's learn from our past and win.

— October 1990

Funding Fiasco

From 1968 to 1988, based on my discussions with people in the progressive funding community, an estimated $275 million has gone from large U.S. donors into progressive politics, *excluding* subscriber and member gifts, little donations into passed hats, door-to-door gifts, and immense electoral donations. Had the $275 million sat in the bank it would now amount to about $740 million. While money isn't the be-all and end-all of left activism, why does the U.S. left have nearly no self-sustaining infrastructure?

Leftists can't organize their way out of a paper bag? Leftists haven't worked hard? No. Given their circumstances, movement staffs, volunteers, and supporters have worked their butts off making unbelievable sacrifices and achieving amazing results.

Instead, we don't have much self-financing left infrastructure because funding has been screwed up so badly that all the hard work, devotion, and intelligence imaginable can only yield limited results. Funding happens individually, competitively, and almost never with an eye toward building efficient, lasting institutions that can promote growth.

Despite the dollar deluge, left projects and institutions mostly struggle just to hang on. Everyone operates in splendid isolation, not helping one another, wasting resources because each organization is constantly on the edge of insolvency. Where does money come from and who does it go to? Do donors know the relative accomplishments and failings of organizations? Do participants? Do you? How do donors decide that one over-rated top-heavy organization should get a million dollars yearly and grow while another worthy democratic organization should get nothing and disappear?

Instead of unaccountable competitive incoherence we ought to have a community that protects the diversity and essential autonomy of its members, even as it incorporates collective planning for overall development. Solidarity, mutual aid—good stuff.

But if you want to know what passes for solidarity now, try this: *In These Times* takes out an ad in the *Guardian's* anniversary issue, and then, vice-versa, while each periodical jealously guards the names of funders and avoids mentioning the other periodical to its readers lest some subscribers defect. Exceptions are worthy—or foolish, depending on how you choose to look at it—but they are exceptions. The rule is a competitive market that rewards style, connections, and even past failure, but not collective power, fiscal responsibility, and political impact.

What causes donors-trying-to-help or projects-trying-to-succeed to lack a sense of solidarity and planning? Political differences and the time-pressures of staying alive are part of the problem, but more of it is that "working together" is actually outside the range of behaviors that most left donors and recipients even conceive of as possible, much less productive. We have independent fiefdoms—periodicals, think-tanks, aid agencies, advocacy groups, movements, projects—each with almost no notion of taking responsibility for something larger. Our collective point and political purpose has vanished in a drizzle of check stubs. Our forest is dying (or at least not flourishing) as we each struggle to nurture our one tree by taking water from neighbors instead of figuring the best way to use it jointly. Meanwhile, whether they want to or not, donors decide what lives and what dies, what grows and what stagnates.

The lack of mutual support among movement institutions has a lot to do with the fact that we are all perpetually scrambling for crumbs of money by competing for names and favor of donors. Every fund-raiser I know bemoans what they do as degrading and debilitating even though most of them have a lot of power in their organizations. The context that breeds left competitiveness and fealty is largely a qualitative spin-off of the unaccountable, unanalyzed, closed-book approach to funding that has been in the saddle for at least the past 20 years. No recipient says anything because if we complain we may get less. But maybe the slogan ought to be "better lesser, but better."

Unionists emphasize the need for companies to open their books so that workers can understand policy and budgets and relate sensibly. That makes sense. So why are the left's books closed? Why is there so little accountability about what we and our organizations do with the funds, efforts, and trust placed in us? Why don't various leftists singly or in groups regularly evaluate the projects, organizations, institutions, and efforts of the left in light of the resources they gobble up and their accomplishments? Why couldn't there be an evolving set of criteria that could help everyone learn what works and what doesn't and why? Why don't we even openly discuss the problems?

When big donors decide what to fund, the key determinants can't include a serious assessment of prior payoff per dollar granted since that information is largely unknown. Sure, donors sometimes ask for financial records. But then donors ignore the records they receive because they presume dishonesty on the part of their supplicants. Instead of evaluating information that they don't trust—and what a commentary it is that donors have good cause not to trust it—donors might reason: "If you got money before you must have deserved it, so here's some more." Or if you know someone who knows a funder, you might get to see the funder and the funder may get to know you better and support you over others who he or she doesn't know. Or, in a less benign scenario, you might get funding because you don't say the wrong things about the Mideast, and you have the right kind of people on your board, and you agree to get rid of the gay content, the feminist content, the cultural content, or the anti-capitalist content, or you never incorporate any of this in the first place. Or maybe your fund-raiser is the kind of person funders like, so they decide, "Okay, here's some money for someone like me." But given current attitudes and the lack of reliable, openly evaluated information, making an informed assessment of practice in light of broader political needs is impossible. If you add what we raise from grassroots supporters and other revenues, the left/progressive community easily spends $60 million *yearly* for a net present value of nearly $3.5 billion for moneys spent since 1968—and still, we are where we are.

Do we want to still have to beg the John Kerrys and their ilk to do the right thing in the year 2009? If so, a good plan is to continue to finance the U.S. left in the same anti-strategic way we have up to now.

What determines who speaks at marches? Partly the preferences of big donors. Yet have you ever attended a rally and known that there was no speaker on the Mideast or that a black militant was absent due to funders' preferences? For that matter, do you know who owns the *Nation,* how much he is worth, and what he gives it? Who funds Food First? Whether money given IPS is well spent or mismanaged? Whether *Black Scholar* gets any grants at all? Are there any exceptions to the rule that what grows has big funders and what dies doesn't? Yet when someone claiming to be a progressive donor refuses to support a particularly effective, efficient project because it is too feminist or too anti-capitalist or even for racist reasons, he or she will go uncriticized. Is this fine because, after all, it's his or her money?

Some years back some folks started a journal called *Democracy.* After a time, it folded. Later a left writer wrote about the history of *Democracy* to reveal some lessons, a self-critical task hardly ever undertaken on the left. His article incorporated nothing about the funding of the magazine. Since *Democracy* was started when one particular funder put up a bundle of support and ended when that funder decided he didn't like the magazine after all, didn't the writer omit an important part of the story? Why is talking about funders and their practices off limits? Is it because crossing funders hurts one's health? Why did *Ramparts* and *Seven Days* fold? Why are *Mother Jones* and *UTNE Reader* large? Is it that the latter are economically better organized and editorially better suited to wide audience tastes, or are they just better funded? Do the politics of SANE have a larger constituency to appeal to than those of Mobilization for Survival or does SANE flourish while the MOBE flounders simply because SANE is rich and the MOBE poor?

The problems even trickle down. Consider asking for support from a bunch of not-particularly-wealthy people who have the means to address large audiences via their writing or talking, or the means to help raise funds via their contacts or credibility, or the means to provide publicity through their workplaces or in their classrooms.

If you or I, for example, were at a meeting having this request made to us along with others who can't alone finance organizations but who could together help by other means, even if we agreed about the value of the projects seeking our help, what would we say? Probably that we have made our choices about who to send our money to and see no compelling reason for making new or additional choices. We are doing what we can, and that's that.

Yet that answer misses the point. If we accept that we can only function *separately*, then given our tastes, preferences, capabilities, and (inevitable lack of) knowledge of movement possibilities, each of us is probably already making sensible choices. But what if we could sometimes act more collectively and with greater knowledge on *shared* priorities?

Separate calculations yield policies that don't add up to much. One writer thinking about talking up *Dollars & Sense,* the *Guardian,* the Greens, or CISPES, or writing letters fund-raising for them will in most cases rightly judge that his or her *lone* effort wouldn't make much difference and is too embarrassing to undertake. But 40 activists deciding together on a set of actions they can all undertake in unison would know that their actions would have some collective impact. They would not be embarrassed, but effective. I think that what impedes this from occurring is a bedrock lack of collective spirit.

With all due respect to myself and to you, the fact is that—like the big donors —we too approach support work as individuals. We pay little attention to anything but our own particular inclinations based on vague information about how organizations operate, where our money or energy goes, and the collective needs and possibilities of the left. Suppose tomorrow you get a handful of mail order funding requests. You won't know who has got multi-millionaire backing; who is surviving frugally on membership funding; who wastes money on inefficient organization or bloated office structures; who pours money back into the left as salaries or fees for services to other leftists or as donations of aid. Nor do big funders know this. Information to make informed judgments isn't available anywhere along the chain.

Perhaps instead of left groups having big name boards of directors, groups of donors should have serious boards of activists advising them on how to collectively promote self-sustaining infrastructure. Models include the various community funds like Haymarket operating under the Funding Exchange umbrella. But donors don't give these folks the bulk of their funds and the activists who advise groups like Haymarket generally feel overwhelmed and relatively powerless to do anything other then spread small amounts of money to many recipients without strategic discussion about how to maximize resources for everyone by building self-sustaining institutions.

Maybe donors should impose as a condition for receiving large grants that supported projects indicate how they will help an array of smaller efforts become stronger.

Maybe if donors who like to be known as progressive had to give public reasons for supporting or not supporting projects their awareness and priorities would comply better with the needs and potentials of the left.

Maybe there ought to be some way to collectively and publicly assess work done, needs, and ways of organizing resources to meet those needs. There needn't be homogeneity to have evaluation. We can have more than one set of norms and we needn't all agree.

Maybe groups of recipients should unite into larger mutually supportive networks that raise funds collectively.

I know these aren't comprehensive answers. But I also know that we'd better figure out some improvements soon lest in 2009 we have to ask, again, where did that last $3.5 billion go?

— November 1989

Chameleon Effect

I don't know much about chameleons, but let's assume they have the characteristic we all think they have: They change color to match their environment. The utility of this is self-evident. The chameleon avoids standing out like a tasty morsel thereby surviving longer. The chameleon's change from one color to another is not only automatic, it is always for the good.

The most interesting thing about this, though, is that we think it is only a chameleon capability; in fact, the chameleon effect is ubiquitous in nature. For example, most living things change their energy-using attributes to accommodate changes in temperature. Survival is enhanced and, assuming there is no better survival technique, nothing is lost. So, what's the point? Humans, too, have chameleon effects. I'm not talking about people's ability to change various chemical, glandular, and other features to accommodate changing temperature, nor our adrenal capabilities for dealing with danger, nor anything so automatic. I am talking about the process by which people mold their allegiances, beliefs, values, and behaviors to fit the personality requirements of the contexts they encounter. I have no evidence this is an evolutionary feature selected for the same reasons as other chameleon effects, but we do have it, and it influences how our values, behaviors, and personalities change when we find ourselves in new circumstances; for example, when law school students find themselves on the way to Wall Street and their tastes, values, and habits change accordingly.

Consider the differences between these personality changes, and a chameleon's environment-induced appearance changes.

- First, because personality changes slowly, people do not keep changing willy-nilly like a chameleon. Rather, only significant lasting changes in a person's environment (like becoming unemployed, getting drafted, changing one's religion, becoming a union activist, or becoming a doctor) can spur this type of change.

- Second, the personality chameleon effect does not operate automatically, but only as a tendency. We tend to change to fit the demands of our new job, changed income, new family status, or changed school, but we can consciously overrule the process. The chameleon *must* change and does so automatically.

- Third, unlike the chameleon's color, our personalities have a lot to do with our overall state of being, including how well-off we are and how well we are able to fulfill and develop ourselves.

A person can generally develop and fulfill her/himself with a whole set of possible personalities. On the other hand, there can be countless other personalities that the individual might possess that would impede maximal fulfillment and development. While a chameleon always settles on an appearance from the acceptable set, a person can choose personality traits from the acceptable or the oppressive set.

As an aside, these ideas can even help us define a good institution as one that efficiently accomplishes desired tasks (upbringing, entertainment, production, allocation...) and simultaneously promotes behaviors/personalities consistent with maximal human fulfillment and development. Of course, we assume here that people are not *infinitely* moldable. We have certain innate needs and capacities and will be fully fulfilled and maximally developed only if these innate needs (for food, space, self-management, etc.) are met and these innate capacities (for self-expression, utilization of physical and mental talents, etc.) are developed.

- Fourth, though we automatically tend to alter our personalities to adapt in a new context, we can also decide to change the context to better correspond to us. Doing one of these is be better than doing the other, depending on whether the kind of personality the new circumstances require will benefit us.

We all know we do these things, though we may have never have put it in words. We know that if our idealistic friend goes to an elite law school, she will change or be at war with her surroundings, but we rarely know (or admit) the same about ourselves.

We often let our chameleon tendency do its thing without oversight. We act as if the environment is as immutable for us as it is for a chameleon. And we act as if our personalities are as self-maximizing for us as the chameleon's color is for it, so that the personality effect will always give us a personality suited to our fulfillment and development. But none of this is true.

Consider the recent movies, *Regarding Henry* and *The Doctor*, for a case study of some typical human dynamics.

Early in *Regarding Henry*, we meet Henry, a high-powered, self-centered, egotistical lawyer—a representative of the legal species—and follow him to a corner store, where he walks in on a holdup and gets shot in the brain. The result is amnesia supreme. He doesn't remember his past at all and, on regaining his strength, has to start re-learning everything.

When he leaves the hospital, Henry has childlike values and feelings. He is engagingly honest, outgoing, playful, and caring. As he learns about his prior self, he hates who he was. When he rejoins his law firm, he's nauseated at his former cut-throat personality. In a revealing exchange over a power lunch, he questions some of his partners' grotesque tactics and is told to be quiet since acts like that pay for his lunch (which is, of course, sumptuous). When he quits the firm and the law, he sets right some prior immoral lawyering acts of his own, discovered in his files but not remembered.

In a subplot, Henry's young daughter gets packed off to a snobby private school and we see her suffering through a lecture aimed at molding her into the competitive, egomaniacal creature her father once was. Later, the new Henry removes her from the school, rescuing her from the trajectory of "success" that the old Henry sought for her.

Regarding Henry dramatizes the U.S. legal system as an immoral, anti-social, profit-seeking capitalist business that, like other business in a market environment, requires personalities nearly devoid of caring, honesty, and otherwise natural human attributes. The movie even indicates that the way people come to fit this environment is via horribly constraining schools, or, if that is insufficient, by the pressures (and income rewards) of the job itself. In our terms, the personality chameleon effect does its thing.

For Henry to see his own condition, he has to be shot in the head. (It also helps, of course, that Mrs. Henry is able to make good money, which softens the loss of Henry's income when he walks out on Wall Street.)

The Doctor is similar, though on a different front. This time it is becoming a patient in his own hospital that jerks the film's star out of his prior personality/value system and into a new and much more humane (if not too politically self-conscious) one. And while Henry dumped being a lawyer entirely, our doctor star becomes a good doctor and wages a reformist war with the system.

In *Regarding Henry*, Henry rejects corporate values and the law profession and seeks a different environment. In *The Doctor*, the star rejects the corporatization of medicine, but not doctoring. He works to change his environment while consciously struggling to retain a desirable personality.

So how do viewers react to these films? With very few exceptions, I would guess, the films are not as big a shock to the viewers as the bullet to the head was for Henry. Viewers don't leave the theater and renounce their professions, or, even better, rebuild their value systems and struggle against the institutions they work in. And yet viewers do seem to like the movies. And this is pretty amazing. We applaud films that demonstrate that we are pitiful in our passivity and venality, but we refuse to register that the films are saying we could do something about it and are jerks if we don't.

The upshot is that people often act like chameleons. We take little responsibility for assessing our own personalities to see whether they are beneficial to ourselves and others. We take little responsibility for assessing whether our life circumstances impose personalities on us that we should reject. We mold ourselves to fit, defend our actions, and rarely if ever consider changing our circumstances by opting out or fighting bad conditions. And our self-denial is so great we can even look in the mirror and see ourselves doing this, and yet go on without a moment's pause.

Political organizing in the U.S. includes changing values, behaviors, commitments, and even personalities. It therefore means overcoming the personality chameleon effect as it operates on the rest of us—not just doctors and lawyers—in a capitalist, racist, sexist, homophobic, authoritarian society. Our organizing is going to have to: (1) provide a jolt sufficient to get people to step outside their prior commitments/values and even personalities to see that change might be worthwhile, and (2) provide a new context sufficiently supportive of new kinds of liberating values and behavior to sustain people in choosing these, even while struggling with a largely hostile world.

If our movements are to have lasting impact, our knowledge of the chameleon effect has to become sharper, and our ability to act on that knowledge more effective. Otherwise, in the act of surviving, we will continue to suffer as mutated chameleons whose flexibility allows us to survive but diminishes our food, play, creativity, and everything else that makes for a healthy, happy, fulfilled, existence.

— September 1991

We Can Win!

To retain control of oil prices, forestall a peace dividend, and divert attention from the abominable price of Reagan's war on the poor, Bush threatens to unleash rivers of blood in the Mideast. Only fear of international isolation, potentially hyperbolic geopolitical losses, and spiraling domestic dissent impede all-out U.S. invasion. We cannot affect international opinion or Mideast nation state and corporate jockeying. We can affect domestic dissent.

Boston antiwar rallies in 1964-1965 numbered only a few hundred people who listened to vague talks about the horrors of war. Most students at MIT, my alma mater, ignored the events, although a few eagerly heckled and threw stones at assembled dissidents.

By 1968-1969, Boston antiwar demonstrators reached 250,000 people listening to talks on the imperialist roots of war and the efficacy of resistance. Most MIT students not only regularly participated, but also elected a student body president demanding no more war research, $100,000 MIT indemnity to the Black Panther Party, no more grades or requirements, open admissions, and redistribution of MIT's technical resources equally among local colleges.

In the four intervening years, Boston saw hundreds of teach-ins, dozens of major rallies, and many acts of civil disobedience, building occupations, and the burning of ROTC buildings. Cultural events, classroom takeovers, marches, sit-ins, building takeovers, and late night discussions transformed student life. This trajectory of increasing resistance shows:

* LESSON ONE: Organizing works. It can change people's consciousness, commitment, and values.

As the antiwar movement grew, a demonstration called "Mayday" was planned for Washington, DC, where demonstrators would use mobile civil disobedience to shut down the government. Demonstration organizers like Rennie Davis and Tom Hayden toured the country giving emotional talks about Vietnam, the war, and called on people to storm Washington with the slogan: "If the government doesn't stop the war, we'll stop the government." This was "apocalyptic organizing": (1) Describe reality as careening toward catastrophe.

(2) Urge that we have only one more chance before final disaster. (3) Urge that we can reverse the tide and win justice and victory *now* if everyone immediately drops everything and joins the action. (4) Sparks fly, commitments are given, and organizers leave for the next whistle stop, fists waving gloriously.

Other activists organized for Mayday with a different approach: (1) Explain that the war is fed by institutions that serve political and economic elites, and nurtured by racism, sexism, and manipulative mainstream media. (2) Teach that our task at demonstrations is to strengthen our movement and attract new recruits. (3) Explain that U.S. policy is now catastrophic and that it will remain so until we build a much greater scale and breadth of opposition. (4) Teach methods of discussion needed to spread the word and create local coalitions and organizations. (5) Preserve and combine the sparks to create more heat, channel the energy to avoid waste, nurture the commitment to get longevity, and then move on.

Both approaches favored teach-ins, rallies, demonstrations, and civil disobedience but when apocalyptically-organized demonstrators returned home from major antiwar events, they were unprepared to see the war continue. Recriminations flew, frustration rose, and anger turned inward. Rennie Davis, Tom Hayden, and almost every organizer at one time or another cajoled well-meaning demonstrators who didn't know the detailed whys and wherefores of their actions. Finally, Davis left to support an "Eastern" spiritual guru. Hayden left to enter a "Western" secular party. And hundreds of thousands of apocalyptically-organized activists burned out.

In contrast long-term organizing gave people the insight to look at our movement and not at government press conferences to see signs of progress. Were we getting better at organizing? At building institutions? At reaching out? At causing some decision-makers to begin to take note? Demonstrators aroused by a long-term analysis better understood their actions and knew what indicators of success to look for and what valuative norms to apply.

The argument that because the bombs are falling we require apocalyptic rhetoric and quick, if ill-informed, actions was repeatedly wrong. First, change is nearly always more distant than the next rally or demonstration. Second, elites can distinguish between brief outbursts that can be weathered and resistance that will keep growing and, if repressed, grow still more. Only the latter worries them sufficiently to affect their policy-making. Thus:

- LESSON TWO: Apocalyptic organizing gets short-term results with limited impact. Long-view organizing produces a movement that can withstand the rigors it will face and send a message capable of reversing war policies.

Organizers in the 1960s favored two main focuses. Some said we have to organize only around the war. "If we stick to the lowest-common denominator and avoid controversial stands we will amass the greatest support." Others said we have to organize not only around the war, but also "around poverty, alienation, racism, sexism, and authoritarianism."

Yes, some people who would otherwise agree with antiwar analysis might reject radical stands on poverty, racism, or sexism, so having ways these people can become involved before they become comfortable with wide-ranging analyses is important. Likewise, debates about diverse issues take time. But ignoring non-war focuses has even more devastating costs.

As the 1960s showed, constituencies concerned about domestic issues don't trust an antiwar movement that slights their concerns. Additionally, a single-issue approach delivers a weaker message. It says to elites, "Yes, there is a growing movement, but its attention is narrowly focused on the war. If you tough it out, this movement won't challenge society's domestic class, race, political, and gender inequalities." A multi-issue approach risks alienating some people via controversial stands, but can reach more diverse constituencies and deliver a more threatening message: "If you don't end the war, this movement will not only become more militant and disruptive about the war, it will develop similar strength and commitment regarding racism, sexism, political participation, and capitalism." Thus:

- LESSON THREE: Single-issue organizing appears superficially less controversial and more popular but carries the seeds of its own dissolution and sends a limited message to elites. Multi-issue organizing is difficult to do well, but averts fragmentation, attracts wider support, and sends a more powerful message.

In 1960s organizing efforts, many of us addressed large groups for extended, highly emotional sessions. We would of course explain the criminality of the war for people still clinging to naive views of U.S. foreign policy and corporations. Especially on campuses, we invariably found that with sufficient facts, we could offset such views. Then, however, we encountered more tenacious obstacles to participation.

First, people who agreed that the war was immoral and only in elite interests would then argue that nothing could be done. Immorality was the way of the world. Hate, inequality, servility, and war are in our nature.

Second, after long discussions on everything from human nature to history overcame cynicism about human potentials, people would fall back on cynicism about achieving better conditions. The bad guys have the guns, money, and media. We can't beat them.

Third, even when we convinced people that in the short term we could force decision-makers to reverse their war policies by raising costs, and that in the long term we could change basic institutions, the final impediment turned out to be distaste of left behavior and a fear of becoming our own worst enemy.

People would say, "I know you are right that the war is wrong and peace is possible, but your protesting seems to pervert you so that you will eventually sell out your values and become as bad as those you now oppose." Thus, popular responses to organizing reveal that:

- LESSON FOUR: Getting people to join radical opposition requires overcoming cynicism about human nature, fear of losing, and a distaste for what activism seems to entail.

The U.S. did not drop nuclear bombs in Southeast Asia. Limits were placed on U.S. policy. Many aggressive acts were prevented and others reversed. Many civil rights were won and women made major gains. Though permanent change requires transformed institutions, there are many short-run victories.

A look at the *Pentagon Papers* multi-volume documentation of decision-making during the period, and at newspapers and the public record of Congress shows a remarkable fact. Whenever some politician changed from voting pro-war to voting antiwar, or whenever some corporate head went on record against the war, the explanation was always the same. It was never the loss of lives of American soldiers or Vietnamese soldiers or civilians, or economic dislocations of the poor at home. When elite figures announced their switch from hawk to dove, and when the *Pentagon Papers* listed factors assessed in choosing policies, the focus was always the desire to keep down the cost of political resistance—"Our army is disintegrating, our streets are succumbing to militancy, the next generation is being lost to our corporations, the costs we are bearing are too high. I am now for peace."

With minor exceptions, no corporate head or high political official opposed the war because it was immoral or because the human carnage upset them. Nor was there any notion that the war was not "in U.S. (meaning elite) interests." They opposed the war because rising social costs threatened to undermine aims elites held even more important than winning the war: their political power and corporate control. That is:

- LESSON FIVE: Moving people to raise the domestic social costs of war can constrain and reverse hated policies.

So what does this translate to? State and corporate elites are not stupid or subject to moral persuasion. They promote their heinous policies not out of ignorance, but because the results serve their interests. To pressure them effectively, we have to avoid single-issue apocalyptic organizing and opt for a multi-issue long-run orientation. We have to educate about immediate facts and proximate causes, but also about the roots of injustice and the possibility of raising social costs both to win immediate reforms and to eventually restructure defining institutions. We must build a peace and justice movement that builds solidarity.

(1) Every antiwar speaking engagement or teach-in panel should include at least one speaker addressing the "totality of oppressions." And I am not talking about someone explaining how antiwar work can benefit class, gender, or race struggles. I'm talking about feminists, labor organizers, conversion activists, and antiracist organizers talking about how *their* work is critically important in its own right, as well as how assisting it will benefit the fight against war.

(2) Antiwar demonstrations, rallies, and written materials should have similar policies.

(3) The organization and culture of the antiwar movement must empower diverse types of people.

- Women will not work well in movement defined by the worst male habits of competitive, macho posturing. We have to incorporate feminist principles in antiwar activism.

- Blacks and Latinos will not join a movement defined by the cultural and behavioral characteristics of white intellectuals. We have to incorporate Black, Latino and other minority culture in the antiwar movement.

- Workers will not lead a movement characterized by the condescension familiar from workers' relations with managers, lawyers, and doctors. We must have a way of organizing that incorporates working-class priorities in antiwar organization.

- Gays and lesbians will not join a movement embodying sexual assumptions familiar from daily encounters with homophobia. We must incorporate respect for sexual diversity in antiwar work.

A multi-constituency movement that inspires lasting commitment will have to be multi cultural and disavow the oppressive features of gender, race, and class relations. We can't attain perfection overnight and shouldn't even try to make a movement that only the most culturally "perfect" human being could feel comfortable in, but we must make steady, substantial progress.

(5) To promote the strongest possible resistance and to give the movement a positive rather than negative orientation, antiwar marches, rallies, and civil disobedience should target diverse sites and make multi-issue demands. For example:

- at the corporate headquarters of major war contractors, demanding an end to war and the reallocation of resources to the production of food, shelter, and infrastructure;

- at drug hangouts and treatment centers, demanding an end to war and creation of massive drug rehabilitation programs;

- at Congress, demanding an end to war and financing full-employment programs, massively progressive "soak the rich" tax reforms, state financed election funds, and binding public plebiscites on policies;

- at army bases, demanding an end to war and conversion of the bases to industrial centers to build quality low-income housing with the first units given to GIs from the base who decide to stay on as employees at the new construction firm;

- at TV stations, demanding an end to war and massive funding for the arts and for independent radio and TV under community control;

- at rape crisis and day care centers, demanding an end to war and massive funding for day care and affirmative action programs for women;

- at inner-city sites, demanding an end to war and funds for rebuilding infrastructure, enhancing housing, and providing jobs;

- at inner-city schools, demanding an end to war and massive funding for education to allow our youth to become more than mercenaries for a garrison state;

- at hospitals, demanding an end to war and conversion of resources to construction of new hospitals and local health centers and the adoption of universal free medical care.

(6) Local, regional, and national antiwar organizations should seek coalition support for antiwar actions from groups organized around gender, race, and class, but should also give material and organizing assistance to groups, projects, and events organized around gender, race, and class whether explicitly requested to do so or not.

This time we should not sacrifice all other agendas to the antiwar agenda, thereby weakening every effort *including* the antiwar effort. We should, instead, share intelligence, energy, skills, and money among many activist fronts.

People will ask, "What could you do that would be better?" and we have to develop answers that do not stop at solely describing how bad the system is, or "Bring the troops home," or "Letting the sanctions and international diplomacy work," or "Strengthening the UN, democratizing it, and making everyone, especially us, subject to its will."

People are going to realize that if capitalism breeds imperialism breeds war, then unless we get rid of capitalism, war will recur and we will need to be prepared to fight. And if we say, OK, we eventually have to get rid of capitalism too, they will remind us how East Europeans and Russians have recently rushed back to capitalism.

In reply we need to present a new post-capitalist vision encompassing economics, politics, gender, and race. To build a large, lasting movement we need to describe activities that can promote lasting change and show that our movement is sufficiently humane, participatory, and sensitive to come through uncorrupted.

You may say revolution is not on the immediate agenda, so why develop long-run revolutionary answers? You may say we aren't trying to get lifelong commitment, we are only trying to get people to fight for peace now, so why worry about long-run aims? If so, you miss the point.

People know serious dissent can change their lives. They know that if they admit U.S. crimes, they will either have to become radical with possible loss of friends and jobs, or else turn their backs on morality. People need long-run answers to believe the long-run struggle will be worthwhile and therefore worth joining now.

People need faith in what they are doing, especially if it entails sacrifices. Building a new sense of self around hatred for war is not sustaining enough and tends to create bitter people unlikely to be effective organizers. To become radical requires jettisoning one's old self-image and it is hard to do this and maintain one's humanity without understanding where one is headed.

Think about it. People who have been effective activists for decades believe in human potentials, in a better society, in the possibility of winning, and are sustained by these positive beliefs, not solely by hating a specific injustice. To try to get others involved as deeply without helping them attain positive vision is ignoring our own politicization.

—December 1990

Index

Index

237

Index

Index

Hartman, Chester, 204
Hatch, Orrin, 26, 27
Hayden, Tom, 229, 230
Health care, 12, 34, 184-85
Heilbroner, Robert, 104, 106, 107
Hierarchical division of work, 35-36, 147, 148
Hill, Anita, 24-29
Hill and Knowlton, 73
Hill-Thomas hearings, 24-29
Homelessness, 12-13, 38, 183, 203
Homosexuality, 11, 145, 146, 188
Housing: and capitalism, 13, 37-38; change strategies, 183, 203-4; federal policy, 17, 18; homelessness, 12-13, 38, 183, 203
Human rights, 55-56, 117. *See also specific topics*
Humanism, 92
Hungary, 112, 123. *See also* Eastern bloc transformations
Hussein, Saddam. *See* Gulf War

I

IMF. *See* International Monetary Fund
In These Times, 155, 183, 217, 220-21
Indonesia, 61, 64, 173
Innovation, 164-65
Institutional racism, 185
Institutional theories, 85-87, 88-89
The Intellectuals on the Road to Class Power (Konrad & Szelenyi), 105-7
Inter-American Development Bank, 132
Intercommunalism, 117, 119, 141-42
International Bank for Reconstruction and Development (World Bank), 41-43, 46
International Court of Justice. *See* World Court
International human rights organizations, 55-56
International Monetary Fund (IMF), 52

Intifada, 178

Iran: coup, 66-67, 173; hostage crisis, 84, 85; war with Iraq, 61-62, 64, 65, 173
Iran-Contra scandal, 84, 85
Iraq: "ecology wars," 196; and Kurds, 62, 64, 178; U.S. aid to, 61-62, 64, 173; war with Iran, 61-62, 64, 65, 173. *See also* Gulf War
Islamic fundamentalism, 61, 62
Israel: Lebanon invasion, 61, 62, 63, 173; and Palestinian issue, 178

J

Jackson, Jesse, 137, 198-202; and Gulf War, 180; and Hill-Thomas hearings, 27-28; strategies for, 199-202, 203-7. *See also* Rainbow Coalition

K

Kennedy, Edward, 175
Kennedy, Joe, 175
Kennedy assassination theories, 88, 90-91, 99-102
Killing train, 75-77
King, Mel, 204
Kissinger, Henry, 67-68
Kolko, Gabriel, 79
Konrad, George, 105-7
Krushchev, Nikita, 116, 120, 121
Kurds, 62, 64, 178
Kuwait. *See* Gulf War

L

LA Weekly, 183
Latvia. *See* Baltic Republics
Lebanon, 61, 62, 63, 173
Left Greens, 183
Left movements: and anti-rationalism, 90-96; classism in, 202; confusion among, 218-19; and end of Cold War, 112, 179; funding, 33, 220-24; and Gulf War, 76, 77, 175-76, 178-

81; infighting in, 217-18; isolation of, 29, 218; lack of pleasure in, 217; Marxism-Leninism among, 129-30, 138, 139-40; and material scarcity, 139; present ineffectiveness of, 214-15; racism in, 30-33; sexism in, 30-33, 189, 190-91; and Vietnam War, 214, 229-30. *See also* Alternative media; Change strategies; Movement goals

LeGuin, Ursula, 160-61

Lehman, John, 68

Lenin, V. I., 108-9, 114, 120. *See also* Leninism

Leninism. *See* Marxism-Leninism; Soviet Union

Levy, David, 158, 160

Libya, 67

Lieberman, David, 73

Literary canon, 78-80

Literary theory, 81-83, 91

Lithuania. *See* Baltic Republics

Looking Forward: Participatory economics for the Twenty First Century (Albert & Hahnel), 156-57, 158, 159, 160, 162

Luxemburg, Rosa, 109

M

McNamara, Robert, 59

Madonna, 187, 188

Marcos, Ferdinand, 50, 173

Markets, 41-46, 147-48, 151-52, 162. *See also* Capitalism

Martin, Roger, 196-97

Marx, Karl, 46, 106, 107-8, 131, 139. *See also* Marxism-Leninism

Marxism-Leninism, 129-30, 138, 139-40, 143

Media: and change strategies, 201-2, 219; conspiracy vs. institutional theories of, 86-87; crime stories in, 10; and cynicism, 106; and Eastern bloc transformations, 112; and Gulf War, 57, 58, 65, 73-74, 174-75, 178, 179; and Hill-Thomas hearings, 28;

and Marxism-Leninism, 130; and participatory economics, 154-55; sexism in, 188, 189. *See also* Alternative media; Television

Mellon, Andrew, 66

Middle East. *See* Gulf War; *specific countries*

Military spending: and capitalism, 13; change strategies, 39-40, 197, 204; conversion, 38-40, 71, 192-97; and drug wars, 17, 18, 195; and New World Order, 72; and participatory economics, 149, 154; and worker militancy, 38-39. *See also* Arms exports

Misogyny. *See* Sexism

Mobil Corporation, 66

Mobilization for Survival, 222

Moldavia, 114

Monthly Review, 155

Morocco, 61

Morris, William, 108

Mother Jones, 183, 222

Movement goals, 18, 138-46; discrete policies, 138-39; feminism, 145-46; intercommunalism, 117, 119, 141-42; vs. Marxism-Leninism, 138, 139-40; participatory democracy, 139-41, 170, 205-6. *See also* Participatory economics

Moynihan, Daniel, 63-64

Multiculturalism: and anti-rationalism, 91; attacks on, 78-80; intercommunalism, 117, 119, 141-42

Multinational corporations, 13-14, 56, 79. *See also* Capitalism; U.S. foreign policy

N

Nader, Ralph, 203

Nagorno-Karabakh, 115, 118

The Nation, 30, 183

National Organization for Women (NOW), 29, 183, 190

NATO. *See* North Atlantic Treaty Organization

Index

NBC, 19-20, 52, 174. *See also* Media
NCIPA, 183
Netherlands, 68
New Perspectives Quarterly, 104
"New World Order," 70-72
New York Times, 19, 67; on Gulf War, 70-71, 177, 178; on Panama invasion, 51, 52. *See also* Media
Nicaragua, 51, 61, 133; and international law, 63, 64, 173; Iran-Contra scandal, 84, 85; and Left movements, 53, 204
Nixon, Richard M., 67
Nobel Prize, 47-49
Noriega, Manuel, 50, 51, 60, 173
North Atlantic Treaty Organization (NATO), 112-13
North, Oliver, 17, 84
Norton, Eleanor Holmes, 206
Nove, Alec, 156
Nuclear industry, 84, 85, 93
Nussbaum, Karen, 204

O

Oil, 61, 66-69
OPEC. *See* Organization of Petroleum Exporting Countries
Oppenheim, V. H., 67
Organization of Petroleum Exporting Countries (OPEC), 67, 68, 69

P

Pacifica Radio, 183
Paine, Thomas, 38
Palestinian issue, 65-66, 178
Panama, 50-53, 60, 62, 173
Participatory democracy, 139-41, 170, 205-6
Participatory economics, 143-45, 147-55, 156-66; and competition, 152-53; vs. coordinatorism, 105, 150-51; efficiency of, 45-46; incentives in, 163-65; and intrusiveness, 160-62;

and markets, 147-48, 151-52; media in, 154-55; and military spending, 149, 154; planning in, 105, 148, 156, 157-60, 161, 162-63; priorities of, 162-63; as real socialism, 105, 134; scale of, 153-54; and specialization, 148-50; and worker militancy, 35-36. *See also* Movement goals
Patriarchy. *See* Sexism
"Peace dividend," 38, 39, 71, 192-97
Peace movement. *See* Left movements
Pentagon Papers, 232
Perestroika, 123-29
Perestroika (Gorbachev), 125-26
Personalities, 225-28
Philippines, 173, 204
Pinochet, Augusto, 173
Podhoretz, Norman, 71
Poland, 112, 123, 124-25, 128, 137. *See also* Eastern bloc transformations
Political correctness, 78-80
The Political Economy of Participatory Economics (Albert & Hahnel), 156-57, 162
Political science, 81, 82
Post-modernism, 81-83, 91
Poverty, 12, 17, 184, 188. *See also* Homelessness
Powell, Colin, 71
Private ownership, 143, 147. *See also* Capitalism; Property
The Progressive, 155, 188
Property, 37-38, 48. *See also* Capitalism; Private ownership

R

Racism: and affirmative action, 19, 22; alternative media exclusion, 30-33; and capitalism, 12; change strategies, 183-86; extent of, 169-70, 174; institutional, 185; literary canon exclusion, 78-80; and Panama invasion, 52; Republican Party manipulations, 88; in science, 91; U.S. vs. South Africa, 182-83
Radical America, 155

TV Guide, 73, 74

U

Unemployment: change strategies, 184, 204-5; and military conversion, 38, 192-93; and worker militancy, 36-37, 192-93

United Nations: and change strategies, 55, 56; and Gulf War, 58, 62, 63, 69-70; and Israel, 61, 62, 178; and Panama invasion, 62

U.S. foreign policy: and capitalism, 153; change strategies, 53-56, 204; and drug wars, 17; "ecology wars," 196-97; and economic domination, 13-14, 51, 56, 61, 79; Grenada invasion, 60-61; and international law, 62-64, 173; and national sovereignty, 60-62, 173; "New World Order," 70-72; and oil, 66-69; and Palestinian issue, 65-66; pollution exports to Third World, 41-43. *See also* Gulf War; *specific countries*

Universities, 78-80

UTNE Reader, 222

Uzbekistan, 114

V

Vietnam War, 61, 74, 179; and Kennedy assassination, 90-91, 99-102; opposition to, 214, 229-30

Village Voice, 183

Voice of America, 64

W

War at home, 72, 174

Washington Post, 19, 121, 177, 178. *See also* Media

WBAI, 183

Weisner, Jerome, 4

Weisskopf, Tom, 161

Western Sahara, 61

Whitman, Walt, 35

Whole Earth Review, 30

Will, George, 63

Winpisinger, William, 204

Wise, Leah, 204

Wollstonecraft, Mary, 36

Women. *See* Feminism; Sexism

Workers: and coordinatorism, 105-6, 108, 137; Cuba, 134; militancy, 34-40, 192-93; and profit maximization, 44-45; and Rainbow Coalition, 199, 201. *See also* Capitalism; Participatory economics

Workplace democracy. *See* Participatory economics

World Bank, 41-43, 46

World Court, 64

Y

Yemen, 70

Z

Z Magazine, 155, 160, 217

Zambia, 196

ABOUT SOUTH END PRESS

South End Press is a non-profit, collectively run book publisher with over 180 titles in print. Since our founding in 1977, we have tried to meet the needs of readers who are exploring, or are already committed to, the politics of radical social change.

Our goal is to publish books that encourage critical thinking and constructive action on the key political, cultural, social, economic and ecological issues shaping life in the United States and in the world. In this way, we hope to give expression to a wide diversity of democratic social movements and to provide an alternative to the products of corporate publishing.

Through the Institute for Social and Cultural Change, South End Press works with other political media projects—*Z Magazine;* Speak Out!, a speakers bureau; the New Liberation News Service and the Publishers Support Project—to expand access to information and critical analysis. If you would like a free catalog of South End Press books or information about our membership program, which offers two free books and a 40 percent discount on all titles, please write to us at: South End Press, 116 Saint Botolph Street, Boston, MA 02115.

OTHER SOUTH END PRESS TITLES OF INTEREST

Looking Forward: Participatory Economics for the 21st Century
by Michael Albert and Robin Hahnel

Liberating Theory
by Michael Albert, Leslie Cagan, Noam Chomsky, Robin Hahnel,
Mel King, Lydia Sargent, and Holly Sklar

Sisters of the Yam: Black Women and Self-Recovery
by bell hooks

Year 501: The Conquest Continues
by Noam Chomsky